Global Cases in Logistics and Supply Chain Management

Global Cases in Logistics and Supply Chain Management

Teachers' Manual

David H Taylor

INTERNATIONAL THOMSON BUSINESS PRESS
ITP An International Thomson Publishing Company

London • Bonn • Boston • Johannesburg • Madrid • Melbourne • Mexico City • New York • Paris •
Singapore • Tokyo • Toronto • Albany, NY • Belmont, CA • Cincinnati OH • Detroit, MI

Global Cases in Logistics and Supply Chain Management: Teachers' Manual

Copyright © 1997 David Taylor

First published by International Thomson Business Press

I(T)P   A division of International Thomson Publishing Inc.
        The ITP logo is a trademark under licence

All rights reserved. No part of this work which is copyright may be reproduced or used in any form or by any means – graphic, electronic, or mechanical, including photocopying, recording, taping or information storage and retrieval systems – without the written permission of the Publisher, except in accordance with the provisions of the Copyright Designs and Patents Act 1988.

Whilst the Publisher has taken all reasonable care in the preparation of this book the Publisher makes no representation, express or implied, with regard to the accuracy of the information contained in this book and cannot accept any legal responsibility or liability for any errors or omissions from the book or the consequences thereof.

Products and services that are referred to in this book may be either trademarks and/or registered trademarks of their respective owners. The Publisher/s and Author/s make no claim to theses trademarks.

British Library Cataloguing-in-Publication Data
A catalogue record for this book is available from the British Library

First edition 1997
Reprinted 1997

Typeset by Kim Allen, Faringdon, Oxon
Printed in the UK by Antony Rowe Ltd, Chippenham, Wiltshire

ISBN 1-86152-236-3

International Thomson Business Press	International Thomson Business Press
Berkshire House	20 Park Plaza
168–173 High Holborn	13th Floor
London WC1V 7AA	Boston MA 02116
UK	USA

http://www.itbp.com

Contents

Structure and Use of the Teachers' Notes   vii
Table 1 Summary of main issues raised in each case   ix

Part 1	**Logistics and Supply Chain Strategy**	1
Case 1	BASF: *Logistics Operations in South and East Asia*	1
Case 2	Brother International: *European Distribution Strategy*	4
Case 3	Gillette: *Creating a European Logistics Strategy*	14
Case 4	Hasbro Europe: *Developing European Logistics Strategy*	16
Case 5	NIKE: *Developing European Logistics Strategy*	16
Case 6	Valkerie: *Global Supply Chain Management*	24

Part 2	**Purchasing and Supplies Management**	27
Case 7	Filton Aerostructures: *Procurement and Supply Management*	27
Case 8	Westland Helicopters Ltd: *Relationship Strategy Development*	32

Part 3	**Manufacturing Logistics**	39
Case 9	Fiat Auto Spa: *Restructuring the Logistics System in Response to Changing Customer Requirements*	39
Case 10	Kalon Paints Ltd: *Strategic Logistics Management*	46
Case 11	Trico: *Manufacturing and Logistics*	54

Part 4	**Distribution Planning and Strategy**	57
Case 12	Goman Marketing Co: *Delivery Vehicles for the Warsaw District*	57
Case 13	Palmer and Harvey Ltd: *Transport and Customer Service Options for the Distribution of Small Orders*	63
Case 14	Pepsi Cola International: *Distribution and Pricing Policy in Ukraine*	67
Case 15	Rank Hovis Macdougall Plc: *Evaluation of Contract Distribution Tenders*	70
Case 16	Scottish Brewers: *The Restructuring of a Depot System*	78
Case 17	Zimbabwe Dairy Marketing Board: *Distribution Planning in a Developing Country*	83

Part 5	**Warehouse Planning and Operations Management**	89
Case 18	British Airways Avionic Engineering: *The Development of an Automated Storage and Retrieval System*	89
Case 19	Britvic Soft Drinks Ltd: *Development of a Major Distribution Centre*	93
Case 20	The Discount Shop: *Warehouse Planning and Operations*	100

Part 6	**Inventory Management**		107
	Case 21	Medisupply: *A Review of Stockholding Policy*	107
	Case 22	St James's Hospital and Lucas Engineering Systems: *Collaboration in Business Process Re-engineering: Purchasing and Supplies*	113
Part 7	**Transport Management**		123
	Case 23	Almarai Ltd: *Transport Safety Analysis*	123
	Case 24	O K Tedi Mining Ltd: *Road Transport Operations in Papua New Guinea*	128
	Case 25	Perfecta Beds: *Improving Transport Productivity*	134
	Case 26	The Port of Melbourne: *Planning Port Capacity*	140
	Case 27	Santos Ltd: *Oil Recovery by Truck or Pipeline*	142
	Case 28	The United States Department of Environment: *The Transport of Nuclear Waste*	145
Part 8	**International Logistics/International Market Entry Strategies**		149
	Case 29	Eastman Kodak Singapore: *Managing International Logistics*	149
	Case 30	Exel Logistics: *Internationalising a Distribution Brand*	153
	Case 31	Hershey Goes Home: *International Market Entry Strategy*	162
	Case 32	Polymedic: *Modal Choice Decisions in International Transport*	164
	Case 33	The Rwandan Refugee Crises 1994: *The Logistics of a Third World Relief Operation*	169
	Case 34	Woolworths Plc: *Sourcing Retail Merchandise from South East Asia*	175

The Structure and Use of the Teachers Notes[1]

The aim of this manual is to make it as easy as possible for teachers to use the cases in the main text and to gain maximum understanding of the cases and their teaching potential.

The notes have been designed to allow teachers to **quickly** :-

- choose a case which is relevant to the subject being taught
- review the overall content and issues raised by each case
- understand the teaching and learning objectives envisaged by the case author
- understand the main issues raised and possible solutions

Table 1 is the starting point in choosing a case. It summarises the main issues raised in each case and also indicates secondary issues. However it must be pointed out that this categorisation is given only to ease the case selection process. The holistic nature of logistics means that most cases in the book require consideration from the supply chain perspective rather than from a particular functional pidgeon hole. Indeed the same point applies to the categorisation of cases into the eight sections within the case book and it should be stressed to students that they should look well beyond this categorisation when analysing cases.

The notes for each case have been structured in the following standardised format for ease of reference:-

SECTION 1 CASE SYNOPSIS

Outlines the context, key features and main issues raised.

It is intended to allow teachers to quickly get a feel for the case when deciding whether or not to use it and to quickly review the case when returning to it at a subsequent point.

SECTION 2 TEACHING/LEARNING OBJECTIVES

These are usually couched in terms of:

- what students are expected to learn from the case

and/or

- what they are expected to do in terms of analysis or activity.

---

[1] The teaching notes for all cases in this book have been prepared as a basis for class discussion rather than to illustrate effective or ineffective handling of administrative situations

SECTION 3 MAIN ISSUES RAISED

The main issues and problems are clearly identified and discussed, together with an outline of the approach or solution that could be adopted. The suggested approach might be the one actually adopted by the company or a 'model' answer.

SECTION 4 SPECIFIC QUESTIONS/STUDENT ASSIGNMENTS

A variety of questions are included for each case.

There is usually a reiteration of the major issues or problems faced by the managers in the case stated in the form of a question(s).

There may also be a list of supplementary questions which address secondary issues or highlight particular teaching points that can be brought out from the case.

These questions can if necessary be used to guide students through the case, although in fact, the text of each case is written in such a way that no specific questions need be given.

It is envisaged that post-graduate or advanced students should not need the guidance of specific questions as the first part of the analysis process is to clearly identify the key questions and issues.

Where ever possible model or indicative answers are given. Where the 'model' answer is assumed to be that adopted by the company it will be described in Part 5.

The questions and approaches given are clearly not exhaustive and there is clearly plenty of scope for cases to be used in ways other than those suggested.

SECTION 5 DESCRIPTION OF ACTUAL DEVELOPMENTS IN THE COMPANIES SUBSEQUENT TO THE CASE

In as many cases as possible a full description is given of the actual approaches adopted by the managers in the companies in solving the problems presented.

A description of developments in the company subsequent to the period of the case has also been included wherever possible.

If required these descriptions can be analysed as a subsequent exercise by students and the question asked 'was this the best or most appropriate approach?'

SECTION 6 SUGGESTIONS FOR USING THE CASE, TEACHING APPROACHES, SUITABLE AUDIENCES

Case authors and /or the editor give suggestions as to:

- how the case might be used
- the level of student to which it might appropriate
- teaching suggestions, time required.

My hope is that this manual will allow teachers to very quickly reach a point where they have sufficient information and understanding of the cases to teach them with authority and thus enable students to gain maximum possible benefit.

Table 1 Summary of main issues raised in each case

NOTE
1 = Primary issue
2 = Secondary issue

	Logistics & SCM Strategy	Organisational issues & control of the SC	Partnerships with suppliers	Information managm't & systems	Demand forecasting	Operations managm't	Inventory managm't	Purchasing/ In-bound logistics	Manufacturing strategy, planning & ops	Transport planning & ops	Warehouse strategy, planning & control	Retailing	Distribution planning & control	Distribution channels	Customer service	Logistics costs	Marketing & logistics interface	International issues	Bench-marking
Section 1																			
BASF	1	1		2															
Brother	1	1		1	2												2		
Gillette	1	1		1			2		2	2	1		2		1	1	2		
Hasbro	1	1		2			1			1							2		
Nike	1	1	1	2			2		2	1			2		2	2	2	1	
Valkerie	1	1				2	1		2										
Section 2																			
Filiton	1	1	2	2	2		2	1							1	1	2	1	
Westland	1	1	1			2	1	1	2	1									
Section 3																			
Fiat	1	1		1	1	1	1		1	1							1		
Kalon	2	2			2		2	2	1						1				
Trico	2	1				1	2	2	1	2			2		1	2	2		1
Section 4																			
Goman							2	1		1			1		2	1	1		
Palmer And Harvey		1								1			1		1				
Pepsi Cola					2					1	2			1		1			
Rank Hovis MacD'				1			1			2					2	2			
Scottish Brewers										1	2		1			1			
Zimbabwe D.M.B.										1	2		2			2	2	1	
Section 5																			
BAAE							2	1		2			1		2				
Britvic			2	2			2	1		2	1				2				
The Discount Shop	2						1			1		1							
Section 6																			
Medisupply			1		1		1												
St James's		1													1				
Section 7																			
Almarai						1			2	1									
O K Tedi Mining		1				1				1			2			1			
Perfecta Beds						1									1		1		2
Port Of Melbourne					2											1			
Santos								2		1			2						
Section 8																			
US Dept of Environ't	1	1		2			1	2	2	2									
Eastman Kodak	1	2	2				1	2		1					1			1	
Exel Logistics	1									1					1		1		
Hershey	1								2			2					1		
Polymedic	1	1					2	1			1		1			2			
Rwanda	1	1					1	1											
Woolworths	1	2	2	1			1					1		1					

Part 1

Logistics and Supply Chain Strategy

Case 1

BASF

Logistics operations in South and East Asia

John Oska, *Regional Logistics Manager BASF SE Asia*

SECTION 1 CASE SYNOPSIS

The case is about the development of strategic logistics plans in an adverse environment. The evolution of logistics in the Asian environment is well behind that of more advanced geographic regions such as Europe or the United States. In this context, strategies that may be logical in these regions are not necessarily appropriate in Asia.

The case describes the situation in BASF within Asia as existed in the early 1990's – fragmented companies each struggling to come to grips with modern logistic ideas with little or no central co-ordination or assistance. While the company had adopted advanced techniques throughout the world, this was not so in Asia. At the same time, there was a growing realisation that management should be decentralised or devolved from Germany so that customer service could be improved. To cope with this change, logistic operations had to be improved.

The company was structured around a powerful centralised logistics system to which each group company's logistics operation reported. At the regional level there was little input on logistics matters. In late 1993, a regional logistics manager was appointed to rectify the existing shortcomings. The case describes the situation the new incumbent found as it existed in late 1993 at the central, regional and company levels.

SECTION 2 TEACHING/LEARNING OBJECTIVES

The learning objectives of the case include:
- To give students an awareness of the need to consider geographical, cultural and demographic differences in undertaking management activities.

- To demonstrate the realities of scarce resources in developing a strategic plan (i.e. how long does it take one person to investigate, research and review plans in such a large area) and implementing the plan (i.e. given the scope of the changes required and the cultural difficulties in implementing change, how is the change to be implemented).
- To give students an indication on the number of factors that must be taken into account in developing a strategic plan and the levels of the organisation that will be effected by the plan.
- To broaden the students understanding of logistics in an environment outside those considered to be more advanced.

SECTION 3 MAIN ISSUES AND PROBLEMS RAISED BY THE CASE

The main issues and problems raised in the case include:

- The cultural difficulties in attempting to rationalise, standardise or centralise an operation that has been fragmented in the past, together with the same cultural difficulties in bringing about any change.
- The lack of educational resources throughout Asia for logistics necessitated either in-house training or bringing in teachers from outside Asia. This further exacerbated the problems regarding change management as "new ideas" from outside Asia are often more vigorously resisted.
- Given the number of countries and the geographical dispersion, the time taken to review the total operation, including gaining the trust of the people in the companies, was significant. In all about two years was required to establish the requisite level of knowledge and trust to prepare a strategic plan.
- The development of a strategic plan could not be achieved without the participation from representatives of the group companies, particularly in the Asian environment. However, in order to gain this participation, the people themselves had to be educated and convinced of the need to change.

SECTION 4 SPECIFIC QUESTIONS

1. Describe the factors to be considered in the development of a strategic logistics plan.
2. Outline the persons to be consulted and the involvement these people would have in preparing the strategy.
3. Prepare a timeline for development and implementation of the strategy.
4. Outline a training plan for personnel in the region to be educated in logistics techniques including the resources needed to conduct the training.

Model answers

1. Factors to be considered:

   - Time available is limited by restriction on personnel numbers; for example, simply visiting every company for a period of two days each would take up to six months; in reality this could take two years.
   - An assessment of the logistics infrastructure and resources available is required; this would include currently utilised assets e.g. warehouses, transport, information resources, telecomms etc. and potentially available resources in each country.
   - An assessment of the experience and professional standard of existing staff is necessary to evaluate what training or recruitment is available or needed, together with training resources within the region.

- An appraisal of regional requirements is required to assess whether there is potential for standardising or centralising processes in areas where synergies or cost savings are available. These might include regional distribution centres, centralised forecasting and production planning, coordinated raw material purchasing etc.

2. Persons to be consulted:

- Staff in each company from various levels, including management and non management from all the key areas including logistics, marketing, finance and production.
- Staff from within the regional head office with a knowledge of each country's differences and particular requirements and from within specialist functional areas to gain insight into potential project areas and developments, for example, information system proposals.
- Staff from within the corporate head office logistics division to determine logistics policy and future developments and to solicit assistance for particular developments, for example, providing training specialists.

3. In some cases specialised workshops or seminars targeting particular groups could be utilised, for example, shipping managers, to develop particular solutions.

4. Timeline:

EVENT	Q1	Q2	Q3	Q4	Q5	Q6	Q7	Q8
Gain familiarity with position	■							
Visit group companies	■	■	■	■	■	■	■	■
Visit head office in Germany			■		■			
Prepare & publish staretgy					■			
Develop training needs analysis				■				
Conduct reviews in select companies				■		■		■

5. Training plan:

- Managing directors: broad overview including gaining support;
- Senior management: broad overview including some understanding of modern logistics;
- Senior management with frequent logistics contact, for example immediate superiors of logistics managers: detailed understanding of logistics management including recent developments;
- Logistics managers: in depth knowledge of trends and developments including exposure to best practice;
- Other managers with frequent contact, for example marketing or production managers: exposure to logistics including benefits available from adopting sound techniques;
- Logistics Dept staff: detailed on the job training including exposure to other logistics areas for future staff development.

SECTION 5 DESCRIPTION OF ACTUAL DEVELOPMENTS

4 Logistics and Supply Chain Strategy

A strategic plan was prepared over a period of two years. This followed extensive discussions within the headquarters, throughout the region and in the head office in Germany. Discussions included workshops, visits and meetings. Each of the companies was visited over the two year period to enable face to face dialogue which is extremely important in Asia.

Some of the factors that were included in the strategy were:

- a plan to review each company's logistics operations to establish the best organisational structure, to review the processes and procedures of the company and ensure the best personnel were available by way of transfer, recruitment etc.;
- a plan to establish the training needs of personnel in the region at all levels of the company and to allocate resources to conduct the training;
- development of a standardised logistics data processing and information system to be compatible with other activities such as production, marketing and finance;
- a plan to establish benchmarking in the region, including appropriate performance measurement criteria for each company based on the needs, structure and operations of each company;
- publication of policies and guidelines to standardise operations and provide guidance to the companies on the performance standards expected;
- a plan to investigate the feasibility of establishing a regional logistics concept to include activities such as regional distribution centres, coordinated raw material purchasing, coordinated regional shipping, centralised production planning etc.

SECTION 6 AUDIENCES/USES

Suitable for final year under-graduate or post graduate courses in logistics or supply chain management.

Also suitable for courses in international business and organisational behaviour to indicate cross cultural organisational difficulties and issues.

Suitable for class discussion or as an assignment/examination question.

Case 2

Brother International

European Distribution Strategy

David Taylor, *University of Huddersfield*

SECTION 1 CASE SYNOPSIS

This undisguised case describes the situation and problems in the parts supply system used by Brother International's European sales operation.

In the 1980s Brother had expanded through Europe by building a network of independent national sales offices in 13 countries and, as in many multinationals, these offices acted as autonomous profit centres with considerable independence in the development and control of their individual operating policies including that of parts acquisition. The company's sales of finished products (photocopiers, printers, PCs) had grown rapidly in the 1980s but the systems to supply parts had not kept pace. By the end of the decade the company was experiencing increasing problems with parts availability which was having a detrimental impact on the level of after sales support.

To address the issue Martin Crossley was appointed to the newly created position of European Parts Manager and the case presents the results of an audit of the situation which he carried out in the first six months of his appointment. It is based around 4 major issues :

- the creation of a pan-European logistics system;
- the need to develop a rational inventory management policy on a European basis;
- the need to develop a European wide information network to allow control of the parts system across Europe;
- the importance of developing and promoting policies in such a way as to gain acceptance from the managers of independent subsidiaries within a multinational corporation.

The case can be used at a strategic level requiring students to identify the problems and develop an overall policy or at a more detailed level particularly in relation to the analysis of inventory data and development of suitable inventory policies.

SECTION 2 TEACHING/LEARNING OBJECTIVES

- To require students to develop a policy for the improvement of the supply chain of a parts operation.
- To enable students to identify critical success factors in developing a coordinated European logistics policy across independent operating subsidiaries of a multinational company.
- To enable students to analyse inventory data and subsequently develop an inventory strategy and inventory operating policies and procedures.
- To enable students to appreciate the importance of an efficient parts supply system to a company's overall competitive position.

SECTION 3 MAIN ISSUES AND PROBLEMS

3.1 Issues to be addressed through the case

The main question arising from the case is what should Crossley do now that he has completed his situational review of the company and compiled data from the UK sales office. Advanced level students could be presented with the full task of developing a strategy, devising operational policies and implementation plans. If required, more detailed guidance could be given as to the type of issues to consider or the task split into its various component parts.

The following separate issues could be addressed through the case.

3.1.1 Logistics strategy issues

- Formulating the operating strategy for a complex multi-site operation.
- Consideration of major strategic decisions such as centralisation v decentralisation of stock; local control v central control.
- Consideration of the pros and cons of trying to develop an integrated European logistics system by reorganising on a pan-European basis the parts supply of autonomous operating units of a multi-national.

- The role, function and authority of the European coordinating office as an intermediary between European sales offices and the Japanese headquarters and factories.

3.1.2 Development of logistics operating policies and systems

There are 2 key issues which are central to this case: inventory management and information management.

Inventory management
The strategic issues of the case revolve around inventory problems and how to improve customer service and at the same time reduce inventory levels and costs. If required, there is sufficient detail on the inventory situation in the company to focus student attention entirely on the analysis of inventory without consideration of the wider strategic issues. Columns A to L in Exhibit 3 can be used for a strategic review primarily through Pareto analysis. The additional information in Columns M to X will however permit more detailed consideration of inventory issues such as stock holding costs, stock availability and service levels, obsolescence, stock-turn efficiency, etc. As with most real data not all the information provided is necessarily useful and it is a valuable exercise for students to identify the key parameters and sift out less relevant data.

Information management
The lack of reliable and relevant data at all points in the supply chain is a major issue. There is a requirement to devise an information system to control and monitor the parts supply system and this will involve specification of the required data for daily operation of the system (order processing, order tracking, etc.) and for the data required to monitor and control the system efficiency (stock levels, transport costs, etc.). There is also the question of the specification and development of the required software and hardware systems and the integration networks across Europe and if required, students could undertake an exercise specifically addressing this issue.

3.1.3 Logistics management and organisation issues

One of the key issues in practice in this case was the need to 'sell' the proposed solution to managers and staff at all levels in the company in order to get approval for changes in procedure and to gain support to make the changes successful. It was one thing for Crossley to devise a new operating strategy and in many respects this was relatively straight-forward; it was quite another to get cooperation from other people in the company to allow the strategy to be implemented. On the one hand he had to persuade his European chairman (a Japanese national) and the Japanese senior management at HQ in Japan that any proposed changes were and affordable within the context of a £5m p.a. parts operation; on the other hand he had to gain cooperation from highly autonomous LSO managers in 13 European countries to firstly cooperate in giving him data and then to accept the changes he proposed, which implicitly highlighted the inefficiency of their previous management of the parts system.

The need for 'cultural diplomacy' and 'selling the benefits of logistics' are key issues which students need to consider if the proposed operating strategies are to have any hope of success.

3.2 Analysis of problems

3.2.1 Poor customer service

Although no-one in the company had clearly identified the parameters with which to measure customer service, nor rigorously quantified customer service performance, staff and management were aware that service levels were unacceptable and deteriorating. Poor customer service is the key issue with this case, as the entire 'raison d'être' of the parts and spares system is as a service adjunct to the main product offerings of the company.

3.2.2 Unnecessary costs of operating the parts service

In appointing the European Parts Manager the company was not primarily aiming to save costs but was looking to improve service levels. No-one had ever identified the true costs of the European parts system as these costs were spread around the local offices and largely hidden within overheads and general staff costs and in any event were considered to be insignificant in relation to total company turnover. However when Crossley had completed his audit of the system, he quickly realised there were opportunities for significant costs savings and that if these could be actualised they would translate directly into the increased profit. The case does not contain sufficient data to fully quantify supply chain costs, but it is clear from the data supplied that there was an over-investment in stock and that transport of an increasing amount of product by airfreight was very costly.

3.3.3 Lack of a corporate policy to control and manage spares in Europe

Caused by:

- the company's sales-led philosophy – sale of new products was seen as the key measure of success and insufficient attention was paid to after-sales service in general and the logistics of parts supply in particular;
- rapid growth in turnover in the 1980s – the spares supplies system had not kept pace with the sales expansion and this was compounded because the demand for spares lagged 2 or 3 years behind the demand for new products;
- a key strategic issue at Brother was the failure to realise the importance of spares provision in the company's competitive positioning within the marketplace. Increasingly Brother products such as copiers, printers, etc. had become 'commodities' in that it was difficult to gain competitive advantage through differentiation of product characteristics or quality. By 1992 provision of the level of after sales service was becoming an increasingly important criteria in the customer's purchase (and re-purchase) decision;
- low turnover of the European spares operation £5m compared to £400 million company total turnover meant senior management did not devote much time to the issue;
- offices in Europe acting as independent profit centres meant they traditionally had autonomy in controlling their stock, which tended to preclude the development of coordinated inventory policies.

3.3.4 Information management issues

- The lack of any standardised information systems in Europe in terms of hardware, software or management information output.
- No integration of computer systems between local offices and the European central control in Manchester.
- Lack of real time information on demand levels, order status, product availability, delivery times.
- Lack of management information with which to monitor the effectiveness and efficiency of the parts supply chain
- Inefficient communication between offices, BIE and Japanese factories.

3.3.5 Staff issues

- Stock management was largely the responsibility of the local offices. Managers of these offices were primarily interested in sales and marketing and as a result did not have the time, expertise, or interest to develop the requisite warehouse and stock control procedures to ensure adequate parts management.
- The European parts control centre was grossly understaffed given the routine order processing and fire-fighting tasks which it faced daily. Effectively there was no parts manager at BIE only an administrator.
- Staff at the local offices involved in the parts system were overworked because of inadequate systems and procedures. As a result many were disillusioned and increasingly prone to errors which compounded the difficulties with parts supply.
- There was a great deal of resistance to 'Big Brother' interference from BIE as the LSOs were keen to retain their autonomy.
- However there was acknowledgement that a problem existed.

3.3.6 Operational problems with the parts supply chain

- Large number of lines stored at each location.
- Small number of active lines.
- Under-investment in fast moving lines.
- Over-investment in slow moving lines.
- Poor availability.
- Excessive obsolescence.
- Erratic lead times.
- Long lead times.
- Poor data integrity.
- Lack of information on delivery dates, order acceptance, alternatives and stock control.
- Poor stores management.
- Poor order handling.
- Incomplete lines of communication.
- Large numbers of staff, lacking skills.
- Poor space utilisation.
- High 'on-costs' – freight charges.
- Lack of confidence in the system.

3.3.7 Analysis of inventory data

Some of the more important points emerging from Exhibit 3 are as follows:

(i) 95% of sales by volume (Column L) and 91% of sales by value (Column R) are generated from 2145 lines (9% of lines) (Column C). It is quite feasible therefore to classify all these as 'A' lines and set stock levels so as to guarantee 100% availability.
(ii) There is a high proportion of obsolete stock. All SKUs selling less than one item per month could be regarded as obsolete, which represents 33% of total stock value (Columns D and E). In practice Crossley decided that any SKUs selling less than two items per month could be deemed obsolete (51%).
NB Obsolete here does not imply that SKU should be deleted from the company's product range but that it should be deleted from the European LSO stock holding.
(iii) Stock Turn ratio Column V
Only on 2 SKUs are there reasonable stock turn ratios of 8.31 and 3.52. On the rest of the product range it is below 2 and on the lowest selling SKUs it is below. In the lowest selling categories (<1) stock is turning over once every ten years!
(iv) Column T shows that on average 14% of SKUs were out of stock within some bands 24%. This does not measure those items which were vulnerable to going out of stock.
(v) If current stock is divided by average monthly demand (Column W and X), there are quite a number of instances where there are less than 4 months stock, which was the average order cycle time from Japan. Therefore many of these items are vulnerable to going out of stock.

SECTION 4 SPECIFIC QUESTIONS

General questions

1. Identify the main issues and problems facing Crossley with the existing parts system.
2. Devise an overall strategy for improving the parts supply system.
3. Develop detailed operational proposals for improving the key areas within the strategic proposal.
4. Identify the critical success factors in implementing the chosen strategy.

Specific inventory analysis questions

What are the key inventory performance parameters that should be extracted from Exhibit 3 (See section 3.7 of this note.)

- What policy should be adopted to categorise the company's parts stock? How should this policy be adjusted over time in order to respond to changes in demand patterns?
- Should stock holding and/or stock control be centralised at BIE or decentralised at the LSOs?
- What policy should be developed to determine re-order points and re-order levels? Should this be different for different stock categories (i.e. ABC categories)?
- What policy should be developed in relation to safety stock levels?
- How could you avoid the build up of obsolete stock as demand for parts decreases? How could you avoid out of stock situations as demand for parts increases?
- What should be the policy in regard to the obsolete stock held in Europe?

Approaches to these questions are contained within sections 3.3.7 and Section 5.

Section 5 Review of the actual strategy adopted by Brother

Three major issues were addressed: inventory policy, information policy and management acceptance.

5.1 The parts inventory policy

5.1.1 Pareto analysis

The policy adopted was based on Pareto analysis. Crossley chose the following categories :

Category of Items	Cumulative No of SKUs	% of total demand
A	2100	95.0
B	12000	97.0
C	25000	99.9

5.1.2 Stocking policy

Category A items:	All stocked at LSOs. Stock levels set to ensure 100% availability at each LSO. In addition 'European' safety stock of all A items was kept at BIE in Manchester.
Category B items:	All stocked at a newly constructed European parts distribution centre in Manchester with 100% availability. This significantly reduced the amount of B stock kept at LSOs but at the same time improved the availability within Europe. Some category B items were also stocked at LSOs where LSO managers felt this was desirable.
Category C items:	not kept in stock in Europe but ordered when required from Japan accepting the longer lead time or airfreighting where necessary.

5.1.3 European Parts Distribution Centre (EPDC)

A new European Parts Distribution Centre (EPDC) of approximately 1000 m2 was built in Manchester adjacent to the BIE offices. The storage and picking system was based on four semi-automated horizontal carousels which provided 16500 storage locations. Additionally there was a mezzanine floor with a further 15000 storage locations.

There was thus considerable planned spare capacity as initially the warehouse held only some 14000 SKUs. (2000 A lines and 12000 B lines).

The warehouse operated with a staff of seven and the BIE inventory administration system employed a further eight office staff. The total annual operating cost for both the warehouse and BIE inventory administration amounted to c £300,000 pa.

The EPDC was established as a cost/profit centre: it purchase stock from Japan and sold it on to LSOs with a margin to cover its operating costs.

5.1.4 The stock ordering system

An on-line computer network was developed to link all LSOs with BIE in Manchester. BIE became responsible for coordinating inventory data and stock ordering for all of Europe. The system captures real demand information i.e. actual sales plus orders for parts which are out of stock.

A 'moving' ABC categorisation
Each month the BIE computer calculates the demand profile individually for each LSO. Items are then classified as A, B or C dependent on whether they fall into the 95%, 97% or 100% bands. Each LSO has its own A, B, C categorisation. Demand is calculated as a 12 month moving average. Products thus move into and out of the A,B, C categories each month.

Order quantities
Each month LSOs order stock of 'A' items so as to build up 2 months' stock on the basis of the latest average monthly demand. Thus as the demand for an item rises, the level of stock held rises and as the demand falls the stock level falls, e.g.:

Month 1	Average Demand 50	Closing Stock 40	Order Quantity 60
Month 2	Average Demand 40	Closing Stock 60	Order Quantity 20

This policy guards against build up of obsolescent stock as demand starts to decline and reduces the possibility of being out of stock as demand starts to rise. A similar system was used for B items held by the EPDC.

To protect against sudden unexpected rises in demand and therefore vulnerability to out of stock, the BIE computer produces a daily exception report to show any items where demand is increasing rapidly. e.g. If more than 10% of stock is used in less than 10% of the time to the next stock replenishment, the stock controller can then decide whether to make an early order.

LSOs now carry on average about 2500 'A lines' with perhaps a further 8000 B lines. Their requirement for storage space and warehouse personnel has commensurably reduced as previously they were each carrying up to 25000 lines

Stock control has been changed from a situation where local offices could order any item in any amount, to a situation where BIE is pushing stock to them based on a central forecast of their requirements. Although LSOs can override BIE' s recommendations, in practice they normally accepted it.

All stock orders are placed on Japan by BIE. Monthly shipments are made from factories by sea freight to the EPDC. There is very little use of emergency airfreight. The order cycle time for B items from EPDC to LSOs is 5 days. Crossley was unable to improve order lead times from Japanese factories

5.2 The computer and information systems

Gaining control of the European parts stock first required gaining control of the information needed to control stock. The establishment of an on-line information system was a critical part of the improvement project. BIE employed a computer consultancy to work in the development of the tailored software and hardware systems needed to meet the functional requirements and link the geographically dispersed European operating units. The computer system permitted real time capture of demand, on-line order processing and status reporting.

A wide area network (WAN) was developed which had three major elements:

1. Order processing – capturing demand and processing orders.
2. Enquiries – order status, stock levels, expected delivery dates, etc.
3. Communications – between all the European sites.

The total cost of the new system from development through to installation was approximately £300,000.

The new computer system permitted centralised information control, which was the key to the development of rational operating policy.

All local offices in Europe had their own stand-alone systems which operated their business and of which stock control/order processing was just a part. It would have been too disruptive and too expensive to try and replace the 20 local systems with one standardised system. Therefore the new order processing/stock control system was designed as module that could be 'bolted on' to the systems existing in each local office- a critical feature in gaining its acceptance.

5.3 Management/organisational issues

Once Crossley realised the scope for improvement in the European parts system, his first job was to convince the Chairman of BIE of the potential benefits. This is never easy for a new manager, without any internal track record or previous concrete results.

It was compounded by the fact that the Chairman was Japanese and Crossley had to become accustomed to the different cultural business norms and in particular the difficulty of getting a straight 'yes' or 'no' answer to any proposal. He was however able to secure the Chairman's support for his data collection exercise which meant that the European managers of the LSOs were reluctantly obliged to cooperate with this new 'logistics whiz kid' from the European head office. However most managers left him in no doubt as to their lack of interest in his activity and scepticism as to any possible benefits.

Once he had devised the new system on paper, he had to spend a considerable amount of time and effort in educating the LSO managers in the benefits of better stock control and in the advantages of the system he was proposing. Again cultural differences and inter-European rivalries had to be overcome. A variety of techniques were employed including news-letters, seminars, and most importantly visits to all LSOs to speak to managers and warehouse staff.

A final and very important issue in terms of the proposed improvements was that the investment costs required to achieve the changes had to be recoverable in a relatively short pay-back period.

Two major capital expenditures were required:

1. the development of a new central European distribution centre at Manchester:
   - capital cost including building, computer hardware; and materials handling equipment
   approx £1.2m
   - Value of stock held   £1.0m
2. the development of the WAN computer systems
   - cost approximately   £0.3m

The new stock policy resulted in savings in acquired obsolescence alone of £500,000 pa and there were also savings due to reduced overall stock-holding. A significant but unquantified benefit resulted from the freeing of warehouse space at LSOs which was turned over to more profitable showroom space.

5.4 Achievements of the new policy

- Increased stock availability.
- Reduced back orders.
- Reduced stock holding.
- Reduced obsolescence.
- Improved age profile.
- Improved data integrity.
- Improved information flow.

- Reduced space utilisation for warehousing at LSOs.
- Improved financial control.
- Reduced use of air freight.

Although the customer service and financial performance of the LSOs was significantly improved, the local managers were reluctant to give more than a grudging acknowledgement that the new policy and operating system was beneficial.

Similarly Crossley received little direct thanks from the European chairman, although once the new system had been successfully instituted, he was asked to take responsibility for developing a European plan for the supply of accessories and was soon after appointed as European Logistics Manager. As such he became the first person recognised as a logistics manager in Brother's world-wide operation.

5.5 Footnote on centralisation of stock

In order to gain control over inventory Crossley felt it necessary to channel all stock through Manchester where he was based and also to have physical control over the items stocked in the EPDC. Two years after the EPDC was established he was of the opinion that maybe it was not so necessary to keep the physical stock adjacent to the information for stock control. As he approached his next task of reorganising the European accessories business (toner cartridges, typewriter ribbons, etc.), he felt that, as the WAN was in place throughout Europe, it might be preferable to centralise the control of stock in Manchester but to have physical stock not located in the EPDC but dispersed around the LSOs with an efficient system to transfer required stock between LSOs, if required. In other words there would be centralised European stock control but decentralised of the physical inventory.

SECTION 6 AUDIENCES/USES OF THE CASE

The case is suitable for use by students of logistics or operations management at Masters level, final year undergraduate or management development programmes.

It may also be useful on courses dealing with international business, cross cultural conflicts and organisational behaviour.

To fully appreciate the issues involved it will require 2 or 3 hours study prior to any class discussion or presentation.

The case can be used in a number of ways

- as a logistics strategy exercise
- as a detailed inventory analysis exercise :- analysis of the inventory data presented and development of specific operational suggestions for inventory management can be undertaken as a stand alone exercise based on Exhibit 2.
as a vehicle to discuss the development of cross cultural organisational structures

Case 3

GILLETTE

Creating A European Logistics Strategy

Martin Christopher,[1] *Cranfield University*

SECTION 1 CASE SYNOPSIS

The case looks back at the changes that have taken place in the logistics strategy for Europe at Gillette. The company originally was organised very much on a country-by-country basis with little integration between them. With the coming of the Single Market and the stated aim of the company to become global in its products and its marketing, the decision was taken to integrate logistics planning at a European level.

The case is based upon the reflections of the Director of Materials Management for Europe, David Harland, as he looked back over the seven years since he joined the company with the specific responsibility for bringing about an integrated logistics system.

A number of hurdles had to be overcome and these are highlighted in the case. Specifically these issues relate to (i) people and their reluctance to accept change, (ii) information and planning systems and the problems of systems implementation at a Europe-wide level, and (iii) customer service and the need to maintain ever high levels of performance with demanding retail customers.

SECTION 2 TEACHING/LEARNING OBJECTIVES

The case was written with the following objectives in mind:

1. To show how global companies are increasingly seeking to develop logistics strategies which will provide substantial cost economies yet will be better able to service the needs of local companies.
2. To highlight the obstacles that often stand in the way of achieving cross-country logistics integration.
3. To generate a wider discussion about the pros and cons of centralised, global logistics management.

SECTION 3 MAIN ISSUES AND PROBLEMS RAISED BY THE CASE

A number of issues are contained within the case:

1. The importance of centralised planning as a way of improving stock availability and forecast accuracy whilst reducing total stock holding. An opportunity exists at this point for the teacher to

---

[1] © Cranfield School of Management, February 1996. All rights reserved.

introduce the 'square root rule' which tells us that an approximate estimate of the reduction of inventory in a centralised system is given by:

$$\sqrt{\frac{nc}{no}}$$

where nc = number of stock locations in centralised system
        no = original number of stock locations.

Thus, for example, a reduction from 16 country warehouses to 4 regional warehouses might be expected to achieve a stock reduction of one half – whilst still providing higher stock availability through 'risk pooling'.

2. Whilst the marketing environment in Europe for Gillette's products is not discussed in any detail in the case, students can be encouraged to consider what the implications of the growing power of the European retailer might be for Gillette. In particular the desire by retailers to reduce their stock-holding, thus forcing suppliers to move to a 'just-in-time' delivery basis, can have serious ramifications for a centralised distribution strategy. A further implication is that if local stocks are no longer maintained, then replenishment lead-time from a central supply point may well be longer and there may be a loss of flexibility in response as well.

3. The problems of change management in logistics are a further issue in the case. By its very nature, attempts to integrate logistics activities across countries will involve significant change within the organisation. Individual country management will often be loath to give up decision-making power. Local sales management will also be concerned that a move to centralised distribution might significantly effect their ability to provide their customers with competitive service. This issue is a real one for many companies and the challenge is to find ways in which the local direct contact with the customer can be maintained and delivery performance enhanced whilst gaining the efficiency advantages of central distribution and purchasing.

The need for cross-functional working on a team basis is one aspect of change management that is relevant in this case and a useful discussion can be generated around this issue.

SECTION 4 SPECIFIC QUESTIONS

1. What are the implications of Gillette's experience for companies contemplating developing an integrated European, regional or global logistics strategy?
2. What are the pros and cons of centralised distribution for fast moving consumer goods companies like Gillette?
3. What role could a third-part logistics service company play in assisting organisations like Gillette to achieve their goals for European logistics integration?
4. How should large-scale change in logistics be managed? What are the human resource and organisational issues raised by this type of logistics change?

SECTION 5 FURTHER DEVELOPMENTS

Gillette has continued to extend its centralised strategy for Europe. They intend to reduce further the number of European warehouses down to five. They have the objective of making more use of 'cross dock' distribution centres, perhaps looking at shared use with other suppliers and making more use of third party logistics service providers.

They are achieving big cost economies through centralised purchasing. They have also been focusing attention upon opportunities for consolidating inbound and outbound shipments through return loads wherever possible and for consolidated delivery with other parts of Gillette.

In information systems they are moving from main frame computers to client servers. The use of EDI links with customers has grown and they are now forecasting and planning all demand replenishment centrally.

The view of Gillette is that logistics management has contributed greatly to the continued improvement in return on investment. In what is in effect a mature market, Gillette's financial performance has clearly benefited from the cost reductions achieved through logistics integration.

SECTION 6 AUDIENCES/USES OF THE CASE

This strategic case is suitable for post-graduate or advanced under-graduate students on courses in supply chain management or Business strategy.

Cases 4 and 5

HASBRO EUROPE AND NIKE

Developing European Logistics Strategy

Martin Ashford, *Head of Logistics, The Financial Times, London*

SECTION 1 SYNOPSIS

Both of these cases concern multinational corporations moving from national structures in Europe to more integrated or centralised logistics. They are both real cases and the data is genuine, although inevitably much has changed in the time since Touche Ross Management Consultants undertook the projects.

The cases can be addressed in largely qualitative ways or – particularly Hasbro – lend themselves also to quantitative analysis. The emphasis is not on detailed number crunching but on developing an understanding of how costs behave as you apply varying logistics scenarios and of the relative importance of the different cost headings.

The main issues evoked by the cases include:

- What are the key drivers behind the development of a pan-European logistics strategy? How does such a strategy impact on the organisation, its people and its customers?
- The importance of inventory as a key cost driver. Arguably, if you cannot achieve significant stock reductions it is not worth even considering rationalisation of European operations.
- The hidden cost of product obsolescence in seasonal and volatile markets.
- The differences between the 'best' solutions to two apparently similar situations, dependent upon the nature of the products, markets and service requirements faced by the businesses concerned.
- The downstream impact of long production lead times. Although the consultants were not allowed to develop this theme, there might be an interesting argument for suggesting that some of the money spent on downstream warehousing could have been better invested in shortening production cycles.
- The difficulty of managing long supply chains stretching from factories in the Far East to shops in Europe. This is a situation faced today by almost all producers or retailers of consumer goods.

- Other issues surrounding the cases, although not developed in any detail, include the development of systems to support European logistics, the choice between in-house and contracted operations and the human and cultural obstacles to large-scale corporate change.

SECTION 2 TEACHING AND LEARNING OBJECTIVES

The cases should enable students to:

- familiarise themselves with the issues surrounding European logistics strategies, as outlined in the previous section;
- demonstrate an ability to 'see the wood from the trees' by sifting through quite a lot of data and information in order to identify the key elements;
- analyse and understand the behaviour of logistics costs as you vary the number and location of distribution facilities;
- consider the practical implications of a 'strategic' decision and appreciate some of the hurdles that may have to be overcome in order to implement it;
- realise that there is no single answer to a question like 'how many distribution centres should I have in Europe'. To say that 'it all depends on your business' is neither original or exciting. It happens, however, to be true.

To get the most from the cases, students should read both of them in outline, although time may allow them really to work only on one. For that one case they will need adequate preparation time fully to understand the information presented in it, before either coming to their own conclusions or contributing to a discussion.

There is scope for some significant quantitative analysis and this is important if the full benefit of the cases is to be achieved. In the case of Hasbro, students should attempt to estimate the costs of the various scenarios for their European distribution, by making some sensible assumptions and extrapolations from the partial data given in the tables and exhibits. In the case of NIKE, the case provides the first-cut comparison of operating costs as calculated by the consultants. However, students should work out for themselves the costs of stockholding and close-outs and should be encouraged to explore the impact on these of varying the underlying assumptions.

SECTION 3 MAIN ISSUES AND PROBLEMS

3.1 Hasbro

Students deserve a black mark if they miss the fact that one of the key issues here is language-specific packaging! This is important because each language-variant has to be treated as a separate SKU. If two warehouses, say in France and Germany, are combined you would normally expect a benefit in the provision of picking faces (one face required per SKU) and in the inventory level (less buffer stock for a single inventory than for two partial inventories). However, if the SKUs are country-specific, this will not happen. Without such savings, it is difficult if not impossible to justify centralisation. In this case, Hasbro accepted the need to move, gradually, towards multi-lingual packaging for some kinds of products but no dramatic change was considered possible or desirable, particularly for products such as games where the contents themselves (gameboards, cards) are often language-specific.

Even without this, it is debatable how much stock reduction would follow from centralisation. Most inventory theory assumes a situation of reorder and replenishment. However, for Hasbro, there is only very limited scope to reorder on the factory. The inventory is built up during the summer and then run down rapidly in peak season. The usual analysis of cycle stock and buffer stock is hard to apply here.

Another issue concerning the product itself is its bulkiness. The cost price is stated in the text to be $430 per cubic metre. This can be contrasted with NIKE's product: using the data from Exhibit XIII, the average cost price for footwear was $2,550 per cubic metre and for apparel $6,000. The higher the value per cubic metre, the less significant is the cost of transport and the greater is the benefit of stock reduction through centralisation.

There is a potential issue on customer service. Given the rapid replenishment expected by retailers at peak times, would a single European distribution centre be able to cope? Students may be able to estimate over how much of Europe it is feasible to offer deliveries within 24 hours, 48 hours or 72 hours. In practice, this probably would not have been a serious constraint. From a location in (say) Benelux, 48 hour delivery is possible to most areas, excluding remote locations such as Southern Italy, and 24 hour service can be had to the 'core' areas of the UK, France and Germany without having to resort to expensive express services.

Factory lead times are a critical issue, although not one that the consultants went into in any detail. Hasbro set an objective of trying to improve warehouse stock turns from four to six, and it was hard to see how this could be achieved without real reductions in factory cycle times. It is worth considering where Hasbro might best invest its money: in building storage space or in installing improved production lines. Another angle would be to consider how control over inbound goods might be improved (tracking, better information on expected dates of arrival, etc.) to enable better planning and avoid unnecessary delays.

The choice of technology for the warehouse(s) is not a simple one. The plans put forward for Soest by the German subsidiary included very sophisticated automated storage, but this was hard to justify in a situation where capacity had to be installed for peak volumes which only occurred for a few weeks in every year. Simpler, more labour-intensive solutions were proposed by the consultants. From a practical standpoint, however, one needs to be concerned at the size of facility that would be required if all stock were centralised: Exhibit VII shows a "low bay" solution totalling 119,000 square metres which is extremely large by any standards.

A further thing to bring out is the way in which different parameters drive different parts of the logistics cost profile:

- the sizing of a pick cell is driven largely by the number of **SKUs**;
- the sizing of a storage cell is driven by the volume of **stock**;
- the mechanical equipment used in a distribution centre will be determined by **peak** throughput volumes, whereas staffing will generally be based on **average** throughputs with some use of seasonal or temporary labour.
- transport costs may be driven by the **order** profile as much as by distance.

The options for Hasbro's logistics structure included:

- Complete or partial centralisation of the operation in Europe. This is discussed below;
- Use of European factory sites as warehousing locations. Potentially this could minimise stocks and avoid wasteful double movement of product. However, none of the current sites were particularly well provided with storage facilities or land for expansion. If they were to be used in this way, would they still be used to replenish national 'satellite' warehouses or should they deliver direct to customers?
- Holding stock back in the Far East. The consultants did not look at this in any detail, but there could be advantages in holding stock close to source and shipping it to Europe only just in time for the peak season. If this were done, how should the supply chain be controlled? Culturally, it would be difficult to persuade European management to leave 'their' inventory on the other side of the world.

The consultants' modelling revolved around the existing warehouse locations. A single site at Creutzwald would be conceivable, although very large. Increasing the number of sites to 4 adds in facilities in the UK, Spain and Italy, leaving Creutzwald to service the central parts of Europe. One problem which starts to emerge is that, for optimal transport, a site at Valencia would naturally service parts of Southern France. From a warehousing point of view, however, this would involve a substantial increase in the number of SKUs to be held there and it should be prevented for that reason.

Adding a fifth warehouse causes further problems of this kind. Ter Apel is preferable, on cost grounds, to a site in Germany but the transport model then tries to split Germany between Ter Apel and Creutzwald. Again, the model has to be overridden to prevent this. Only for a six warehouse solution is a site added in Germany (Soest) and this reduces Ter Apel to a minor role.

The data in the case is sufficient to allow some estimates of cost to be made for these solutions. Ignoring stockholding costs, the actual results obtained by the consultants were as follows:

$ million per annum	Inbound transport	Warehouse	Outbound transport	Total
One European distribution centre (Creutzwald)	10.05	22.77	16.88	49.7
Two DCs (Creutzwald/Newport)	10.08	23.56	13.19	46.8
Three DCs (Cr, Newpt, Valencia)	10.18	24.11	11.36	45.7
Four DCs (Cr, Newpt, Val, Milan)	10.34	24.71	11.01	46.1
Five DCs (Cr, Newpt, Val, Mil, Ter Apel)	10.19	25.39	10.48	46.1
Six DCs (Cr, Newpt, Val, Mil, TA, Soest)	10.26	26.47	10.48	47.2

This shows that complete centralisation was not viable for Hasbro and, moreover, that the decision was very marginal in the range of three to five distribution centres. Partly on pragmatic grounds (existing infrastructure, avoidance of problems in serving Southern Italy) the consultants concluded that a four distribution centre strategy would be the best. However, even the six centre solution only increased total logistics costs by $1.5 million per annum (3 per cent). Hasbro favoured this approach, which enabled all the main countries to retain their 'own' warehouse while avoiding 'putting too many eggs in one basket' by using Creutzwald as the single centre for the core of continental Europe.

3.2 NIKE

In the case of NIKE, the outstanding issue which students must pick up on is the potential impact of centralisation on inventory levels and close-outs.

From the data supplied in the case (Exhibit XIII) the following costs can be calculated ($ million per annum throughout):

STOCK	Footwear	Apparel
(Annual volume * cost price/stock turns * interest rate)		
National structures	13.66	7.97
Single European DC	12.13	6.98
Two DCs	12.13	7.44
Three DCs	12.13	7.44
CLOSE-OUTS		
(Value of sales @ full price * % unsold * % discount)		
National Structures	63.50	33.36
Single European DC	42.33	16.68
Two DCs	42.33	24.33
Three DCs	42.33	24.33

If these figures are added to the total operating costs shown in Table 4, the following total cost profile is obtained:

TOTAL COST $ millions	Footwear	Apparel
National structures	135.3	70.3
Single European DC	108.2	43.8
Two DCs	109.0	53.6
Three DCs	108.5	56.1

This analysis was done by the consultants for the November 1992 workshop. It shows very clearly not just that there was a strong case for centralisation but also where the greatest savings lay: in reducing the anticipated level of close-outs! Cynics might, at this point, wonder what point there was in the consultants building elaborate transport models whose impact on the final result was far less than that of two simple numbers (percentage of close-outs and percentage discount) which were virtually plucked from the air. In practice, this result led to a lot more hard thinking about what NIKE would need to do in order to drive down both current inventory and the level of unsold goods.

What is particularly interesting about this is that the key number – the 'opportunity cost' of unsold goods – is not a figure that ever appears on the profit and loss account, let alone in the logistics manager's reports. Discounts are generally deducted from revenue at a very early stage and are a truly 'hidden' cost.

Based on these figures, the consultants recommended to the November 1992 workshop that NIKE should centralise apparel but consider a two-warehouse strategy for footwear, based on Belgium and Southern France. The latter was chosen for its potential for importing through Marseille, although the poor industrial record of most Mediterranean ports gave rise to concern. The figures were, however, extremely sensitive to variation in the input assumptions on inventory and close-outs. The underlying assumption in NIKE's own estimates was that two or even three footwear warehouses could be run as a single inventory without any increase in stock levels. For apparel, knowing the problems that the business experienced in managing these products, the assumption was that there were further savings to be had from a single physical location. These are clearly debatable points.

Students should not find it difficult to appreciate that the stockholding issues are the key to the NIKE strategy. Once this has been grasped, various other issues need to be considered, including:

- The impact of the futures programme on flows. This is in many ways good news for the logistics manager and for a centralised strategy, as it enables bulk deliveries to be pre-programmed and sent out on relatively relaxed lead times. It also means, however, that good information on incoming goods and expected availability is vital to the management of the business.

- Service standards to different parts of Europe. As noted for Hasbro, delivery of goods within 48 hours is possible from Benelux to much of the 'core' of Europe. However, if there had been a more substantial requirement for 24 hour service, or if 48 hour delivery had been the norm even to remote regions, there might have been a different outcome to this case.
- Service to Scandinavia. The 'EFTA'[2] countries were, at the time, considering membership of the EU. Serving Scandinavia from Benelux would then become feasible, although service times might be an issue especially for the Northern regions. An alternative would be to have all bulk stock in the central warehouse and a 'satellite' in Scandinavia.
- Customs. There are clear benefits to a business such as NIKE in holding goods under Customs bond until they are required. Fortunately, this is becoming easier although the authorities are more flexible in some countries than in others.
- Logistics management. One of the biggest hurdles facing NIKE was to create a central management team capable of achieving the inventory reductions and other savings which would give the strategy its payback. There had to be a measure of centralisation of purchasing, sales order processing, inventory management, allocation of product to customers, etc. To back this up, major new systems were required. For example, a salesman in (say) Italy, in order to confirm an order to a customer, would need to know in real time if there was product available in the central warehouse. This need implied major networks spanning the whole of Europe. Putting the networks and local systems in place was a massive task for NIKE even with a single-site development. Their IT people warned that it might be impossible to achieve it within the planned timescale if several distribution centres were to be brought on-stream at the same time.

SECTION 4 SPECIFIC QUESTIONS

Some suggested questions are as follows:

4.1 Hasbro

- What options for Hasbro's distribution network should the consultants include in their analysis?
- Use the data in the case to estimate the operating costs of a centralised strategy based on a single warehouse, compared to the six-warehouse base case and to other options that you feel should be considered. Which strategy would you recommend, and why?
- What features of the product range are of most significance to the logistician? Assess the issues for stock management within Hasbro.
- Do you believe that there is a need for improvements to the upstream logistics (i.e., sourcing, manufacturing and shipment to European warehouse)? What changes would you recommend?
- Discuss how changes to the logistics network might impact on the service provided to customers. Suggest how the benefits can be maximised and the pitfalls avoided.

4.2 NIKE

- Use the data in the case to estimate the effect of complete or partial centralisation on the holding cost of inventory and on the loss of revenue resulting from close-outs. What impact do these factors have on the total logistics costs? How sensitive are your conclusions to changes in the underlying assumptions shown in Exhibit XIII?
- What strategy should the consultants recommend? Is complete centralisation the best solution?
- What options exist for the design of NIKE's new warehouse(s)? Which technologies and handling methods should be analysed for handling footwear and apparel (different solutions may

---

[2] European Free Trade Area, now disbanded.

apply to the two types of product) and what would be their respective advantages and disadvantages?
- Consider in outline the implications of your recommended strategy on the information systems requirements of the business. What systems would management need in order to run the future operation?
- How would you set about creating a pan-European transport network to service the new strategy? Do you believe that a single carrier could handle the traffic from a central warehouse to all parts of the continent?
- NIKE's General Managers, in each country, were previously running their own quasi-autonomous businesses. If they are to lose part of their operational responsibility, how would you 'sell' this to them? What are the potential advantages to them?

SECTION 5 WHAT ACTUALLY HAPPENED

5.1 Hasbro

As already seen, the consultants reached the conclusion that four warehouses would be 'optimal' but that six represented a practical solution which fitted with the company's existing infrastructure at relatively slight additional cost. On this basis the key tasks were to integrate the fragmented operations in Germany and France.

Hasbro accepted this recommendation. The German management put forward a financial proposal for a new warehouse on the site at Soest, which was accepted: the new building opened early in 1994.

Meanwhile, the French subsidiaries were combined managerially and some rationalisation took place, using the Creutzwald site as a basis. In all countries, Hasbro continued the full integration of the previously separate Hasbro and Kenner Parker businesses. The business remains structured primarily on a national basis but with considerably enhanced central coordination at the European level. The factory at Ter Apel closed at the end of 1994 as part of the ongoing restructuring of the business, but warehousing for the Benelux countries continued on the site after production ceased.

5.2 NIKE

True to its slogan ('Just Do It'), NIKE moved forward at top speed. The November 1992 workshop was used to obtain 'buy-in' from key managers from both Europe and the US, primarily for the centralisation of apparel. The consultants suggested a 2-warehouse strategy for footwear, but this was less clear-cut and was left for further review.

The work of the consultants continued after the workshop. Detailed site selection was carried out, leading to the purchase of a site at Meerhout, Belgium, close to the Dutch border and very well served by highways and other infrastructure. The apparel strategy model outputs were reviewed in detail and full comparison made against the incremental cost of upgrading and modifying existing infrastructure (this was to respond to some criticism of the 'greenfield' basis of the analysis). Detailed warehouse specification was undertaken for the apparel facility.

By mid 1993 construction was underway, with Touche Ross still acting as project managers. The new facility began receiving apparel in September 1994 and delivering to customers in January 1995. By this time a complete European transport tender had been undertaken and carriers selected, and major new IT systems had been developed in-house by NIKE. The central organisation had been greatly strengthened, with a new role for purchasing, stock control and carrier management at the central level. National warehouses began to be wound down.

While all this was happening, the consultants reviewed the strategy for footwear. The assumptions on stock turns and close-outs were reassessed and it became hard to justify the second proposed distribution centre in Southern France. A number of hybrid approaches were investigated, including the continuing use of the Paris facility. Finally, however, it was decided that footwear should also be centralised on the same site as apparel (this possibility had been allowed for in the design of Phase 1). This second stage construction started receiving footwear in the summer of 1995 for shipment to retailers in January 1996.

The total cost of the project to NIKE, including systems, was well over $100 million but it had an expected payback of under two years. Some outline details of the new European distribution centre are:

- high bay warehouse (semi-automated bulk storage): approximately 14,000 square metres, with a height of 28 metres;
- low bay picking and packing module for apparel: approximately 23,000 square metres with mezzanine for picking and extensive conveyor systems to take picked orders to value-added and packing areas prior to despatch;
- low bay for footwear: approximately 27,000 square metres including an automated carton sorter for individual pairs of shoes;
- office block: approximately 9,000 square metres.

In all, the building measures around 75,000 square metres and sits on a 32 hectare site with extensive landscaping.

SECTION 6 USES OF THE CASES

The cases have been presented deliberately as a pair, since they lend themselves to a discussion of the similarities and differences between them. While each is complete in itself, it is recommended that they be used together. The best way of doing this, assuming that class numbers allow, will be for the students to be divided into at least two groups such that half of them can work on Hasbro and the other half on NIKE. They could then either work individually before the case is discussed in class, or work in groups to come to a collective version for presentation to the class.

The range of issues, and the combination of qualitative and quantitative elements, makes the cases very suitable for use as a group assignment. Either case, on its own, could be used as an individual written assignment although this should be supplemented with class discussion to ensure that the contrasting nature of the two businesses is adequately explored. It is not recommended, however, for individual students to be asked to work on both cases at once ('compare and contrast') since this is likely to lead to superficiality. The comparison is much better made through class discussion.

In view of the length of the cases, and the amount of material to be digested, they are not really suitable for use in examinations.

Case 6

VALKYRIE LIGHTING

Global Supply Chain Management[3]

Daniel F. Carr, *Hewlett-Packard Corporation* and **Philip B. Schary**, *Oregon State University*

SECTION 1 CASE SYNOPSIS

This disguised case is based on the situation facing a division of a major US corporation which manufactures lighting equipment. It is designed to introduce the concepts of supply chain design and implementation. The progression of supply chain development is from structure to organization to process. The content takes the structure of the supply chain as given.. The supply chain is global, both in terms of sources of supply and of finished product distribution. The case requires users to identify and prioritise the main problems with the supply chain and then to develop a workable model for supply chain operation. A critical issue relates to the relationship with a key supplier.

SECTION 2 TEACHING/LEARNING OBJECTIVES

1. To allow students to consider the main problems and issues in a large scale global supply chain
2. To examine the relationship with a key components supplier and how this can be managed to facilitate wider improvements in supply chain operations
3. To consider appropriate methods of entry into foreign markets and how these will impact on supply chain structures and operations
4. To highlight the importance of the relationship between supply chain management, sales/marketing management and production management

SECTION 3 MAIN ISSUES AND PROBLEMS

The dominant problem is the relationship with a key supplier Sunshine. If that could be solved, everything else might be solvable, albeit with certain trade-offs. The main problem is that Sunshine if not a dominant partner is at least independent enough that they are not a satellite of Valkyrie. At the same time, they create several problems for Valkyrie's production planning: erratic delivery, lack of open communication and inflexibility in their own production. Valkyrie needs Sunshine's technology but is limited by their production schedule.

---

[3] This case is based on a real situation but the names of the companies and individuals concerned have been changed for reasons of commercial confidentiality.

There are also other problems in the wings:

1. intense competition, particularly by the new rival,
2. product proliferation, resulting in costly inventory investment,
3. erratic sales caused by
   - customer behavior and
   - sales policies (or their lack),
4. computer and communication compatibility,
5. the need for production flexibility,
6. overseas expansion with its choice of methods of entry and the issue of third party provider control.

The competition will gain over Valkyrie if they can get their own supply and quality problems solved. This makes the supply chain solution into a strategic answer. It also places a time imperative on any solution.

Product proliferation could be solved in several ways: restricting the number of products, getting the sales force to encourage sales concentration in a few items, or by developing modular products which can be assembled at the last moment.

The first cause of erratic sales may not be solvable. In fact, it looks like it could be getting worse as retailers assert their power, and contractors ask for more responsive delivery. The second one can be remedied by a combination of modifying policy and giving sales reps access to the production schedule.

Computer compatibility ultimately relates to the relationship with Sunshine. This could include the EDI problem. It may be impossible to get Sunshine to change its entire system for compatibility with Valkyrie. The alternative is either to live with this situation by investment in inventory, or create a cell within Sunshine with computer operating and data systems matched to Valkyrie's.

Flexibility can be achieved to some degree by product design modularity. It could also be reduced by reducing the need for flexibility through reduced variety. The real solution could lie in the Sunshine relation. If Sunshine could be made more flexible through production and procurement changes, or by modularizing Sunshine's own component products, the problem could be eased. There is also a need to look at Sunshine's own procurement policies to see if their suppliers could become more flexible and short the 60 day lead time.

SECTION 4 SPECIFIC QUESTIONS

The two main questions raised by the case are as follows :

1. Define, categorise and prioritise the main problems facing the supply chain planning team
2. Develop a specification of the key requirements and operational features of the supply chain from sources of supply, through manufacturing, to distribution.

Other more specific or supplementary questions might include :

3. What should be the teams' objectives in terms of the management of the relationship with Sunshine ? Consider how those objectives might practically be met .
4. Evaluate the various methods by which Valkyrie might enter the European Market. Which method would you recommend and why?
5. Consider the relationship between supply chain policies and marketing / sales policies. To what extend should these policies be jointly planned
6. Is it feasible for either Valkyrie or Sunshine to operate a low inventory production system, when some of Sunshine's components are sourced in the Far East? If so how should the international logistics pipeline be designed and operated.
7. To what extent can and should Valkyrie's production policies be modified as part of the new supply chain approach ?

SECTION 5 A POSSIBLE SOLUTION

5.1 The relationship with Sunshine

The key problem is Sunshine. Development of a closer relationship is desirable. This could be accomplished by offering to finance a new production line like Falkner suggested, backed up by independent production planning, perhaps by Valkyrie itself. This line or lines would be completely under the control of Valkyrie. This line would be supported by a separate computer and EDI system directly connected to Valkyrie's plant in Denver and which would also interface with Sunshine's own system. The Sunshine procurement system is a little less clear. Is it possible to make it more responsive, or is its behavior determined by the pattern of past business practices? Organizations have institutional memories and these older practices might be difficult to overcome.

How would Sunshine be motivated to make this change? Perhaps the prospect of steady business might be successful, coupled with some financial inducement in addition to Valkyrie's investment in the Sunshine line and computer. The additional cost would be equated against the net value of additional sales made possible through increased flexibility.

5.2 Marketing and sales policies

At the same time, sales policies could be changed to encourage long-term contracting with retailers with more stability in the ordering pattern. Standard products could be produced and shipped directly to customers as needed. Contractors are a more difficult problem. Their need for JIT delivery could be turned to competitive advantage. A pattern of delivery could be developed so that early signals of construction delay could be turned into changes in the production schedule.

5.3 Production policies

Production scheduling could commit a portion of capacity to standard lines which would be produced on regular schedules. Other products could be designed for modularity and assembled on demand.

The complete problem of product line proliferation and flexible production is not solvable without drastic change, such as licensing Sunshine's designs and technology and producing in-house. This would avoid the lead time delays from transportation from Taiwan to Denver. The flexibility problem then devolves to production system and product design. This of course would have higher cost, but it may be necessary with the competitive environment.

SECTION 6 AUDIENCES/TEACHING SUGGESTIONS

The case is suitable for final year undergraduate or masters level students on courses in logistics, supply chain management or operations management

It would also be useful for courses dealing with marketing or international business

For realism, a sense of time urgency could be added to reflect management pressures.

The role playing approach could be used, with participants taking on the functional orientations of individual team members.

Part 2

Purchasing and Supplies Management

Case 7

FILTON AEROSTRUCTURES
Procurement and supply management

Peter Hines, *Cardiff University Business School*

SECTION 1 CASE SYNOPSIS

This true case describes the changing situation facing the Filton Aerostructures company as it sought to make improvements to its Procurement function. The Bristol (England) based company was a second tier supplier to the European Airbus Consortium that manufactures aircraft.

Filton Aerostructures, like most other firms in the industry, was facing a period of rapid change involving the downsizing of their operations and in particular their staff numbers. In addition to this the company was also seeking ambitious improvements in terms of cost reduction, stock turn, production lead times and overhead costs. All of this has had a serious impact on Procurement with sizeable staff reductions.

The Procurement function fell in size from 58 in 1993 to 38 in 1995. These staff were organised in a traditional manner under John Ramsay, the Procurement Manager and his four managers representing: purchasing, expediting and scheduling, administration and change management. As such a fairly hierarchical command chain was in existence within Procurement.

The function was facing many difficulties in its daily operations, not least because of a history of poor relationships with its internal customers and external suppliers as well as poor organisation within the function itself. The essence of the case as it can be used with students is to identify a way out of the problems faced by John Ramsay. The case is perhaps typical of a company going through major change with an initial traditional approach to management. As such it offers students abundant opportunity to try to understand a common, real world scenario, analyse its problems and seek to not only build a solution but also an implementation plan to take John Ramsay and his staff towards this desired outcome.

28 Purchasing and Supplies Management

SECTION 2 TEACHING/LEARNING OBJECTIVES

1. To provide students with the opportunity to understand a case of major change in a real company and its implications for the Procurement function.
2. To provide scope for analysing the problems inherent in the existing Procurement function.
3. To review how organisational structures within Procurements can be radically changed if circumstances dictate.
4. To help students to understand how to plan strategic change and its subsequent implementation.

SECTION 3 MAIN ISSUES AND PROBLEMS RAISED BY THE CASE

1. How to cope with the reduction of staff numbers in Procurement.
2. How to introduce 'lean' ideas into an industry that has traditionally been over staffed.
3. How to achieve better customer satisfaction in the Procurement function.
4. How to improve internal and external communications.
5. How to improve supplier performance.
6. How to improve relationships with suppliers and customers.
7. How to reduce inventory levels.
8. How to achieve better demand forecasting.
9. How to ensure a continual improvement of suppliers.
10. How to survive in a rapidly changing industry.

SECTION 4 SPECIFIC QUESTIONS

1. What are the major problems and issues facing John Ramsay as he seeks to develop the Procurement function?
2. Review how the company should reorganise its Procurement function in the light of the redundancy programme and the changing needs of its internal and external customers. Explain why this approach is likely to be successful.
3. What other programmes or changes may be required to gain competitive advantage through Procurement and the supplier base?
4. What planning process should the company go through to decide upon its strategy and subsequently implement it?
5. Describe how Filton Aerostructures may go about implementing the changes outlined in questions 2-4. What potential problems will the company face and how can these be overcome?

SECTION 5 DESCRIPTION OF ACTUAL DEVELOPMENTS IN THE COMPANY

This section will summarise the response that Filton Aerostructures made to the situation as described in the case.

5.1. Procurement reorganisation

After a detailed review process (described in 5.3 below) a completely new structure for Procurement was arrived upon as depicted below (Figure 2.1). This structure moved away from the more traditional split between purchasing, expediting, administration and change to one that was more customer focused. Thus the function was split into customer focused teams which included specialists from each of the traditional sub-functions, but working as a group in a dedicated way. In addition these teams were co-located with their internal customers so that the Procurement function took on a 'virtual' nature as they were no longer one large central, but remote function. Thus, for example, a team of four people including the group leader would work in the fabrication area of Filton Aerospace. This team would carry out all of the traditional Procurement tasks for its internal customers in the fabrication job shop which makes a wide range of complex assemblies using cellular manufacturing methods.

The other customer focus teams were distributed among the other significant, but different, operational manufacturing areas within the business. Thus the other manufacturing areas had five Procurement staff allocated to each of them. These other areas included the machining shop, the bonding shop (where metal adhesion is carried out), the assembly shop as well as manufacturing services (where a range of jigs are made specific for individual customers).

The advantages of this were that staff were on the spot to solve potential problems for their customers and hence help them to avoid difficulties with, and disappointments to, external customers. Each of the value stream groups was headed by a group leader rather than a traditional manager showing a cultural shift to a more TQM style approach. As such teamworking and multi-skilling were being encouraged. This meant that when the team had to respond to, for instance, a purchasing problem, this could be done either by the purchasing specialist or by any other team member. Thus the suppliers have a clearer view of who they were selling to and could therefore be more responsive and enter into closer communications and were thus more likely to be encompassed in a closer relationship with Filton Aerostructures.

New Procurement Organisation 1/5/95

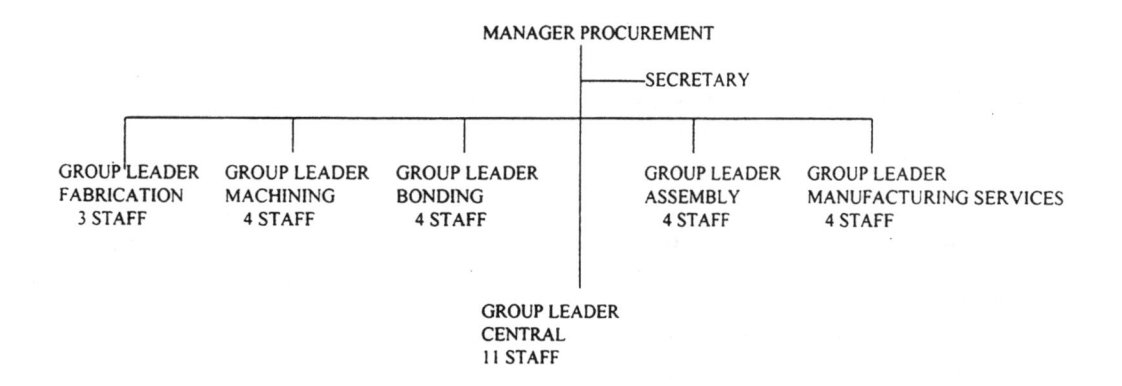

```
                        MANAGER PROCUREMENT
                               |
                               |———SECRETARY
    _____|_____
    |            |             |             |            |
GROUP LEADER  GROUP LEADER  GROUP LEADER  GROUP LEADER  GROUP LEADER
FABRICATION   MACHINING     BONDING       ASSEMBLY      MANUFACTURING SERVICES
3 STAFF       4 STAFF       4 STAFF       4 STAFF       4 STAFF
                               |
                         GROUP LEADER
                         CENTRAL
                         11 STAFF
```

Figure 2.1 New procurement organisation

The second part of the new structure which is noteworthy is that a Central Procurement Group was created. The reason for this is that some tasks are better dealt with in this way than in the dispersed teams. Examples of these tasks would be: training, supplier coordination, supplier development and purchasing of consumables. This Central section together with the group leaders was also charged with looking for ways of improvement and further development of systems and supplier linkages.

5.2. Other changes

One of the reasons for the organisational change was to support a move from operational status of the function to a more strategic role which was capable of planning, initiating and running improvement programmes for Filton Aerostructures and the suppliers alike. There are three key areas that were addressed in order to achieve this, the first showing benefits in the short term, the second building from the short term to major benefits in the long term and the third largely in the long term:

5.2.1 Improved forecasting/JIT implementation

Before the changes the forecasting system was not providing suppliers with a good forward vision of requirements. This often resulted in shortages or high stocks. As a result forecasting improvements were undertaken coupled with a move to JIT delivery. Although a PC based forecasting system was in operation it was felt necessary to forge closer relations with internal customers and so help improve the accuracy of schedules. This was largely achieved through the co-location of Procurement staff with the internal customers so that information flow could largely be verbal and so fast and direct. This therefore avoided misunderstanding between Procurement staff and their internal customers. In addition raw materials such as aluminium were changed from purchases based on last months usage to a system based on scheduled usage, with rapid call off from suppliers, rather than on large scale stock holding.

This approach meant that suppliers given a week's lead time are now achieving near 100 per cent on-time delivery rather than the previous 60-70 per cent. This resulted in the requirement for less safety stock and speculative purchasing meaning that accountable purchased stocks fell by 50 per cent with an improved level of service to internal customers. This change happened in a period of just over a year.

5.2.2 Continual improvement programme

A continual improvement programme called 'CIP Lifeline' was introduced in order to encourage suppliers to adopt a kaizen approach within their organisations. The Charter associated with this move stated:

> Through working with suppliers & customers, Procurement will consolidate and improve upon their competitiveness in the market place. The benefits of CIP will be shared between customers and suppliers, thus increasing profitability through the elimination of waste. The CIP philosophy will ensure no adversarial relationships exist.

This initiative was driven by the Central Procurement team as well as other functions within Filton Aerostructures. The basic process by which it worked was to benchmark the individual suppliers so that a datum point can be created and the opportunities for improvement estimated. The individual supplier was then given a presentation on the findings by the cross functional customer teams. Then, depending on resources, suppliers were invited to a CIP workshop usually carried out at the supplier's premises.

These CIP events were designed to be cross functional in nature for buyer and supplier alike. They involved open and frank discussions about how team working could be introduced or improved, the assistance the customer could give, how to carry out improvement programmes, how to cost improvements, as well as the provision of various cost improvement techniques.

The benefits of these improvements were then shared between buyer and supplier.

5.2.3 Customer-supplier relationship development programme

The CIP programme described above was designed to help make specific improvements to individual suppliers. However, in addition to this there were several areas of internal development that many, if not all, of the key suppliers benefited from. Examples of this included set-up reduction, shop floor layout and introduction of Statistical Process Control methods. Coupled to this a mechanism was felt necessary for co-ordinating the activities of suppliers so that inter-company waste could be removed. This waste involved the fact that strategies were not aligned between the customer and the various suppliers. As a result there were many areas where waste was occurring, for instance in differing transport systems, communication systems and quality systems. As a result the Customer-Supplier Relationship Development Programme was developed.

This approach was basically a Supplier Association whereby a group of about 40 key suppliers were brought together on a regular basis at a series of seminars where Filton Aerostructures shared its strategic direction and consequently areas for improvement could be discussed. At a more detailed level a number of more specific workshops were held in regional groups to pencil in the fine detail of how these improvements could be undertaken. The findings of these groups were then brought back to the next seminar for discussion and agreement of the full group of 40 companies and the customer.

In order to ensure that suppliers were effectively bought in to this process Filton Aerostructures ensured that the first area to be addressed was not problems that the suppliers were causing but problems that Filton Aerostructures was intentionally, or more often unintentionally, causing the suppliers and which resulted in a lower performance than was possible. The first seminar was used to brainstorm these key problem areas with a total of over 50 being discovered. The next series of workshops involved six groups of suppliers who were given an even share of the problems for analysis. The suppliers, facilitated by Filton Aerostructures staff, were then asked to find solutions and report back to the next seminar. At this subsequent seminar the problems were then prioritised and action plans developed for the most important ones.

This approach was intended in the short term to build relationships and trust so that subsequently major step-improvements could be made for buyer and supplier alike.

5.3 The planning process

The planning process adopted by Filton Aerostructures involved using a mixture of internal and external expertise. This was undertaken in a series of off-site discussions facilitated by an outside expert and involving an open and frank discussion of the issues, possibilities and problems of making any changes to the existing system. The outside expert was also able to bring to bear his knowledge from other organisations faced with a similar situation.

The total process involved firstly describing the existing situation, reviewing the necessity for change and in particular the downsizing of staff that was occurring. Then a list of areas within Procurement that were not working well was produced. Following this was a review of what the requirements for any new approach would be. At this point the consultant described a 'straw man' approach that could be taken, i.e. a potential approach; which could be used as the basis for discussion.

Using this model a discussion was undertaken to identify which benefits of the present system would be lost by moving to the new system. This was accompanied by a discussion of the benefits of the new system. Further analysis allowed the initial model to be modified to avoid losing what was already good and to ensure most, if not all, of the difficulties of the existing approach were covered. Next a brainstorming session was undertaken to capture any concerns that still existed.

This last activity was a further fine tuning of the approach. The concerns that were raised at this point included: the potential for duplication, whether the necessary resources were in place to manage the change, where should staff be located, what were the costs of the change, what internal measurement system would be used to gauge the performance of Procurement, how would the new teams become multi-skilled as well as concerns about career structures. Many of these concerns were addressed immediately, whilst others were prioritised for action by the new management team.

In terms of implementation, the problems were mainly due to the speed with which this had to occur due to the short timescale before the reduction in staff to 38. However, the new management team were able to adopt a roll out implementation plan which meant that changes were made within a sensible timescale involving piloting before full changes. The actual implementation did not occur without some difficulties. Primary among these was the need to 'multi-skill' staff which was undertaken primarily through on-the-job training. However, considering that the changes involved a one-off reduction of nearly 20 per cent of staff, the transition was relatively smooth with both suppliers and internal and external customers enjoying the benefits within weeks of implementation.

SECTION 6 AUDIENCES AND TEACHING SUGGESTIONS

The case has been designed so that it can be used at a variety of levels from HND up to Masters level. It is suitable for general logistics courses and in particular those focusing on Strategy, Management of Change and Procurement. It is suggested that it is used as a group exercise with groups of 4–6 students. Students should be allowed around an hour for discussion before each group feeds back its key findings.

Case 8

WESTLAND HELICOPTERS LIMITED
Relationship Strategy Development

Dr Paul Cousins, *Centre for Research in Strategic Purchasing and Supply, University of Bath*

SECTION 1 CASE SYNOPSIS

This case explores three key issues, firstly the structuring of a 'strategic' purchasing function/process; secondly the development of a supplier selection methodology and thirdly the formulation of inter and intra organisational relationships.

The case examines the transition of an organisation from bankruptcy to success and the subsequent implications for effective management of the organisation's supply activities.

It discusses how Purchasing has changed and concentrates on the Colour Display Generator – procurement project. This a project based procurement activity of high strategic and political importance to the organisation, and to the success of their new helicopter – the EH101.

Mr Porter, the newly appointed Director of Material, has to develop a new approach to this procurement exercise and he seeks the advice of consultants (The University of Bath) to help him develop a 'new' procurement strategy to encourage partnership relationships. Several models are suggested in the case, particularly a multi-attribute approach.

This case is based on a real example from the author's research work. The CDG is an actual part, as is the EH101, however some names and various commercial information have been altered. The case took place in 1993 and is on-going through to production in 1997. Currently, WHL and the chosen supplier are forming a joint venture to market a new technology which has developed from the collaboration. The partnership has proved hard work, but very successful.

SECTION 2 TEACHING AND LEARNING OBJECTIVES

Students are expected to learn the following from this case:

1. To understand the complexity of inter-organisational relationships. It is not simply a case of forming relationships with suppliers – the internal relationships and measurement systems need to be in place first.

2. To understand that different skills and competencies are required in order to operate in a project as opposed to a functional bases.
3. To think about the complexity of choosing a 'partnership' supplier.
4. To develop a methodology for the process of selecting a preferred supplier.
5. To consider how to measure the relationship, based on a multi-attribute modelling process (AHP).
6. To understand that process is necessary in order for relationships to form effectively.
7. To understand that in order to change the types of relationships, the firm (WHL) needs to show the suppliers that a different method of working is being employed.
8. To understand that relationships are not based on 'love' on 'trust', but on sound business sense.

SECTION 3 MAIN ISSUES AND PROBLEMS

The case raised three main problems which are separate but related. Lecturers may decide to focus on one or more of these problems. These are broadly:

3.1 Purchasing strategy and structure

How should the purchasing function be structured and measured to encourage strategic behaviour. At present the function is measured tactically, therefore personnel behave in that manner. If a strategic focus is required, a team based approach will have to be adopted. (see Carlisle and Parker- mandate teams) Therefore consideration will need to be given to this issue. Also, how should the function be structured, the issues of centralisation and decentralisation are pertinent here. Issues such as the 'clan' structure can be employed. Finally, consideration must also be given to the types of competencies that are needed to develop successful relationships – what skills do they currently possess? What skills would be required?

3.2 The need to develop a systematic and comprehensive approach to the supplier selection process

There is a need to develop a more rigorous and coordinated approach to supplier selection than had hitherto been used in the company . This is as much to do with changing internal approaches within WHL such as inter-departmental rivalries and the non – strategic perspective of the purchasing function, as it is to do with the actual mechanism for supplier selection. Section 5 below outlines the Vendor Management Model which was used by the consultants to address this issue.

3.3 Relationship definition, strategy, measurement and management

What do we mean by 'partnerships'? How can they be defined? Measured? and managed? These issues are addressed in the second part of the case. Various models are put forward for consideration. The use of a multi-attribute approach, combined with the selection of inter-organisation cross functional teams is suggested (this also works in practice). Ten attributes are put forward, not all of these are necessary, students should consider their definition i.e. what do we mean by price, delivery, quality etc. Specifically, what do we mean by 'culture'. This is a very difficult concept to grasp, how do we measure it? The answer is that it should be used as a precluding and NOT predicting variable. For example, it is easier to say we can't do business with this organisation for whatever reason, rather than we feel that we can do business with this organisation.

The choice of the relationship type is only one element. Students must then consider how the relationship could be measured? How should the suppliers be interviewed? Should they be debriefed etc.

SECTION 4 SPECIFIC QUESTIONS

1. Analyse the existing purchasing function at WHL and determine what resources are required; what skills and competencies are needed; and what changes in procedures and working practices should be initiated to develop a modern purchasing approach.
2. Develop a methodology to enable Westland to select the best supplier for the current CDG project
3. Determine and justify who should be in the supplier selection and management team. Should these be different ?
4. Develop a strategic plan for the management of supplier relationships.
5. Advise Porter on how he can develop the WHL purchasing function towards a Stage Four in the Purchasing Positioning Matrix.
6. What are the major problems with relationship definition and how would you overcome them?
7. Advise how WHL should develop a 'strategic' collaborative relationship with their chosen CDG supplier and with their suppliers in general.

SECTION 5 THE APPROACH TAKEN

The consultants engaged by WHL recommended the following approach and were instrumental in its in implementation

5.1 Development of a sourcing team

A cross functional selection team was convened. This consisted of two representatives from: Marketing, Purchasing, Production, Design, Quality and Finance. Two members were chosen so that there would be no break in continuity. This became known as the Sourcing Team. The team with the aid of the consultants determined the selection process. This exercise was very important as it was a facilitator to break down the inter functional boundaries that had build up over the years.

The team decided on a four phased approach:

Phase 1 – Determine the appropriate selection criteria
Phase 2 – Reduce the list of ten potential suppliers down to four.
Phase 3 – Choose the 'best' supplier from the remaining group.
Phase 4 – Work with the supplier to develop the relationship.

Phase 1 Selection criteria
The group decided that all ten of the criteria were of relevance to the exercise and then went about rating the overall top level attributes to establish an ideal characteristic.

They then weighted each of the chosen attributes.

The group then went through a lengthy discussion procedure deciding on the sub-attributes for each main attribute. The number of sub-attributes were restricted to five per attribute. For example, the attribute price was sub-divided into: Unit Cost, Non-Recurring Costs, Whole Life Cost and Tooling Costs. Each of these sub-attributes were then weighted by the group, each weight being agreed upon by consensus.

Phase 2 Short listing four suppliers

The 10 suppliers were then sent the attribute lists, but not the weights. This firstly indicated to the supply base that a different approach to business was being undertaken. Secondly, because the weights were not included they did not know which were the most important criteria.

Each supplier was asked into the company for a one day session. They presented to the selection team in the morning and then were interviewed individually in the afternoon. Each team member scored each supplier against ALL of the criteria. These were then placed into a multi-attribute model (known as the Vendor Management Model) and the 'best' overall supplier was chosen. The selection process went from 10 to 4 suppliers.

Phase 3 Selecting the preferred supplier

Detailed investigations, on the same basis were then conducted with the remaining four suppliers This included visits to supplier facilities, interviews with staff at various levels within the companies, reference to existing customers etc. until one was chosen.

All the unsuccessful suppliers were debriefed on the process, and told why they did not get the contract.

The suppliers were interviewed after the event to gauge their feelings, all felt that this was a much more structured, efficient and equitable way of doing business. They also felt that Westland were serious about forming collaborative relationships, based on their actions – the adage *'actions speak louder than words'* is certainly true in this instance.

Phase 4 The management phase

The Sourcing team were required to meet at regular intervals to rate and re-rate the supplier.

There was a gradual improvement in relationships not only between WHL and the supplier but also between the various functional groups within WHL.

At the outset of the new approach there was considerable anxiety and doubt about the process both in terms of the nature of the new relationships with suppliers and also of the required approach to inter-functional cooperation within WHL

All of the functions within WHL were going to have to work together. This appeared to fill most group members with a great deal of anxiety and trepidation. Furthermore, all information concerning the commercial and design proposals for the CDG project were going to be made available to all group members. This would breakdown the 'power of information' approach which was traditionally used by all of the functions involved

The prospect of working jointly with the chosen supplier to complete the remaining two thirds of the CDG design also gave all group members a feeling of uncertainty.

The development of a team approach to sourcing and of a 'partnership' with the supplier slowly evolved as is illustrated by the following extracts of discussions between the Consultant and various members of WHL staff

5.2 Interview points

Perks (WHL Contracts Negotiator): I want to ask the supplier for a detailed breakdown of costs. This is part of what Partnership is about, isn't it?

Consultant: Are you prepared to tell the supplier what your on-profit charge is going to be?

Perks: No, definitely not. That information is confidential

Researcher: Then why should the supplier tell you his costs if you are not prepared to reciprocate? You must both have something to bring to the table.

Perks: OK, I guess you're right. We haven't really got a Partnership yet have we? It is just an improved business relationship.

The group was very receptive to the relationship strategy approach and felt that the purchasing partnership philosophy was working well. Changes had also been made to the way in which business was conducted within WHL.

The design function now felt that it had much more access to information that, although it was not vitally important to their jobs, it was indeed useful (i.e. commercial proposals or cost listings).

Designer: It's great now that we have access to commercial proposals. We can use the information when putting together our design. It's not essential but it shows that Purchasing trust us with the information. This makes us feel more like a team as opposed to autonomous departments.

Purchasing: Yes well, we realise that as far was your job goes this information is not vital. However, we do require a view on it from you and also expect you to help us accordingly in terms of cost reductions now that you are in full view of the facts.

Designer: One of the interesting things that I have found with this philosophy is how long and how much dedication it takes to put it into practice. For example, no sooner do I convince one manager that it is a good idea and it is working than another tries to put a block on it! The process of persuasion then has to begin again.

5.3 Outcome

Overall from WHL's point of view the use of the VMM has been very successful. The company found that this new and original method of supplier selection and management had enabled them to achieve a far better design than they originally expected within a significantly reduced time-frame.

The process has been extended on a project by project basis. It has also been extended in several relationships to measure the improvement in relationship strategy by using a positioning tool. (See Figure 2.2).

The tool has further been used for suppliers to assess the buyer and for the final customer to assess the buyer (supplier), with very interesting results. The idea of the tool is for the supplier and buyer teams to examine the distances between the perceived and actual performance levels and then to minimise these gaps.

SECTION 6 AUDIENCES AND USES OF THE CASE

This case is suitable for final year and postgraduate students on a variety of courses including

- supply chain management,
- purchasing
- organisational behaviour
- general management e.g. MBA

Students need to be aware of the concepts of strategy and relationship theory before attempting the case.

It is suggested that the teacher splits the class into groups of around 4-6 students and they should then be asked to give a presentation on how they would solve this problem.

It is also possible to form role playing of the different members of the cross-functional teams, this works better in post-graduate audiences where students are from different functional disciplines. This can emphasise how different functions view/interpret the different attributes. Main level attributes can then be subdivided into sub-attributes for definition, these will need to be weighted. The weighting of the attributes is a very interesting and difficult process and is worth experiencing.

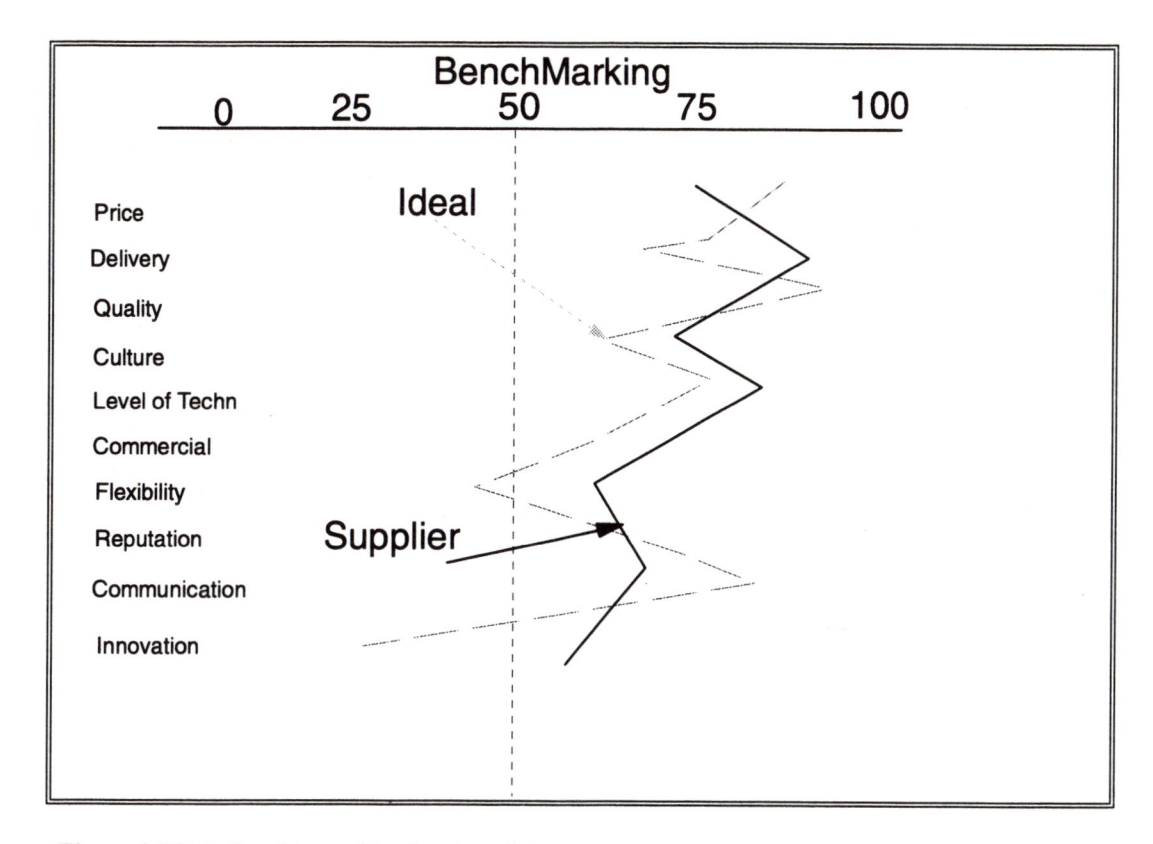

Figure 2.2 Relationship positioning template

Source: Cousins, P.D. (1996b).

Part 3

Manufacturing Logistics

Case 9

FIAT AUTO SpA

Restructuring the logistics system in response to changing customer requirements

Paulo Bianchi, *T Kearney, Milan*

SECTION 1 CASE SYNOPSIS

At the beginning of 1991, Fiat Auto SpA was facing a difficult transition from its current and ageing product range to a completely new one, involving an investment of $25 billion and a major turnaround of the company, encompassing engineering, manufacturing, relationship with suppliers, sales and logistics. In this frame Fiat saw outstanding customer service as a key competitive weapon for the future and also as a necessity to support the old models during the transition to the new range. Fiat's CEO established bold service objectives:

- Delivery time for cars sold from inventory 1 week (previous average 2–4 weeks).
- Delivery time for cars made to order 6–8 weeks with 95 per cent reliability (previously 10–15 weeks with no commitment on delivery date).
- Conformance to initial customer requirements 100 per cent (previously 40 per cent).

An inter-functional team of fully dedicated middle managers supported by an international manageement consulting firm was set up to design and implement the new logistic model. The team examined the European sales structure, the information system, and the logistic process of Fiat, to understand the technical and political constraints.

It also conducted a benchmark on European and Japanese competitors, to understand the current state of the art. The team learned that the best logistic processes exploited the unique characteristics of each car producer and of its customers, and that three main types of logistic processes existed:

- the Traditional European – leveraging on the need for a stable production plan and on the propensity of customers from Southern Europe to buy from inventory;
- the German – leveraging on a strong product and on the rigidity of customers from Northern Europe and of customers of luxury cars;

- the Japanese – leveraging on the rigidity of production, on the close linkage between car producers and dealers, and on the ability to make reliable forecasts.

From this, the team concluded that Fiat needed a tailor made logistic process. The case is real; only the names of the team member and some sensitive information are disguised.

NB The case contains a very useful description of the alternative logistics processes and systems adopted by some of the world's major car manufactures.

SECTION 2 TEACHING OBJECTIVES

The student learning objectives are:

1. To understand the requirements and difficulties of co-ordinating logistics across the whole supply chain from dealers, through manufacturing to suppliers.
2. To understand the nature of the various supply chain and customer service models used by different car manufacturers.
3. To appreciate the need to develop workable supply chain solutions within the constraints of existing organisational (political) structures and existing fixed operating systems, in particular production and information systems.
4. To understand how logistics can be used as an effective weapon by a weak competitor in a very competitive market and how it can contribute to position a product in the market place.
5. To appreciate the importance of inter-functional teams in designing 'out of the box solutions' and in building the consensus of the extended enterprise (company, dealers, suppliers) about them.

The student action objectives are:

1. To identify the reasons why the current Fiat logistics system is incapable of delivering the required higher customer service standards.
2. To develop an appropriate design for Fiat's new logistic concept.
3. To identify the factors which will be critical to successful implementation of any proposed solution.
4. To identify the constraints within which the logistic planning team must work.

SECTION 3 MAIN ISSUES AND PROBLEMS RAISED BY THE CASE

There were a number of factors critical to the successful development of a new logistics system.

3.1 The need to avoid incorrect behaviour by the dealers

The new model developed by Fiat works if the dealers:

- Order the 'right' number of cars i.e. the cars they will sell.
- Pool a sufficient number of cars in the 'global logical inventory', i.e. they make available to other dealers a sufficient number of cars ordered by them, but not yet customer tagged (see also Section 4 Description of actual development in the company).

Possible incorrect behaviours are:

- A dealer does not enter orders in the system and picks the cars it needs from the global inventory.
- A dealer 'blocks' all the cars ordered to avoid them being 'stolen' by other dealers

To avoid this, Fiat:

- Implemented an extensive training and support program to change the behaviour of Fiat personnel and dealers. This involved workshops and courses to several thousand people, the establishment of a task force which visited the dealers to use the new process and to solve operating problems (e.g. use of new information tools), and the establishment of a hot line with Fiat.
- Used various economic incentives, e.g., cars pooled in the global logical inventory had longer terms of payment, the periodic bonuses to the dealers were based both on the cars ordered and on the cars sold.

3.2 The need to develop a European-wide computer based communication system

This allowed:

- Weekly (as opposed to monthly) order gathering and confirmation.
- Real-time search for the car required by the customer, inclusive of the respecification of a car already planned for production.

Fiat leveraged on existing plans to connect all the European dealers to its information system. A simple and user friendly interface, residing on a personal computer in each dealership, was implemented and installed. It was not necessary to link in real time the dealer information system with the production planning system in Fiat's plants, since the respecifications compensated statistically up to 95 per cent. So, consistently, with some reasonable constraints, the respecifications are always accepted.

3.3 The need to win the support of senior management

Senior management support was required in such functions as production, sales and purchasing. In 1991 the automotive industry was rigidly organised by functions, whose heads were on average very technically competent, and very jealous of their fiefdoms.

To overcome this problem:

- Fiat assigned full time to the project very respected and experienced middle managers from all the functions involved. In this way every function had a representative in the project team, who in turn was able to 'sell' the recommendations of the team to his original function. On the other hand, the full time involvement set a clear priority for the team members.
- Great attention was given in keeping the senior management of Fiat, the key middle managers, and the dealer associations involved in the development of the recommendations. In this way their consensus was built step by step and useful suggestions incorporated in the solutions.

3.4 The need to convince the management of the subsidiaries that to have their own market inventory was not only not critical, but counter-productive to their success

- A model was developed to show how much cash flow could be freed by eliminating the market inventory and how the availability of cars and the delivery time could be improved using a pan-European inventory.
- Meetings with dealers in each market were set up to demonstrate the model, to show understanding of the problems of the subsidiaries and to answer the questions posed by them.

3.5 Other factors critical to project success were

- After the completion of the project the team members obtained key positions in the areas most influenced by the recommendations. (e.g. Mr Le Mele became logistics and information system manager, Mr Marsili was put in charge of the purchasing of transportation services outside Italy). This provided both a reward to the effort of the team members and champions of the new model in the most critical areas.
- The investment in information systems was negligible: the existing dealers hardware and network was used. The development of software required about 15 man years.
- The effectiveness of the project was due to the combination of:
  - The knowledge of the Fiat culture and processes by the team members.
  - Their credibility with the senior managers of their original departments and their ability to 'sell' findings and solutions.
  - The external view and knowledge of best practices provided by the consultants.
  - The capability of Fiat personnel and consultants to work as a team.

SECTION 4 SPECIFIC QUESTIONS

1. Why is the traditional European model inadequate to give an outstanding service to the customer?

In this model, the dealer must order the cars at least two months ahead of delivery. However, the average customer is not prepared to wait such a long time to have the required car. So, he is practically obliged to choose a car already existing in the physical inventory of the dealer, which, given the possible combination of major (e.g. engine, ABS, sunroof, air conditioning...) and minor (head lamp washers, special battery) options is unlikely to be very close to his original requirement For very high volume models, there was a probability of no more than 10 per cent of finding the required car. This translates into customer dissatisfaction and financial loss for the dealer, because discounts were usually given to compensate for the non conformance of the car to customer requirements. Moreover, even if the customer was willing to wait for the required car, the dealer was unable to give him a delivery date, because he did not know if the order would be accepted by the car producer, and, even if accepted, the manufacturer could only specify the month of delivery.

2. Why doesn't a high inventory level, both dealer owned and market owned, give a high level of service?

The inventory of the dealer is too small to include all the combinations of options required by the customer. The probability to find in it the required car is about 40 per cent at major options level and no more than 10 per cent at minor options level.

The cars in the market inventory are usually produced in addition to the cars ordered by the dealers to saturate the production capacity. They are the 'easiest' cars to produce based on production constraints and not the cars with the highest probability to be required by the customers. These cars are usually 'pushed' by the market through the sales channel, using heavy promotions, which translates in lesser profits and lower image of the brand.

3. Why is it impossible to successfully adopt the logistic process es of the competition?

A logistic process is successful when it is able to satisfy the requirements of the customer consistently with the constraints posed by the other processes of the extended company (e.g. manufacturing, supply, dealerships).

The requirements of the customers are influenced by the image they have of the car producer and by the kind of car they are buying. For example, the average BMW customer believes he is buying something distinctive, that he likes to customise, and is willing to wait all the time needed to get exactly that car with those options.

On the other hand, the customer of a SEAT (low end brand of the Volkswagen Group) does not care so much about image or options, but wants a cheap car now. In logistics terms, this translates into the need for prompt delivery at Seat, and in the possibility of long lead time for BMW.

From the manufacturing point of view, the logistic process must deal with the flexibility of plants. Some car producers are very rigid to changes in volume or specification, such as the Japanese. Some other, such as Fiat, which can rely, for example, on temporary layoffs are more flexible.

Also the suppliers can be a source of constraints. The Kanban system and the size of the Japanese first tier suppliers makes it very difficult to deviate from forecast on short notice. The Italian suppliers, often small companies with very flexible workforce, can change their production schedule more easily.

All these differences make it very unlikely that the same process would give the same results if adopted by different car producers.

SECTION 5 DESCRIPTION OF ACTUAL DEVELOPMENT IN THE COMPANY

The new logistic model was developed by April 1992. It was successfully tested on the Lancia brand in Italy starting in September. During 1993, it was extended, starting from Italy, to the whole Western Europe. The objectives of Mr Cantarella were exceeded. In 1994:

- Cars made to order were delivered: 40 to 50 per cent within three weeks, 85 per cent within five weeks, 100 per cent within seven weeks (Fiat makes commitment on the delivery week with the final customer). Only models for which the demand largely exceeds production have longer delivery time.
- The reliability of the promised delivery week was 95 per cent and up to 97 per cent for high volume models.
- Conformance to initial customer requirements was 100 per cent.
- In addition, Fiat was able to cut the inventory level (in number of cars owned both from Fiat and the dealers) by 60%, equivalent to $2.5 billion.

The New Model (Annex 3) works as follows:

- The 'out of the box' solution was to decouple the dealer order and the customer order cycle, and to exploit the production flexibility of the Fiat plants, which allows almost everything except the model to be changed upto 2 weeks ahead of production.
- The already existing 'long term planning' (time horizon 12 to 18 months) is used to determine the capacity by family (at Fiat a family is group of versions of a model), and to allocate it to the plant. Based on the long term plan, a weekly volume by family is reserved to each dealer, based on its sales potential. This means that the dealer is sure to receive up to the reserved volume each week.
- Each Monday night, the dealer transmits its orders to Fiat. They are allocated by the system to the first week for which the dealer has not yet saturated the reserved volume (this week is known to the dealer, and as a standard is seven weeks ahead).
- By Tuesday night, the orders are checked against production and suppliers constraints, and clearings are made among dealers to saturate plant capacity. This means that, if a dealer has an order portfolio exceeding, for example, 8 weeks, and another dealer has an order portfolio of 4 weeks, the exceeding volume reserved to the second is used to shorten the delivery time of the first dealer.
- In the 'Wednesday meeting', executives from the logistic, sales and production departments approve the order portfolio, and it is then released to the plants by Friday.
- In week 2, the plants develop the detailed schedule for Week 8 (or the first week not yet planned) and release the material scheduling to the suppliers. The suppliers have already a six month forecast based on the long term planning.

44 Manufacturing Logistics

In this way, a production portfolio is built up, based on dealer orders. Its length can vary, depending on the demand of a given family. The customers pick their car from this portfolio.

When a customer orders a car, he can:

- Take a car from the dealer's inventory, if he wants prompt delivery and does not care about conformance.
- Take a car from the dealer's 'logical' inventory, i.e. cars ordered by the dealer but not yet delivered. Of course, the dealer's inventory is limited and the customer may be not able to find the car he needs, or the delivery time may be too long.
- Take a car from the global logical inventory. When a dealer orders a car, it can define the car as 'blocked' (customer tagged or needed for its own inventory) or 'free'. The 'free' cars, on average 20 to 40 per cent of the total, form the global logical inventory. If the lead time for the first suitable car is too long, another car can be respecified to meet the requirement of the customer.
- The search in the logical inventory, the respecification of the car and the customer tagging are made in real time.

SECTION 5 AUDIENCES/USES OF THE CASE

A major strategic level case suitable for use with post-graduate or final year under-graduate student and undertaking courses in logistics or supply chain management.

Also useful on course in manufacturing and operations management

SECTION 6 APPENDIX

Figures 3.1 to 3.3 show the logistic process implemented at Fiat.

- Every month a share of the production capacity by "Budget family e.g. model, body,...) is reserved to each dealer with a time horizon of eight weeks
- The long term planning allocates also the total capacity by budget family to each assembly plant

The dealer can enter the orders in its system at the time it prefers

| W 1 | W 2 | W 3 | W 4 | W 5 | W 6 | W 7 | W 8 | Weeks

Weekly planning cycle

| D 1 | D 2 | D 3 | D 4 | D 5 | Days

The material scheduling for the next 6 week is released to suppliers (some cars planned for week 3 to 7 may have been respecified)

The orders entered in week 1 are planned for production in week 8

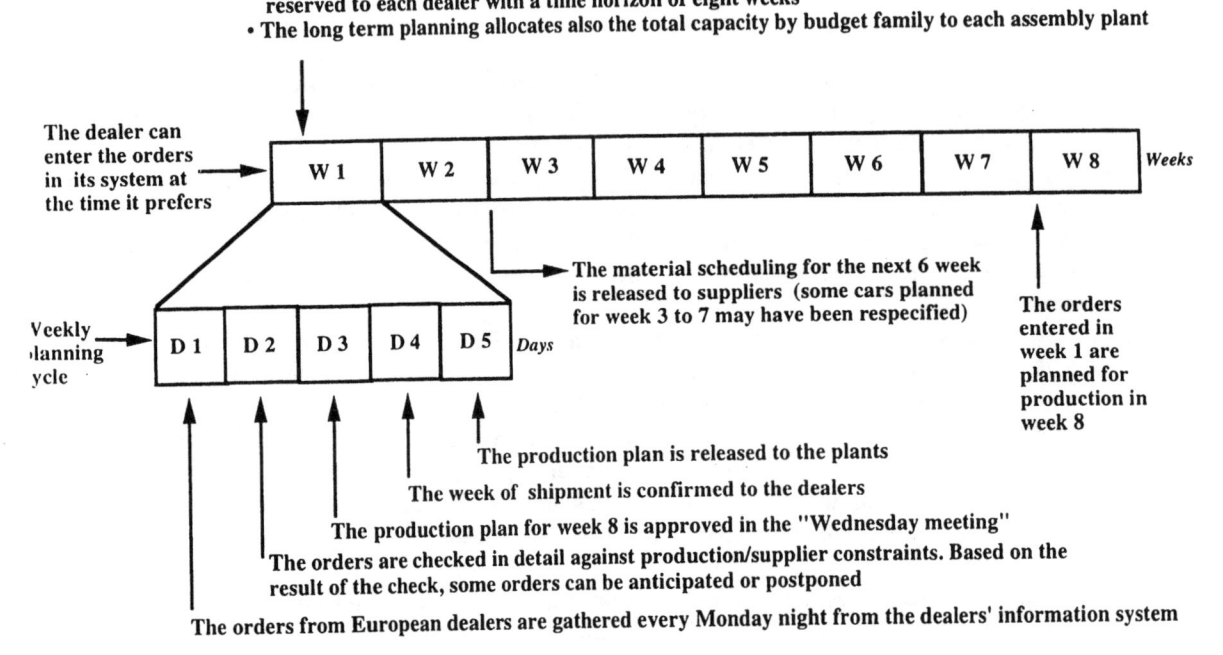

The production plan is released to the plants
The week of shipment is confirmed to the dealers
The production plan for week 8 is approved in the "Wednesday meeting"
The orders are checked in detail against production/supplier constraints. Based on the result of the check, some orders can be anticipated or postponed
The orders from European dealers are gathered every Monday night from the dealers' information system

Figure 3.1 The new Fiat logistic concept – dealer order cycle
Note: Week 8 is the standard; if the order portfolio is short, the orders can be planned for a nearer week; if it is long, for a farther week.

Manufacturing Logistics 45

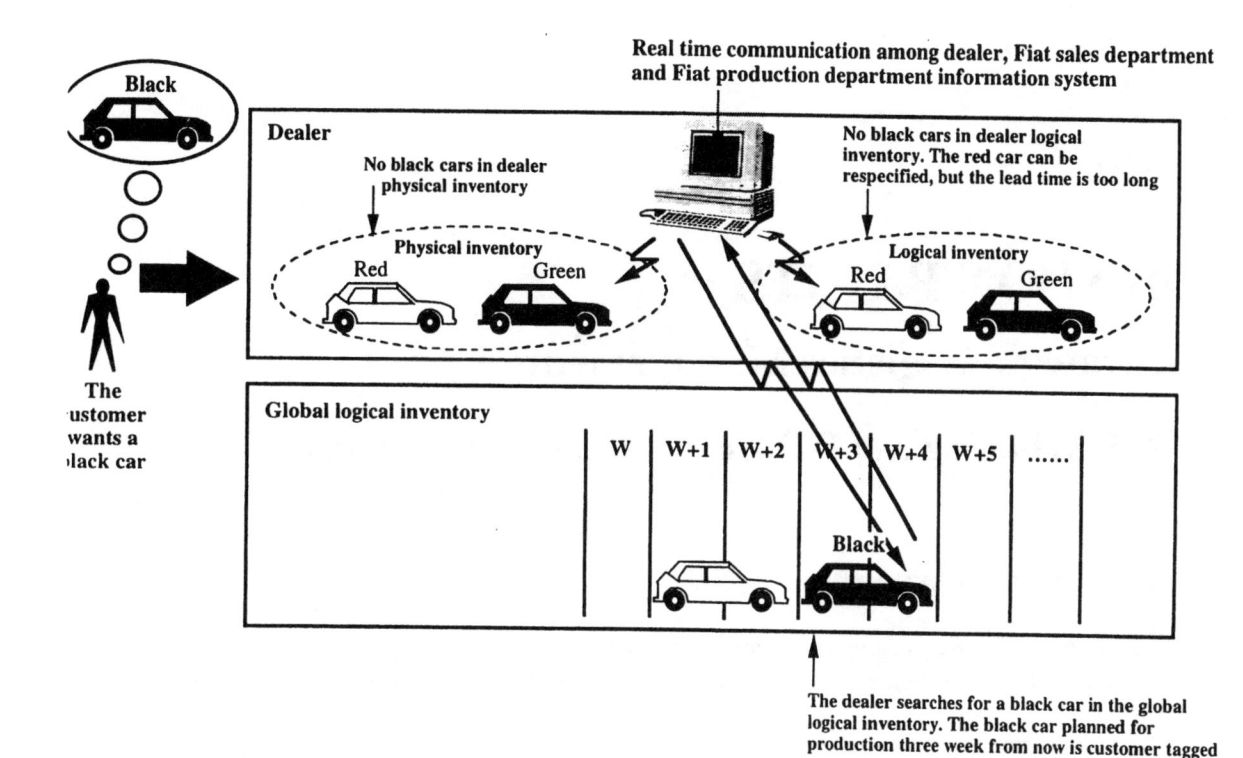

Figure 3.2 New Fiat logisitic concept – the customer's perception is that the dealer can deliver his car with the right specifications in a short time

Prerequisites

- No major changes to existing information systems required
- At least 15% of global pipeline pooled by the dealers in the global logical inventory
- Delays of payment differentiated by blocked (customer tagged) and free (dealer tagged) orders
- Consensus by the dealers (training and support):the success of the concept is based on active participation by the dealers

Actual performances

- Immediate confirmation of delivery date both for cars existing and not existing in inventory
- 40 to 50% of cars delivered within 3 weeks, 85% within 5 weeks, 100% within seven weeks
- 95% reliability of the promised delivery date (up to 97% for very high volume models)

Pros

- Very reactive to changes in mix/volume
- Gives early notice on short term trends
- Puts relatively small pressure on the single dealer
- Allows to match customer requirements also having a complex product range (many models and many options)

Cons

- Requires mechanism to incentivate the dealers to order also in weak markets
- In extreme case can require more flexibility to mix/volume by production

Figure 3.3 Features of the new Fiat logistics process

Case 10

KALON PAINTS
Strategic Logistics Management

A E Whiteing and **P D Corns**, *University of Huddersfield*

SECTION 1 CASE SYNOPSIS

This factual case study examines the logistics system of a major paints manufacturer, and relates logistics management to the strategic management of the company involved. The recent history of the company is examined, and the development of the company's successful strategy is set against the background of the paint industry in the UK

The study examines the company's progress in two key market segments – the supply of branded paints to the professional decorators' market and the supply of own label products to the major UK do-it-yourself retailers such as B&Q. The contrasting logistics needs of these two sectors are drawn out, and a range of problems relating to the logistics systems used to service each sector are identified.

The study takes a holistic approach to the company's logistics system, covering many aspects of purchasing and supply, production planning and scheduling and the physical distribution system. Within the latter section, considerable attention is paid to issues relating to transport management, inventory and warehouse management, packaging and order processing.

The case raises a wide range of questions relating to the efficiency of each component of the logistics system and the effectiveness of the system as a whole. It also raises issues relating to appropriate distribution channels and desirable levels of customer service in each of the two key market segments under consideration, and the logistics cost impacts of decisions in these areas.

Although the case study can be used for an appraisal specifically of the logistics system of the company concerned, it is intended primarily for the investigation of the relationships between logistics management and strategic management. For example, it can be used to illustrate the logistics management and cost implications of strategic management decisions, or to appraise how logistics considerations might constrain the range of future strategic directions open to senior management.

SECTION 2 TEACHING/LEARNING OBJECTIVES

1. To provide students with an opportunity to explore the relationships between strategic management and logistics management in a manufacturing company.
2. To provide students with an opportunity to evaluate the total logistics system of a manufacturing company, to identify logistics trade-offs throughout the organisation, and to suggest potential improvements.
3. To provide students with an opportunity to evaluate existing strategies for the various elements of the logistics system such as transport, warehousing, inventory management, order processing and production planning, and to suggest possible improvements.

4. To show how market segmentation can be used to advantage, and to examine the logistics implications of such market segmentation decisions.
5. To provide an opportunity to explore appropriate marketing and logistics channels for each market segment.
6. To explore the logistics implications of various customer service policies in each market segment.

SECTION 3 MAIN ISSUES AND PROBLEMS

Kalon has undoubtedly been successful in developing its business in two distinct market segments – the supply of branded paints to the professional decorators' market and the supply of own label products to major UK do-it-yourself retailers. This success is due both to astute strategic planning on the part of senior management and to the effectiveness of the company's logistics system. Having said this, there are a number of problems that remain to be resolved.

3.1 The future strategic direction

The over-riding consideration is to determine the future strategic directions of the company – it is not sufficient to simply project present strategies into the future. In terms of logistics, although total logistics costs as a proportion of sales value have been reduced significantly, there remain a number of relatively high cost areas. Perhaps more significantly, there are a number of potential bottlenecks to the smooth flow of goods through the logistics system, and these bottlenecks might well become critical if the present relatively low level of factory capacity utilisation could be improved.

There are also issues to be resolved in relation to the appropriateness of the company's distribution channels for each market segment and in relation to the high levels of customer service provided in each segment.

3.2 Potential weaknesses in the Kalon logistics system

A number of potential weaknesses can be identified:

- There is relatively low utilisation of production capacity
- Manual detailed production planning would become impractical if capacity utilisation was to increase significantly
- Materials procurement is largely by traditional methods rather than modern systems involving partnership sourcing and supplier rationalisation, and there are potential problems relating to materials quality
- The lack of a comprehensive warehouse stock location system causes picking stock replenishment delays and increases the dependence on manual stocktaking
- Warehouse allocation by customer rather than random location reduces cube utilisation
- The company does not use a transport routeing and scheduling package
- Various customer service elements impose relatively high costs. Examples include the 'black band' special labelling service, the order top up system and the tote box small item picking operation for B&Q
- The dedicated pallet system leads to relatively high costs which seem to be 'lost' somewhere in the transport or warehousing cost headings.

3.3 The scope for state-of-the-art logistics solutions

A useful approach to the identification of solutions to these problems is to consider the extent to which Kalon can implement state-of-the-art logistics solutions. In general, there is some potential for information technology driven solutions such as:

- warehouse management systems;
- inventory control systems;
- vehicle routeing and scheduling packages;
- demand forecasting systems;
- production planning tools;
- requirements planning systems.

State-of-the-art logistics strategies such as JIT production, partnership sourcing and contract logistics also provide useful starting points for the generation of solutions. However it must be pointed out that the paints industry, with its very large product ranges, essential batch production, lengthy production times and seasonal demand profile offers relatively little scope for true production to order. Therefore feasible solutions involve production for stock for most product lines, but with various modifications to the present system so that production becomes somewhat more flexible and demand-responsive than at present.

The case also offers the opportunity to discuss other topical logistics issues, such as:

- The advantages and disadvantages of factory rationalisation in the wake of acquisitions;
- The relative strengths of 'own account' transport versus contract distribution;
- The arguments for and against a regional depot network, as used by Kalon's main competitors.

In the latter two cases, the Kalon strategies seem defensible even though the company is to some extent going against current trends. The relatively low factory capacity utilisation at Birstall is a rather more pressing problem, however.

SECTION 4 SPECIFIC QUESTIONS

4.1 Highlight areas within the Kalon logistics system which may cause bottlenecks and delays in the flow of goods, and suggest changes which might facilitate smoother flow

There are a number of areas in the Kalon logistics system where bottlenecks may occur. Some relevant examples are discussed below.

4.1.1 Quality Testing

Delays occur when products are held in storage tanks awaiting the results of quality tests, which can take many hours to complete. In extreme cases and when production capacity nears capacity utilisation this could delay the start of further production batches.

Given present technology this is a very difficult problem to overcome. The whole process depends upon the drying and testing times for the different products. Kalon are currently investigating ways to reduce drying and testing times and have made some progress on many product lines. For some oil based product lines drying and testing times have been halved.

Some delays caused by the need to make adjustments to the final product could be avoided by ensuring consistent quality of raw materials. If all inputs are of the highest quality then it is reasonable to expect that product quality would also be more consistent. This may call for a reduction in the number of suppliers used and concentration of purchasing on those providing the highest quality This should reduce the need for adjustments to be made and thus will reduce the average time that products are held in the storage tanks.

4.1.2 Filling Lines

Delays will occur if filling lines stop for any reason such as breakdown or cleaning. Holding vessels will not be emptied and this may delay the transfer of further batches from production lines. Significant delays will eventually starve the central warehouse of supplies.

Investment may well be required to reduce the possible problems in this area. Establishment of additional filling lines would increase capacity but would be a relatively expensive option. Greater flexibility would avoid the need to dedicate lines to product types and would allow filling to continue for all products whilst preventive maintenance was carried out, but may increase total cleaning time. The present filling lines are labour intensive rather than highly mechanised, and this offers some advantages. Skill requirements are relatively modest, and coverage for absenteeism or illness is easy to arrange.

4.1.3 Transfer from Birstall Factory to warehouse

Finished products are held in an area immediately adjacent to the filling lines rather than transferred directly to the warehouse. The area concerned is only small and there is definite potential for bottlenecks to occur here. In particular there is only one loading bay for despatch to the warehouse. If a vehicle breaks down here, products will back up very quickly. One relatively expensive solution to this problem would be to add a second loading bay to the building. Another would be to build a conveyor between the factory and the warehouse, but any unreliability would result in the same problem. Production could be cleared immediately to the warehouse by forklift truck, but this solution would alter the flow of work in the warehouse and may require labour to be transferred from other warehouse tasks such as order picking and load assembly. The present system using articulated vehicles allows transfer to be delayed until warehousing staff become available.

4.2 What elements of customer service offered by Kalon and highlighted in the case add considerable cost to the logistics function? What suggestions, if any, could you put forward in order to reduce the impact on logistics costs?

Examples can be found in both market segments – the large orders to DIY chains and the many small orders to trade centres and other customers in the professional decorators' market.

4.2.1 Top up order for trade centres

Top up orders received on the second day of the order cycle impact heavily on order processing and administration at Kalon and put considerable pressure on the warehouse and the load planners. Although the facility is used extensively, it is questionable whether it is really justified. The top up option gives the trade centres an escape route for poor ordering in the first place, and without this fall back option they may well develop skills in getting the order right first time.

4.2.2 Full product range availability to trade centres

The large range of goods purchased by Kalon in order to offer a full range of decorating materials to the professional decorating market must increase the cost of warehousing. The range extends from the smallest of decorating sundries to bulky items such as rolls of loft insulation, and this increases storage complexity compared to the relatively standardised and straightforward task of storing tins of paint. There are also implications for space utilisation both within the warehouse and on outbound vehicles. The effects of this large product range of Kalon's overall profitability requires careful consideration.

4.2.3 Black banding

The black band label system used by smaller customers involves the attachment of labels after order assembly. This is a large operation as over 200 customers use his service. The costs to Kalon imposed by this service are considerable but at present it is offered at no extra cost to the customer.

4.2.4 B&Q tote boxes

The tote box picking operation for the B&Q contract adds substantially to Kalon's logistics costs. The operation requires pickers to be employed full time. The cost of the boxes themselves is also quite considerable. However such operations are increasingly unavoidable as major retailers exert their power in the supply chain and exploit opportunities to push stockholding and elements of the picking operation back down to suppliers.

4.3 Kalon holds a large volume of stock at the central warehouse. As a result warehouse space is at a premium and extensions have been required. However factory capacity utilisation is only 65%. Suggest logistics strategies to enable the warehouse and distribution to cope with possible increases in volume.

If production was to be increased great strain would be put on the already extended warehouse. Various strategies that may well help to reduce the pressure on the warehouse are suggested below.

4.3.1 Production to order

If Kalon could move away from producing to stock to production for order, significant reductions in both cycle stock and safety stock could be achieved. In order to produce in this way, demand forecasting and production planning would have to be improved. In present circumstances, production for order is impossible for most product lines. More flexible production in the future should not be ruled out, because many product lines can be produced relatively quickly. Such increased responsiveness would however call for considerable change in company strategy and management style. The relatively low level of factory capacity utilisation at the time of the case – around 65% – allows some flexibility to alter production schedules at relatively short notice. If utilisation increased significantly in the future, the scope for more flexible manufacturing would be reduced unless more sophisticated scheduling systems were employed.

4.3.2 Warehouse management computer system

If a modern computer-based warehouse management system were to be installed, inventory could be managed much more effectively and utilisation of available warehouse space could be improved. At present, reach truck drivers simply place new stock into an available space in the warehouse aisle appropriate to the customer concerned. A warehouse management system would also negate the need for Kalon to dedicate aisles to customers or groups of customers, which would also promote better utilisation. Dependence on the reach truck drivers' knowledge for stock retrieval could be ended and the drivers could be allocated much more flexibly across the entire warehouse.

4.3.3 Warehouse extension or reconfiguration

Any decision to change the warehouse racking system would not be taken lightly as considerable expense and disruption would be involved. If such a decision were taken, however, a narrow aisle system with appropriate narrow aisle trucks would increase warehouse capacity significantly. Kalon has further land available for possible warehouse extensions, and this option has been used in the past. It can however be argued that warehouse expansion would not address the fundamental problems relating to the high levels of inventory and the associated costs. It would seem more sensible to take a long and hard look at how inventory levels could be reduced across the business without impacting on customer service levels.

4.4 What improvements could be made to Kalon's procurement strategy?

The relatively short production planning horizon means that materials must be purchased in advance of requirements, leading to relatively high materials inventory levels. Many purchased items are fairly basic materials and commodities, and bulk discounts are likely to be obtained.

A case could be made for streamlining the number of suppliers for each type of material used. The main rationale for this would be to improve the quality of materials purchased. Reduced variation in materials quality may help to reduce the need for adjustment at the quality checking stage, and therefore reduce total paint production times.

4.5 What improvements could be made to production planning at Kalon?

Without accurate forecasts of demand it is very difficult to plan production effectively. Kalon's problems in production planning stem from the difficulties in forecasting the volume of paints to produce across the various product ranges. A rather basic four week moving average system is used to forecast demand for each product. These forecasts are then adjusted by an "expert" based on nothing more than his/her knowledge of the market and experience of the previous year.

This system appears to be quite effective in identifying quantities to be produced, but it is then up to a production planner to draw up a schedule manually on the Friday prior to each week. Moreover, once the production schedule is under way, changes may still have to be made to accommodate urgent requirements. This scheduling system is unlikely to optimise production with respect to changeover times, and it would become very difficult to manage at times of very high capacity utilisation. It also relies on ready availability of materials.

Further problems arise when the computer suggests the need for more production in the week than capacity allows. To circumvent this problem, expert judgement is used to decide how to build up stock in anticipation of peaks in demand.

Export orders are not forecast in any meaningful way and are simply slotted into the production schedule as and when possible.

52 Manufacturing Logistics

This entire system would benefit from streamlining, possibly to establish one mechanism for all types of orders. It would also be advantageous to find ways of improving demand forecasting and to try to extend the planning period beyond one week. There is a need to reduce the use of expert judgement, which relies too heavily on relatively few individuals.

The advisability of changing production plans in mid-stream needs to be investigated. Such late changes can cause considerable disruption throughout the supply chain, even though they make the company more customer responsive.

4.6 In what ways do Kalon's preferred marketing channels affect the efficiency of the company's logistics system?

Supplies to the major DIY multiple retailers move through very straightforward logistics systems. Channels have tended to become shorter as the retailers have centralised their inventories. Order sizes and drop sizes are large, and transport in complete vehicle loads has become the norm. Centralisation at B&Q allowed Kalon to reduce its vehicle fleet, and to concentrate on larger vehicles.

Customer service levels in this market segment are necessarily high, as exemplified by the B&Q small order picking system discussed earlier. This increases inventory levels and can call for late changes to production schedules at times of high demand.

Kalon's continued growth in the professional decorators' market has required the servicing of very many smaller customers and the opening of a nation-wide network of trade centre outlets. In this market segment much smaller orders are the norm, increasing the cost and complexity of the order processing system. A large and varied vehicle fleet has to be maintained and vehicle utilisation is much poorer.

The trade centres in particular must be supplied with a complete range of decorating materials and this means that Kalon buy in many lines from outside suppliers. This leads to high inventory levels and increased warehousing requirements.

Main competitors in the professional decorating market tend to operate networks of regional depots. However those competitors are primarily paint manufacturers rather than suppliers of entire ranges of decorating products. If Kalon were to operate a regional depot network already high inventory levels would be increased further, and this option is therefore unlikely to be cost-effective.

4.7 Identify potential strengths of the Kalon logistics system

The system provides relatively high customer service over a large product range without incurring the costs of a regional depot network.

The production scheduling system is reasonably demand responsive against a background of a very large product range and the need for batch production methods, factors which combine to preclude true JIT manufacturing.

Transport efficiency is relatively high given the constraints imposed by the many small drops and the lack of a computerised routeing and scheduling system.

The central warehouse is modern and well equipped in terms of racking and materials handling equipment.

There are EDI order processing links to major customers.

Distribution costs as a proportion of sales value are in line with those in comparable industries and companies.

SECTION 5 DESCRIPTION OF ACTUAL DEVELOPMENTS IN THE COMPANY

The case study makes clear that there is little scope for further organic growth in either of the two market sectors that have given such successful growth since the mid 1980s.

In principle, two possible strategic options can be identified, and given the existing strategy of market segmentation, these are not mutually exclusive:

- development of stronger Kalon brands for the retail market. This would reduce dependence on the own-label products, but would be difficult. Kalon would have to attack ICI Dulux head on and the strategy would need a great deal of expensive marketing support
- further acquisition, particularly on mainland Europe, to strengthen and consolidate Kalon's position as a main contender in its strongest markets.

In the event Chief Executive Mike Hennessy made a very significant move in the latter direction in 1995, when Kalon merged with Euridep, the decorative paints division of the French Total oil company. Euridep owned Manders-Johnstone with two factories in the UK and 14% of the UK trade paints market. This merger gave Kalon 30% of the UK trade paints market and raised the company's position to second in the UK market after Akzo Nobel. Taken together, the recent acquisition with Novodec (as mentioned in the case study) and this more recent merger with Euridep have enabled Kalon to strengthen its position in its two key markets. One Manders-Johnstone factory has been scheduled for closure and production will be switched to Birstall where capacity utilisation will increase dramatically.

SECTION 6 AUDIENCES/USES OF CASE/TEACHING SUGGESTIONS

6.1 Audiences

This case study is suitable for a wide range of applications. The focus on the relationships between strategic management and logistics management make it especially relevant for students at final-year undergraduate level on business and logistics courses, or on a wide range of management postgraduate courses. The considerable amount of information relating to the operation of the Kalon logistics system make it most relevant to students studying transport, distribution management, operations management or logistics. Students without a basic grounding in such areas may obtain less benefit.

6.2 Possible uses

The case has been developed for the investigation of the relationships between logistics management and strategic decision-making, and to explore the logistical impacts of strategic decisions in some depth. Thus the case is not suitable for short seminars or class discussions. In groupwork situations it is recommended that with no prior reading three hours are allocated for reading, discussion, generation of solutions to tasks and reporting (ideally through group presentations).

On appropriate courses the case could be used as the basis for major assignments, either on an individual or a group basis. The bibliography at the end of the case suggests a range of supporting material.

6.3 Teaching suggestions

The case is suitable for teaching methods involving group discussions and presentations. Students can be assigned to competitive groups, which will all study the case in its entirety and prepare solutions to the same question, or else groups can be assigned to concentrate on issues relating to different parts of the case, such as production planning, purchasing or physical distribution. In the latter case it would be possible to highlight areas in which the different groups' solutions were inconsistent as a total logistics solution.

Once students have become familiar with the scenario of the case and with possible solutions, teachers will be able to make regular reference during subsequent teaching sessions.

Case 11

TRICO

Manufacturing and Logistics

Dennis Nettle, *Victoria University of Technology*

SECTION 1 CASE SYNOPSIS

This case is true in substance, though the sequence of some events has been modified to make the case more readable. The case describes the changing situation facing Trico, a manufacturer of windscreen wiper assembles. The case represents a synopsis of a ten year period over which the company came to grips with its competitive problems through a range of reforms which allowed it to focus more on customers and products, and hence to develop the integration between JIT distribution, manufacture and purchasing -which is at the centre of the logistics concept.

Firstly, the case describes how Trico was typical of the situation of many auto-components suppliers in Australia -one of dependency on their large customers and on the local domestic market. It describes how this market dependency was reflected in operations in terms of distribution, production and purchasing, and also innovation. Short term horizons in terms of car company ordering, lack of JIT and in process quality control, were major causes for high finished goods and raw material inventory costs at Trico.

Secondly, the case describes how Trico's high inventory costs were also due to the poor organisation of the production process: in particular the existence of a bottle neck operation -the 200 tonne press which was central to all the processes. Functional organisation of the production process was also a problem because it contradicted the actual flow of production, resulting in extensive material handling.

Thirdly the case describes the difficulty Trico management had in dealing with these problems due to the functional nature of the factory organisation. Despite the integrated cross functional nature of the problems, there was a lack of an operational coordinating function at the management level. On the other hand the functional organisation of the process impeded cross-functional involvement by employees.

SECTION 2 TEACHING/LEARNING OBJECTIVES

1. To provide students with an understanding of the importance of a systematic approach to logistics which includes the manufacturing function.
2. To provide students with an understanding of the strategic, social and organisational conditions which impinge on the development of a systematic approach to logistics.

SECTION 3 MAIN ISSUES AND PROBLEMS

1. The linkage of JIT in manufacturing to JIT distribution.
2. How to manage the process of introducing just-in time concepts into manufacturing; the importance of team based approaches.
3. The problem of the strategic context, and the factors in the market place which may impede reform.
4. The problem of where to start a JIT improvement process within manufacturing.
5. The role of quality management in JIT

SECTION 4 SPECIFIC QUESTIONS

1. What does the case tell us about the role the external environment plays in the development of an integrated logistics strategy?
2. What role did the organisational context play in the problems and solutions to Trico's problems?
3. Describe and explain the sequence of reforms within the production process.
4. JIT is only about introducing Kanban. Discuss

SECTION 5 DESCRIPTION OF ACTUAL DEVELOPMENTS IN THE COMPANY

It is important to observe that the problems faced by the company did not focus on a single set of operationally defined choices. There was a longitudinal sequence of changes which needed to be made both operationally and strategically.

Firstly it should be observed that because of the symbiotic relationship between Trico and its major customers, the ability of Trico to change its manufacturing strategy depended to a large extent on the car companies changing their relationship with their suppliers. More broadly the ability to make these changes was also facilitated by changes in government policy, and changes at the corporate level. It is important to observe how like many foreign owned companies in Australia, Trico's capacity to develop a more independent exporting role was impeded by head office corporate policy. Trico's ability to develop its own internal organisational competencies, and tackle the non-OEM market, could not be resolved without these changes in the environmental context.

Secondly it is important to observe how even given these changes in the external environment, the ability of Trico to tackle the JIT and quality requirements of the car companies, required changes in the organisational/social context. The problems of functional organisation resulted in a sequential approach to operations which belied the interrelated nature of operational problems. Gearing the organisation horizontally in relation to the logistics channel required firstly improving the coordination of all the aspects of distribution, manufacturing, and purchasing. It also required a cross functional team organisation at the operational level. The involvement of unions and the guarantee of job security were key factors in gaining employee commitment. Increased employee commitment had numerous benefits in terms of the company's JIT strategy. Many problems were uncovered and resolved, of which managers had little knowledge.

Finally it is important to observe the actual sequence in which the JIT program was undertaken. Press shop set-up times was the first obstacle which had to be resolved before other problems could be addressed. In other cases the reforms undertaken promoted a reorganisation of the process away from a functional layout towards a layout more in accordance with the flow of the process. Resolving these problems of layout were crucial in turn for the reforms made to the organisation of inwards goods inventories and their location at assembly points.

SECTION 6 AUDIENCES/USE OF CASE/TEACHING SUGGESTIONS

6.1 Audiences

Suitable for undergraduate, and post-graduate courses in operations management or logistics. Could also be used by general management students.

6.2 Possible uses

Suitable for half hour discussion. Could also be used as an extended example in lectures.

6.3 Teaching suggestions

Students can read the first half of the case study, and consider the review questions; or they could read through the whole case.

It is important to note that the key thing about the case is to focus on the interrelated contextually conditioned nature of the problem and therefore the interrelated and hence long term nature of any solution. Rather than giving the students a well defined problem which is within the competence of a particular manager to solve, the aim of this case is to show the range of decisions (some of which were external to Trico) that were required to bring about change.

Part 4

Distribution Planning and Strategy

Case 12

GOMAN MARKETING CO.
Delivery Vehicles for the Warsaw District

Grzegorz M. Augustyniak, *Warsaw School of Economics* and **Professor Fred Beier**, *Carlson School of Management, University of Minnesota*

SECTION 1 CASE SYNOPSIS

Goman Marketing Co. is an import and distribution company with warehouses throughout Poland and was established based on a mixture of Polish and foreign capital.

One of the company's customer service goals is to deliver complete orders within 48 hours. Because this goal was achieved for only 75 per cent of Goman's orders, the company is considering several changes to its delivery process. The primary decision faced by Goman is whether the current delivery vehicles should be replaced with larger vehicles. In addition, a new order assembly ('bucket') technology, which would be feasible with larger vehicles, is under consideration.

SECTION 2 TEACHING OBJECTIVES

This case can be used to illustrate the importance of physical distribution and logistics management. In addition, the issues presented in the case emphasise the need to maintain a cost effective logistics system and deliver expected customer service. The case also provides an opportunity to analyse financial investment criteria. Three specific teaching objectives addressed are:

1. To introduce students to the logistics functions of warehousing, inventory management, order processing, and transportation,
2. To illustrate the trade-offs between customer service and delivery costs,
3. To assess specific delivery process modification alternatives using cost and benefit information.

58 Distribution Planning and Strategy

SECTIONS 3 AND 4 MAIN ISSUES AND POSSIBLE ASSIGNMENT QUESTIONS

1. Should the company buy the larger vans for its Warsaw warehouse? If so, why? If not, why not?
2. What other recommendations would you make in order to make Goman's delivery process more efficient (regardless whether students would buy the new vans or not)?
3. What additional information would you like to have?

3.1 Analysis and discussion of questions

Before discussing case questions a teacher should encourage students to identify the main limitations faced by Goman, which are:

1. Small trucks – which limit the number of boxes to be loaded and delivered to customers.
2. Order processing – which takes too much time.
3. Hours when the stores of Goman's customers are open.

Class discussion may be organised around these three problems, while questions to the case may be used to help students to prepare for the discussion before the class. Below one can find answers to the case questions which provide necessary information and solutions to lead a class discussion.

3.1.1 Should the company buy the larger vans for its Warsaw warehouse? If so, why? If not, why not?

The decision regarding the purchase of new vans leads to an assessment of the costs and benefits of the van alternatives. Although the costs of the new vans can be determined from information provided in the case, the benefits are more difficult to determine. Table 4.1 provides a summary of the information from the case.

Table 4.1 Van cost and benefit information

	Van size		
	10–12 m^3	20 m^3	30 m^3
Costs (PLN)			
Van*	31,500	46,500	82,500
Bucket technology	N/A	1,500	1,500
Operating cost (per month)	200	200	200
Driver (per month)	650	650	650
Benefits			
Loading time (minutes)	90	90	?
Capacity (No. of orders)	25	36	?
Capacity (No. of deliveries per day)	20–25	36	36

* depreciated over 3 years (36 months); current vans are two years old.

At the very beginning, it might be useful to estimate Goman's current delivery capacity and the number of late orders. By assuming that the goal is to deliver 100 per cent of its orders within 48 hours, we may make the following calculations:

Delivery capacity = number of vans x number of deliveries
 = 3 vans x 25 deliveries/day x 20 days/month
 = 1500 deliveries/month
Late deliveries = number of deliveries x 0.25
 = 1500 x 0.25
 = 375 deliveries/month

Considering each of Goman options:

— adding an additional 12m^3 van at the Warsaw warehouse,
— replacing all 12m^3 with 20m^3 vans, and
— replacing all 12m^3 vans with 30m^3.

In each case the incremental increase in delivery capacity exceeds the number of late deliveries. Table 4.2 provides a summary of the cost of each option, and suggests that purchasing new 20m^3 vans leads to the lowest cost per delivery and the lowest cost of incremental delivery capacity. Some students may be encouraged, based on the arithmetic analysis, to recommend that Goman should buy larger vans. However, it is appropriate at this point to apply financial criteria to the discussion and ask if this would be an appropriate use of Goman's money.

Table 4.2 Analysis of options for Warsaw warehouse

	Total cost (per month) (PLN)	Total delivery capacity (per month)	Total cost/Total delivery capacity	Incremental increase in cost[a] (PLN)	Incremental increase in delivery capacity	Incremental cost/ Incremental capacity (per month) (PLN)
Options						
Add 1 12m^3 van	6,900[b]	2000	3.45	1,725	500	3.45
Purchase 3 20m^3 vans	6,425[c]	2160	2.97	1,250	660	1.89
Purchase 3 30m^3 vans	9,425[d]	2160	4.36	4,250	660	6.44

Notes:
[a] Incremental increase in cost = Total cost (per month) − Current cost (see Table 4.1) = Total cost − [(31,500/36) + 200 + 650] x 3
[b] Total cost (per month) = [(31,500/36) + 200 + 650] x 4
[c] Total cost (per month) = [(46,500/36) + 200 + 650] x 3
[d] Total cost (per month) = [(82,500/36) + 200 + 650] x 3

Assuming that students will come to a class with already prepared calculations, it is obvious that the choice is basically between the existing small van or a larger van with bucket technology. Savings come in two types, from the reduced equipment cost per stop and the reduced labour cost per stop. The savings then should be related to the *difference* between the two investments.

First of all students should be asked to identify the advantages and disadvantages of buying larger van.

The main benefits are:

- Increased capacity up to 36 deliveries.
- More effective use of labour.
- Use of efficient delivery technology (buckets).
- Reduce of errors in delivering process.

The main disadvantages are:

- Price of the larger truck (46,500 PLN).
- Cost of the buckets (1,500 PLN).
- High depreciation (over 36 months).
- Possible increased fuel consumption (the case does not provide any information about it, but it may be easily assumed).
- Higher maintenance cost (the text of the case assumes that cost to be the same for all kinds of vans, but it might be questioned by students).

Having identified the pros and cons of buying larger van one may come to some calculations (all figures rounded up to 0.00).

Currently used $12m^3$ vans
The Warsaw warehouse operates three $12m^3$ vans each of them having the capacity of making 500 stops per month (see the beginning of this section).
Then:

the ownership cost is	31,500 PLN/36 months	875.00 PLN
maintenance cost is	200 PLN per month	200.00 PLN
total cost per month (excl. labour)		**1,075.00 PLN**
total cost per stop (excl. labour)		**2.15 PLN**
cost of labour per stop per month	650 PLN/500 stops	1.30 PLN
total cost per month per stop		**3.45 PLN**

Considered $20m^3$ van
The number of stops per month increases to 720 (36 stops per day x 5 days a week x 4 weeks a month).
Then:

the ownership cost is	46,500 PLN/36 months	1,291.67 PLN
maintenance cost is	200 PLN per month	200.00 PLN
total cost per month (excl. labour)		**1,491.67 PLN**
total cost per stop (excl. labour)		**2.07 PLN**
cost of labour per stop per month	650 PLN/720 stops	0.90 PLN
total cost per month per stop		**2.97 PLN**

Then, the net saving per stop using a larger van is **0.48 PLN** which means that annually (720 stops per month x 12 months = 8,640 stops per year) Goman may save up to **4,147.20 PLN** (or 12,441.60 PLN when replacing all smaller vans with larger ones). It means that the investment in larger vans will be paid back in over 11 years (compared to 3 years of full depreciation of the vans!).

3.1.2 Conclusions

The main conclusions are:

- Goman should not replace its smaller vans with larger ones.
- If Goman needs to buy and extra van, it should consider purchasing a $20m^3$ one.
- Since the analysis is simplified, some students may raise some additional questions or make their own remarks to presented calculations like:
- The fuel consumption and the maintenance cost of a larger truck would be probably higher than of smaller ones.

- The analysis does not take into consideration the opportunity cost of purchasing new vans (high rate of interest, possible investments which may bring higher profit etc.) which make this option even less feasible.
- The cost of purchasing new vans would be partially covered from the sales of existing vans – which may revitalise that idea again, etc.

The final conclusions are not affected substantially by these remarks and the attempt to put too much emphasis on quantitative analysis may focus students' attention to unimportant issues.

3.2 What other recommendations would you make in order to make Goman's delivery process more efficient?

Despite purchasing new van(s) students should be encouraged to propose several other actions which might improve Goman's delivery process. These include:

- Allow each salesperson to telephone or fax orders to the warehouse when they are received (it would also require changing the working hours of employees, because faxing orders when nobody is in the warehouse does not make any difference).
- Assemble orders and load trucks during the evening to save 90 minutes of loading time in the morning and increase the number of deliveries that can be made each day.
- Standardise the labels on all products to facilitate order assembly and verification by the customers.
- Orders could be repackaged to reduce the number of cartons per delivery and therefore simplify the driver's job of reassembling the order.
- Drivers might be authorised to pick up orders while delivering products to customers.
- Goman might discuss with its clients the possibility of establishing 'turn-key' deliveries (orders with accompanying invoices could be distributed in the night and left in a separate room to which drivers would have access). That would be very much a question of trust.

3.3 What additional information would you like to have?

Information which would facilitate a more efficient delivery process and help in the decision to purchase larger vans includes the following:

- Information about the late deliveries.
  - How are late deliveries distributed among days of the week, months of the year, and warehouses?
  - What are Goman's goals for on-time delivery?
- Information about the likely increase in demand and implications for needed delivery capacity.
  - Are sales expected to grow? At what rate?
  - Does the need for delivery capacity increase as sales increase?
  - Is the number of customers expected to increase? At what rate?
  - Does the need for delivery capacity increase as the number of customers increases?
  - Will larger warehouse require additional delivery capacity?
- Information about the cost of late deliveries.
  - Do late deliveries lead to lost sales?

62 Distribution Planning and Strategy

SECTION 5 DESCRIPTION OF ACTUAL DEVELOPMENTS IN THE COMPANY

Between September 1992 and February 1996 the company, along with its logistical system, changed significantly.

The proportion of Polish products rose to over 60 per cent. Goman had also increased the number of SKU's offered (200), but the customer base did not increase significantly as was expected.

The system of distribution had also been reorganised. The warehouse in Pozna_ had been expanded and become a distribution centre, from which almost all products were distributed to customers through all eleven of Goman's branches (warehouse plus sales office). The new warehouses had been located in Lublin (East), Sosnowiec (moved from Katowice), Rzeszów (south-east) and Bia_ystok (north-east).

Deliveries to Poznan and from Poznan to branches were arranged through public transportation companies. Branches, on the other hand, were served exclusively by Goman's own fleet of vans.

Goman finally decided not to buy larger vans, but to add more small ones. The largest ones were of 1,800 kg maximum load (about 15m^3). Warsaw warehouse in particular operated four vans and two pick-up cars.

Orders were collected as they had been before, however other forms of ordering (like faxing or mailing) were introduced. Sales people were no longer required to collect payments in cash, since the majority of customers had switched to money transfer instead (deferred payment was the most common form of payment). Goman had also installed an information system assisting in demand forecasting.

Orders were assembled the day before and loaded into the trucks next morning at eight o'clock. Orders inside a truck became more consolidated and better organised (usually in form of one to four plastic-wrapped packs). It did not however eliminate the need to compare the delivery with the invoice by a driver.

As the result of all those changes, the customer service level offered had been significantly improved: almost all orders were delivered within 24 hours.

SECTION 6 AUDIENCES/USES OF CASE/TEACHING SUGGESTIONS

6.1 Audiences

This case is the most suitable for logistics or distribution classes offered to undergraduate students. For more advanced the instructor should place more emphasis on discussion of question two.

6.2 Teaching suggestions

The discussion of this case should take around 60–75 minutes.

It is recommended to assign the case questions before class. The purpose of the first question is to encourage students to identify sources of savings in Goman's logistics system and to quantify them. In the process of discussing the quantitative aspects of the case it is important to bring out the capacity constraints which Goman currently faces.

The more robust discussion occurs in question two. In effect, this discussion should examine two aspects of Goman's operation, i.e., how can the current constraints be removed (as in organising a turn-key delivery system) and what can be done to improve Goman's logistics system independent of van decision. The discussion should be conducted as brain storming session where students are encouraged to express ideas freely.

Case 13

PALMER AND HARVEY LTD

Transport and Customer Service Options for the Distribution of Small Orders

Colin Bamford, *The University of Huddersfield* and **Eddie Dennis**, *Palmer and Harvey McLane Ltd.*

SECTION 1 CASE SYNOPSIS

This case is derived from the particular experience of Palmer and Harvey Ltd (P&H) a major UK wholesaler. The data contained in the case is real – it is derived from information obtained by the co-author from the company itself and from a first-hand customer service survey carried out in 1992.

The case considers three particular issues:

- how the company should respond to the distribution of small orders to customers and in particular, whether it should provide different types of transport and customer service level for such customers.
- how to carry out a customer service survey of small order customers.
- how to use this information in order to determine an optimum transport strategy to meet customer needs.

In arriving at an appropriate outcome, P&H recognised that there were particular trade-offs in so far as the cheapest transport alternative was not necessarily the best one in terms of its effect on customer service.

SECTION 2 TEACHING/LEARNING OBJECTIVES

On completion of a study of this case, students will be able to:

1. Understand how to incorporate original customer service data and information on possible transport options into the development of a coherent logistics policy which will enable the company to compete as a major player in a highly competitive and changing market place.
2. Understand how data from a customer service survey can be used to meaningful effect.
3. Appraise the methodological and statistical problems of carrying out an effective customer service survey.
4. Evaluate alternative transport delivery options within a wider logistics context.

SECTION 3 MAIN ISSUES AND PROBLEMS RAISED BY THE CASE

The case raises three related issues. These are

1. What should P&H do about meeting the needs of customers who order small quantities of goods to be delivered to their premises?
2. What is the perceived customer service requirement of such customers?
3. How best might such orders be delivered?

The small order problem is one which has not been well documented and researched.[1] An immediate issue which is raised is that of 'how to define a small order'. This clearly depends on the nature of the business and the extent to which there is a trade off between continuing to service small order customers and the loss of revenue and customer goodwill if these orders are refused. Lambert et al suggest seven alternative policies for dealing with small orders, namely:

- channel co-ordination
- standardisation of processing of small orders
- volume discounting
- order consolidation
- automated order handling
- minimum order quantity
- higher than break-even minimum order quantities

After careful consideration, including an analysis of their customer base, P&H applied a 'minimum order quantity'.

The customer service survey which was carried out followed a conventional pattern.[2] There was though a very deliberate attempt to focus on those variables of particular reference in P&H's markets and at the same time, to seek to compare the perception that P&H's customers had of the company's main competitors. The price of delivered products was clearly over-riding – this of course was of importance to P&H in looking at transport options, where there was a strong argument for minimising direct transport costs.

The five transport options raised in the case were carefully assessed by P&H. Option (i) (a mixed fleet) was ruled out at an early stage on the grounds that it increased direct transport costs; Option (ii) (van sales) had little relevance on account of P&H's diverse product range. Option (iii) merited more consideration.[3] P&H though were concerned about the limited flexibility, loss of control and the poor level of customer service likely to be forthcoming from the use of a contractor and therefore, this option was discounted. Franchising (Option iv) was an interesting and in some respects, innovative approach. Although not applied it could remain a realistic future possibility for the company to adopt. The Safe Option (do nothing) was the logical short term outcome, not least as costs are known and service levels can be controlled by P&H. This option was the one which was adopted by P&H to deliver to small order customers and represented, no particular change in transport terms to current operations.

---

[1] For more information, teachers and students should read Lambert, D. M. et al. (1987), 'Solving the Small Order Problem'. *International Journal of Physical Distribution and Materials Management*, 17(2) and Lambert, D. M. et al (1990), 'Small Order Problem' *Management Decision*, 28(3).

[2] For more details see Christopher, M., *The Customer Service Planner*, Butterworth - Heinemann, 1992.

[3] See Walters, P. J., 'In or Out, The Contract Logistics Dilemma', *Distribution Dynamics*, 1994.

SECTION 4 SPECIFIC QUESTIONS

Three additional, more specific questions, follow from the discussion of the Main Issues and Problems raised in the case. These are:

4.1 What criteria might be applied in order to determine a minimum order quantity?

There are various possibilities, largely dependent upon the type of product and nature of the business. Some obvious alternatives to the volume measure applied by P&H are

- value of order;
- profitability of order;
- the extent to which customers normally order above the minimum order quantity;
- the extent to which a customer is from a single account or one outlet from an important multiple account;
- differential pricing depending on the quantity ordered.

4.2 How reliable was the customer service survey carried out by P&H?

This is an important question, not least as strategic decisions are being taken on the basis of evidence from the customer service survey.

A discussion of this might include reference to:

- the adequacy of the sample size
- the estimation of sampling errors
- an appraisal of alternative forms of data collection to an interview survey
- the potential to stratify the customer base in order to enhance the statistical reliability of the information provided.

A further set of issues could cover:

- whether there would be value in carrying out an identical survey of how P&H's competitors were perceived by P&H customers;
- how such comparative information could be used to competitive advantage by P&H.

4.3 What are the particular advantages and disadvantages to P&H of franchising or contracting-out transport sevices?

4.3.1 Franchising transport services

The franchising option is particularly interesting, not least as it

- reduces the capital needed by P&H for vehicle purchase;
- would involve little change to present working practices;
- service levels could be clearly specified.

4.3.2 Contracting-out transport services

On the other hand, franchising may present new distribution issues such as

- On what basis should franchises be determined?
- Will franchises make an adequate rate of return? How can P&H business be effectively integrated with other delivery work?
- Is the loss of direct contact with customers of any significance?

The contracting out option is one which many businesses like P&H have pursued over the past 10–15 years in the UK. The arguments for and against have been the subject of on-going argument and review. In favour are issues such as

- Contracting out allows a company to concentrate upon its core business.
- Capital can be released for divestment into core activities.
- Costs are known and can be easily incorporated into financial budgets.
- There are no labour relations problems for the customers of contract logistics operators.

Alternatively, as P&H concluded, contracting out could be inadvisable due to

- a lack of service flexibility;
- the immediate customer interface would be lost;
- the nature of the small order business would not be an attractive proposition to a contractor;
- customer service levels might fall.

SECTION 5 DESCRIPTIONS OF ACTUAL DEVELOPMENTS IN THE COMPANY

As a consequence of this particular investigation, P&H

1. Introduced a 20 outer minimum delivered order quantity
2. Decided to retain its own existing fleet of delivery vehicles.

The outcome of this was that

(a) Some customers were lost – they transferred their businesses to other competitor wholesalers or bought direct from 'cash and carry' outlets.
(b) Other customers remained with P&H but ordered less frequently. Like customers in (a) above, they used competitors and 'cash and carry' outlets to purchase stock, mainly for topping up purposes. The business of such customers remains vulnerable.

SECTION 6 AUDIENCES/TEACHING SUGGESTIONS

This case is suitable for use by

1. Final year undergraduate/MSc students specialising in logistics management.
2. Marketing students who wish to study the practical application of a customer service survey.
   Transport Management students who wish to study the decision criteria in transport choice.
   The volume of data contained in the case makes it particularly attractive for detailed analysis and investigation by (1) above.

Case 14

PEPSI COLA INTERNATIONAL
Distribution and Pricing in Ukraine

David A. Menachof, *University of Plymouth*

SECTION 1 CASE SYNOPSIS

Pepsi has been doing business in the Former Soviet Union for over 20 years. Bottling and distribution of their product is done in major cities throughout the CIS via franchise agreements. This case examines Pepsi Cola International's current distribution methods along with resulting product pricing outcomes. As the economic transformation of this part of the world continues, is a change in the distribution methods currently in place advised or warranted?

A situation has occurred whereby the final product's distribution and pricing it out of PCIs control. Local product varies in price from city to city. It also competes with 'imported' Pepsi that is considered superior by the local population. Regaining control of the distribution pipeline is plagued by three overriding factors:

- Infrastructure (Existing Channels of Distribution)
- Political and Fiscal Instability, and
- the 'Soviet' Mentality

SECTION 2 TEACHING/LEARNING OBJECTIVES

- To enable students to understand some of the realities facing Western companies doing business in the former Soviet Union.
- To encourage the student to identify the problems involved in doing business in an unfamiliar environment. To put their self-reference criterion aside and understand the need for patience in this environment.
- Try to get the student to imagine how different their actions would be if they based their actions on the 'Soviet' pattern.
- To bring up the issue of business ethics (in light of a business climate that fosters bribes and 'mafia' activity).
- To encourage the student to make the connection of logistics activities with retail pricing.
- To give the student the tough task of gathering information from a part of the world where information is scarce. The student will be forced to make a decision with drastically less information than desired.

68 Distribution Planning and Strategy

SECTIONS 3 AND 4 MAIN ISSUES AND SPECIFIC QUESTIONS

3.1 Regarding product distribution, specifically what channel of distribution should be used and who should control the distribution at its various stages on its way to the final consumer

Currently, PCI controls the distribution of the concentrate to the franchisees, while local distributors distribute the final product. In Russia, PCI has several company-owned routes in St. Petersburg and Moscow, but in general, final product distribution is left to local operators. It may be suggested that as bottling capacity increases, there may be better reason to control the final product distribution, but until production capacity is able to meet demand, it doesn't make financial sense for PCI to attempt to control final distribution or even attempt to further regulate franchisees. In addition, the haphazardness of product distribution caused by 'grey market' sales, mean that any control attempt at this point in time would be futile.

3.2 Regarding pricing, what changes, if any, should be made to the retail price policy of Pepsi. The standard product currently being the .33 litre returnable bottle. How should this price compare to a .33 litre can of Pepsi imported from Israel or Greece, for example?

Currently, PCI can only attempt to regulate the price of Pepsi sold by the franchisee. Anything beyond that is out of PCIs control. Due to the number of participants in the final product distribution chain, there is nothing that can be done regarding the varying retail price of Pepsi at this point in time. Only as the market reforms develop and a more stable business climate occurs will it be possible to attempt to monitor the number of retailers selling the product.

The reason for the price differential between domestic and imported Pepsi is based on perceived quality by the local consumer. In this case, a marketing campaign to assure the population that domestically-produced Pepsi is manufactured to the same high quality as Pepsi around the world might be one possibility to remove some of this grey market shifting of the bottled product.

3.3 Explain what other issues or problems are of major concern to you as you make your recommendations on the preceding issues. (This question should provide the student the opportunity to bring up the uncertainty and 'real' problems involved in doing business in Ukraine (and other CIS countries).

Infrastructure (Existing Channels of Distribution), Political and Fiscal Instability, and the 'Soviet' Mentality are the overriding problems that face Pepsi Cola International or any multi-national attempting to do business in this part of the world. Anyone attempting to do business in the Former Soviet Union must take the time to find honest, reputable partners and be willing to stick it out for the long haul.

SECTION 5 ACTUAL DEVELOPMENTS

Although these developments are not in Ukraine, they are occurring in the Commonwealth of Independent States. Pepsi Cola International continues to expand its presence in the CIS as evidenced by the following recent agreements. Pepsi recently signed a long term lease in Podolsk (15 km south of Moscow) for a company-owned bottling operation that should have two lines operational in the Summer of 1996, while running a company-owned distribution operation as of

15 November 1995. A joint venture in Sochi, Georgia where Pepsi Cola International will have management control will have a 2 liter PET line operational in December 1995.

DSD (direct store delivery) efforts continue to be hampered by the three overriding factors mentioned earlier: Infrastructure (Existing Channels of Distribution), Political and Fiscal Instability, and the 'Soviet' Mentality. The focus remains on Distributor Sales as a key arm to product distribution.

Since most of the distribution is undertaken by local distributors and out of PCI's direct control, shipments from other countries will continue to occur for the time being, but is expected to taper off as Pepsi Cola International opens more company-owned or joint venture facilities in the CIS.

The overall outlook is good and growth is expected to continue and accelerate as the privatisation process in Ukraine takes hold.

SECTION 6 TEACHING SUGGESTIONS

When this case was tested on a group of Finnish undergraduate business students during the Spring of 1995, they gave suggestions that would be perfectly valid and acceptable in developed economies, but failed to take into account, or rather were unaware of the difficulties in attempting to do business in Ukraine. I admit that I purposely did not give them much direction except as to the specific questions supplied with this case.

Following that trial, I believe that this case may be best discussed in two parts. During the first discussion, your students may very well come up with the same conclusions as these Finnish students. Following that discussion, introduce the issues of real concern to Western corporations who are doing business in Ukraine, such as bureaucracy, bribery, extortion and banditry, and how to limit exposure to potential loss in such a situation. PCI has solved these problems by only shipping the concentrate to its licensed bottlers allowing the risk to be taken by the local distribution channels.

The universal nature of this case to such a range of product categories and its geographic coverage makes it an interesting and enlightening exercise. All consumer products are subject to the same factors and all of these factors are currently problematic throughout the Former Soviet Union and many Eastern European countries.

Case 15

RANK HOVIS MCDOUGALL PLC
Evaluation of Contract Distribution Tenders

Jane Parkin, *University of Huddersfield*

SECTION 1 CASE SYNOPSIS

Rank Hovis McDougall (RHM) is a leading UK food manufacturer. In 1992 RHM Food Services Division was one of five operating divisions within the Rank Hovis McDougall Group plc. Distribution costs were highlighted as one of the areas where the consolidation of customers, products, fleets, warehouses or facilities could well reduce the overall costs within the Division. Three businesses: McDougalls, RHM Ingredients and Pasta Foods were considered to be ideal candidates for this exercise. At that time the distribution networks of the three businesses were run completely independently.

This case study follows the process of inviting three major national distribution companies to tender for a combined distribution network for the three businesses and of evaluating these tenders.

The main issue covered is that of evaluating contract tenders, both in terms of cost and other factors when the information provided by the different distribution companies is not easily comparable.

This case study is real except that the cost figures have been disguised and the names of the contract distribution companies concealed.

SECTION 2 TEACHING/LEARNING OBJECTIVES

3. To give students the opportunity to evaluate contract tenders and make decisions as to:
   (a) whether to contract out or not;
   (b) contractor selection.
4. To give students the opportunity to discuss how a distribution network can be planned and costed.
5. To allow students to understand key issues in contract distribution.
6. To give students the opportunity to discuss how the 'invitation to tender' process for contract distribution should be managed.

SECTION 3 MAIN ISSUES AND PROBLEMS

3.1 The difficulty of obtaining comparable proposals for a complex distribution tender

The proposals submitted by the two distribution companies were initially very difficult to compare not only because they offered different solutions but primarily because they included different aspects of the RHM operation and left RHM with different levels of retained costs. For example, accepting the Company A proposal would have left RHM to cover more aspects and costs of the trunking operation than the Company B proposal.

3.2 The issue of retained costs

Neither of the two distribution companies highlighted the costs that would be retained by RHM if the contract proposals were accepted.

One of the major tasks facing the consultant was to determine the nature and level of these retained costs.

The retained costs had to be considered at two levels:

- direct operating expenses not covered by the proposals e.g. distribution in Northern Ireland;
- the cost of retaining RHM distribution managers who would be necessary to manage the relationship with the contractors. This is a frequently overlooked cost of contracting out.

3.3 The issue of contract management fee

It was also impossible from the original proposals to determine the level of management fee to be charged by the contractors, and to ascertain whether this fee was included in the costing.

The management fees may have been deliberately or inadvertently concealed or excluded from the proposals; but in any event required the consultant to seek specific and detailed clarification from both contractors. The consultant discovered that the management fees were included in the proposals and were approximately 7.5% of the total contract cost for Company A, and 10% of total contract cost for Company B.

3.4 The efficiency with which RHM managed the Invitation to Tender process

A more specific brief could have been given to the contractors in order to obtain proposals and costings that were more directly comparable. However, many companies considering contracting out their distribution operation are unused to the process and so do not really know what questions to ask of the distribution companies nor what to put in the Invitation to Tender document.

In practice the proposal was complex for the contractors because it required consideration of how best to amalgamate three previously separate operations then costing out the preferred solutions.

Had RHM been more prescriptive in the invitation to tender, the development of proposals by the contractors would have been easier, as would the comparison of proposals, but the solutions proposed may not have been so innovative.

3.5 The approach to evaluating contract proposals

The RHM project team realised that evaluating the proposals was a time consuming and complex task particularly for managers who all had day to day operational responsibilities. It was for that reason that an outside consultant who had experience in contract evaluation and could dedicate time to the task was brought in.

With hindsight it would have been advisable to involve the consultant from the outset of the project and particularly in the preparation of the invitation to tender.

3.6 The initial locations proposed by the distribution companies

72 Distribution Planning and Strategy

Although the distribution companies described their suggested depot locations as 'ideally situated' and 'modern' it was the experience of the working party who visited these that each of the distribution companies had empty warehouses which they were keen to employ for the RHM contract and which were neither modern nor ideally located. RHM thus at an early stage asked the distribution companies to consider alternative locations.

3.7 The type of contract

The proposed basis of the distribution contracts was 'cost plus'. This does not encourage efficiency on the part of the contractor who is guaranteed all costs plus an agreed management fee.

RHM have subsequently included profit sharing agreements in their contracts. A reduced management fee is paid but any savings made by the distribution company are shared in an agreed proportion between RHM and the contractor. This has improved efficiency and practically eliminated empty running.

3.8 Contract performance monitoring

Neither of the two contract proposals made any reference to the detailed criteria by which the contract should be monitored nor of the performance that should be achievable in relation to the criteria.

It is perhaps not surprising that contractors do not include such a 'rod for their own back'; the omission was that RHM should have specified in the invitation to tender a requirement for the contractor to indicate how the contract should be monitored and a penalty clause stating how any poor performance should be paid for.

SECTION 4 SPECIFIC QUESTIONS

1. Devise a spreadsheet to compare the costs given in the contract proposals and the RHM operation.

   Indicate which data is available from the proposals and where additional data is needed in order to complete the spreadsheet analysis.

2. As the consultant what would you recommend to RHM?

3. The cost of closure of current facilities was identified as £260000 for Dunstable and £400000 for Reading. Use discounted cash flow methods to calculate the annual cost of spreading these payments over 5 years using an interest rate of 12.5% pa (the rate quoted by one of the distribution companies) and compare these with the costs given by the contract distribution companies.

Possible approach

Most spreadsheets have several financial functions (these can be discovered by using the help facility). In Excel, for example, the function PMT (periodic payment for an annuity) with syntax:

> **PMT(rate, per, pv)** is used.

To find annual payments (assumed payable at year ends) to cover an initial outlay of £400000, the command in Excel is:

> **PMT(0.125, 5, 400000)** which gives a result of £112342 (this is the figure quoted by distribution company A)

The calculation is more complex using a calculator; any basic level Quantitative Methods for Business textbook will give details.

4. Draw graphs showing the seasonal fluctuations in demand for each of McDougall's, RHM and Pasta Foods. Use suitable calculations to estimate any savings that could be made in hiring extra vehicles to cover peak periods if the three operations are combined.

Possible approach

		Total throughput (pallets)				Average weekly throughput				Weekly throughput as a % of average			
Period	Weeks period	McDougll	RHM	Pasta	Total	McDougll	RHM	Pasta	Total	McDougll %	RHM %	Pasta %	Total %
1	5	6446	4519	4796	15761	1289	904	959	3152	114	97	103	105
2	4	5365	3966	4317	13648	1341	992	1079	3412	119	106	116	114
3	4	5426	3897	4317	13640	1357	974	1079	3410	120	104	116	114
4	5	4430	4444	3837	12711	886	889	767	2542	79	95	83	85
5	4	3382	3540	4796	11718	846	885	1199	2930	75	95	129	98
6	4	4132	3701	3837	11670	1033	925	959	2918	92	99	103	98
7	5	5628	4605	4796	15029	1126	921	959	3006	100	99	103	101
8	4	4440	3653	3837	11930	1110	913	959	2983	98	98	103	100
9	4	4866	3606	3837	12309	1217	902	959	3077	108	97	103	103
10	5	5858	4580	3837	14275	1172	916	767	2855	104	98	83	96
11	4	4094	3592	2878	10564	1024	898	720	2641	91	96	78	88
12	4	4539	4307	2878	11724	1135	1077	720	2931	101	115	78	98
Total Average		58606	48410	47963	154979	1128	933	927	2988				

Average weekly throughput

[Graph showing pallets (600-1400) vs Period (1-12) for McDougall, RHMI, and Pasta]

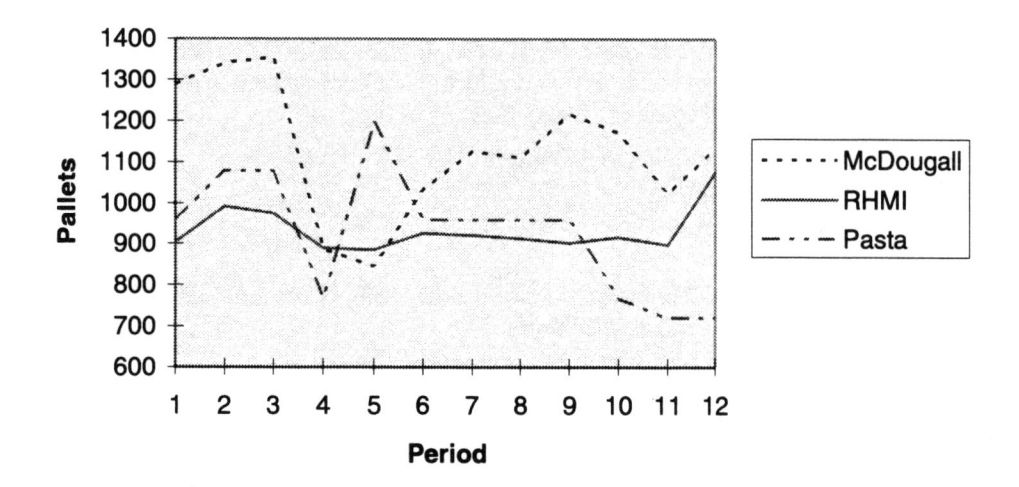

It can be seen from both the calculations and the graphs that the peaks and troughs cancel each other out to a large extent. For example, in period 1, McDougall's is running at 14% above average and to cover this extra vehicles and drivers would have to be hired. However, when the operation as a whole is considered, the throughput is only 5% above average and could probably be covered by the normal fleet and drivers.

Students could be encouraged to discuss some or all of the following issues by working in small groups.

5. How should a distribution network be planned?

6. Who should be involved in the project team?

7. What data is needed to plan a distribution network:
   - over what timescale?
   - what standard units should be used (pallets, etc.)
   - what level of detail is appropriate?
     - what products should be amalgamated?
     - which customers should be amalgamated?

8. How should seasonality be dealt with?
   - should facilities be set at the level of
     - an average week?
     - a peak week?
     - somewhere between the two?

9. How should analysis be carried out?
   - rough outline using a spreadsheet or
   - more detailed using specialist distribution software?

There are several strategic planning packages now available on the market (e.g. Fastnet by Paragon and CAST by Radical). These can be used for the overview of numbers and locations of depots. For more detailed analysis, such as the optimum number and size of vehicles at each depot, a vehicle scheduling package (such as Trandos, Paragon, Truckstops etc.) can be used. It should be emphasised that these packages should only be used as aids to decision making: they are not guaranteed to provide the optimum solution. Packages such as these were used by the two distribution companies in preparing their solutions.

10. How should the cost of different possible solutions be compared?

There are difficulties here with comparing both annual operating costs (of warehouses, vehicles etc.) and fixed costs (such as the cost of closure of existing facilities, initial purchase or lease costs of new facilities, 'one-off' set-up costs). The only way to do this rigorously is to decide on a time scale (e.g. 5 years) and use DCF (discounted cash flow) methods.

11. Decisions over in-house v contract distribution

There are several possibilities here:
- contract out all the distribution
- keep it all in house
- go for a mixture: in house distribution at some depots, contract out at others, contract out the transport but keep the warehousing in-house
- is it preferable to use several different distribution companies?

12. How to decide which contract tender to accept?

This isn't as easy as it might appear: it was certainly not obvious from the original quotes produced which of the distribution companies was proposing the best (cheapest?) alternative, or indeed whether any of them satisfied the working party's criterion that at least £500,000 should be saved over the current operation.

13. What issues other than cost are important?
   - e.g. level of service

14. Contract issues

If a company decides to contract out some or all of its distribution operations, decisions have to be made on the terms of the contract such as:
   - length of contract
   - open book or closed book accounting
   - fixed price or cost plus
   - measures of efficiency (e.g. percentage of orders delivered complete, correct and on time): what the target should be, how frequently these should be measured, how presented, what the penalty should be if the target is not met
   - management/staffing
   - assets: can the contract distribution company take over current buildings, vehicles, staff? What is a reasonable price for these?
   - computer systems: what systems are proposed by the contract distribution company? Will these fit in with current systems? What will the likely cost and timescale be for interfacing computer systems?
   - start-up costs
   - cost of closing down current facilities
   - transfer of undertakings: in the UK there is legislation that states that when a part of a business changes hands, the employees should be transferred together with their associated benefits and rights. In practice this can be a major issue in determining whether contract distribution is a viable option.

SECTION 5 ACTUAL DEVELOPMENTS

5.1 The approach adopted by the consultant and the recommendations

The consultant identified the need to consider four main issues:
- Will any of the quotes for contract distribution work out significantly cheaper than the current operation?
- What issues other than cost need to be considered?
- Should the distribution operations for the three companies be combined?
- If the operations were combined and the operation kept in-house, what analysis should be carried out by RHM to decide on the optimum distribution network? Could an in-house amalgamated system be operated more cheaply than the third party contract solutions?

5.2 Cost comparison of solutions

These results were summarised on a spreadsheet (see Table 4.1). It then became clear that not only were there no substantial savings involved in any of the proposed solutions by the distribution companies, but that the current RHM operation was cheaper than anything else.

Did this mean that there was no possibility of savings by amalgamating the operations of the three businesses?

Looked at in more detail it could be seen that:
- Although Reading was not the ideal location for a Southern depot, the costs of closing this and opening a new depot elsewhere would outweigh any savings in transport costs.
- The cheapest contractor option (company B using a Southern warehouse at Reading) resulted in total costs at a similar level to the current RHM operation. This meant that if RHM were to adopt

this solution and run the operation as efficiently as planned by company B, the only potential for savings would be the management fee included in the quotation. As this was approximately £280000, this figure is below the £500000 minimum given by the working party as necessary to make change worthwhile.

5.3 Recommendations from the consultant

- RHM should not pursue any of the options proposed by the contractors.
- RHM should not consider in-house amalgamation on the basis of a new site for the southern distribution centre.
- RHM should consider further the amalgamation of the three distribution systems on an in-house basis using the current Reading warehouse as the southern distribution centre. Further analysis would have to be carried out on the potential for reductions in stock levels at Reading before deciding whether the current warehouse capacity would be adequate.
- there should be improved management of seasonality if the distribution of the three businesses is combined as the peaks and troughs of each business occur at different times of the year.
- utilisation of trunking vehicles should be improved if the distribution functions are combined owing to the opportunities for backhauling and double shifting.
- there should be scope for considerable savings in secondary distribution costs if deliveries to customers from the three businesses are combined but this would need to be analysed in detail using a vehicle scheduling package.

Table 4.3 Cost comparison of options (all figures in £000's)

	Distribution Company A		Distribution Company B			RHM
	Option 1 Ossett Northants	Option 2 Ossett Luton	Option 1 Ossett Hatfield	Option 2 Ossett Reading	Option 3 Ossett Erith	Current
Warehouse north	918	918	893	893	893	1110
Warehouse south	1650	1812	1803	1542	1280	1421
Total warehouse	2568	2730	2696	2435	2173	2531
Transport north	1284	1284	1136	1136	1125	957
Transport south	2089	2020	1172	1128	1317	841
Transport sub-contract	0	0	1092	1092	1092	2274
Total transport	3373	3304	3400	3356	3534	4072
Total contractor quote	5941	6034	6096	5791	5707	
Additional costs						
Closure Reading (400)	112	112	incl.	N/A	100	
Closure Dunstable (260)	73	73	incl.	65	65	
Start-up cost north	56	56	N/A	N/A	N/A	
Start-up cost south	87	101	24	24	23	
Costs retained by RHM	899	899	748	748	748	
Total cost to RHM	7168	7275	6868	6628	6643	6603

5.4 Subsequent developments in RHM

Nothing ever stands still! In November 1992 just as the consultant was submitting his final written report to the working party, the RHM Group was acquired by Tomkins plc, a conglomerate. The recommendations about amalgamation started to be carried out for two of the three businesses: McDougall and RHM, and savings were made. The first major rationalisation of the RHM group after the take-over reduced the number of Divisions from five to three. The three RHM businesses which were involved in the distribution initiative ended up being allocated to two separate divisions and came under separate Divisional Management control. Thus the complete recommendations could not be carried out.

Further cost reduction projects for distribution are currently taking place.

78 Distribution Planning and Strategy

SECTION 6 AUDIENCES/USES OF CASE/TEACHING SUGGESTIONS

This is a detailed case dealing with strategic decision analysis. As such it is probably most suitable for masters level students, final year undergraduates or middle/senior managers on executive training programmes.

CASE 16

SCOTTISH BREWERS

The Restructuring of a Depot System

Professor Alan McKinnon, *Heriot-Watt University*

SECTION 1 CASE SYNOPSIS

The centralisation of warehousing has been one of the major trends in logistics over the past thirty years. Much of the discussion of this centralisation process in the academic logistics literature has been highly generalised. To appreciate the true complexity of the process one must examine the actual business context within which it takes place. This case study illustrates how industry- and company-specific circumstances can affect the planning and implementation of a depot rationalisation programme. It is based on the experience of Scottish Brewers, the largest supplier of draught beer in Scotland. In restructuring its depot system in 1992–3, the company was not simply following the general trend towards more centralised stockholding, but also responding to a contraction of its core market and intensification of competition in the retail beer market following a liberalisation of beer sales through public houses.

Scottish Brewers' prime motive for restructuring its distribution system was to cut costs and this it handsomely achieved, though not in the manner conventionally portrayed in the logistics literature. There was no trade-off between logistics costs and service quality, for example, as senior management insisted that the standard of customer service be at least maintained. The logistical cost trade-offs were also much more heavily skewed towards savings in manpower and property costs than the textbooks normally suggest. By comparison, the transport cost penalty which the firm incurred was relatively small. In trying to explain why Scottish Brewers' experience of warehouse centralisation differed from the conventional model, one must take account of the related changes that occurred at the same time. The reduction in the number of stockholding depots was part of a wider package of rationalisation measures.

SECTION 2 TEACHING/LEARNING OBJECTIVES

In analysing the case study students might be expected to:

1. Examine the impact of a major change in the external business environment on distribution operations.

2. Explore the cost trade-offs that a firm can encounter when restructuring its distribution system.
3. Reassess the conventional logistics wisdom on the relative costs and benefits of a depot rationalisation programme.
4. Calculate the payback period for this programme.
5. Identify the strategic issues that must be addressed when restructuring a depot system.
6. Review the range of supporting measures than can facilitate the restructuring process and augment the resulting benefits.

SECTION 3 MAIN ISSUES AND PROBLEMS RAISED BY THE CASE

The case ends with a brief summary of four key strategic issues:

3.1 The need to maintain customer service

The sales department insisted that the standard of delivery service be maintained, even during the transitional period. The new system also had to be able to accommodate a growing number of delivery time restrictions. In restructuring its distribution system, Scottish Brewers managed to achieve both these objectives. Contrary to the view expressed in some of the logistics literature,[4] the centralisation of inventory was not achieved at the expense of a reduction in service quality and lost revenue. The standard of service in fact improved, partly as a result of the centralisation of order processing at the South Gyle (Edinburgh) facility. Although, within the new structure, inventory was dispersed to four depots, customer service and administrative functions were centralised at the South Gyle site and upgraded with substantial investment in new IT equipment.

3.2 The scope for reducing logistics costs

Traditional logistics theory suggests that in centralising inventory firms trade-off higher transport cost for lower inventory and warehousing costs, usually achieving a substantial net saving in the process. The main benefit supposedly derives from firms exploiting the so-called 'square root law of inventory', thereby reducing the total amount of safety stock they must hold to provide a given level of customer service.[5] They can also take advantage of economies of scale in warehousing by concentrating storage capacity in a smaller number of larger premises. Conventional reasoning suggests, however, that to enjoy these benefits firms must be prepared to accept an increase in transport costs as centralisation generally increases delivery distances.

The experience of Scottish Brewers deviated from this standard model in several important respects.

First, when calculated on an annual basis, the main cost saving accrued from the rationalisation of warehousing operations rather than inventory. By cutting 50 jobs, most of them management and supervisory posts, the firm was able to reduce labour costs by £1.25 million per annum. Depot closures also yielded an annual saving of £0.4 million on property-related expenses such as rates and maintenance. When set against these cost reductions, the annualised saving in inventory costs of £30,000 seems relatively small.

Second, Scottish Brewers did not benefit from warehouse economies of scale in the conventional sense. The four depots at which the firm concentrated its stockholding and order picking functions did not have to be expanded, for three reasons:

---

[4] Maister, D. H. (1976) 'The centralisation of inventories and the 'square root law', *International Journal of Physical Distribution*, **6**(3), 124–34.

[5] For example Rand, G. K. (1976) 'Methodological choices in depot location studies', *Operational Research Quarterly*, **27**(1), 241–9.

1. The reduction in sales volumes had left them with spare capacity.
2. The 'square root law' effect coupled with tighter stock management substantially reduced the total amount of inventory in the system.
3. Night shifts were introduced at the two largest depots, at Bellshill and South Gyle, moving them onto a 24-hour cycle. In addition to improving asset utilisation, the introduction of a night shift also yielded other benefits. For instance, it permitted greater co-ordination of inbound and outbound deliveries and more efficient allocation of staff time between goods reception and load preparation. It also made it easier to meet the specified order lead-time.

Although the surviving four stockholding depots were not physically expanded, their fixed costs were spread across a much increased throughput.

Third, the centralisation process increased total transport costs by only a small margin. Local delivery costs (outbound from the depots) did increase by roughly £0.25 million per annum, reflecting the longer average distance from depot to customer. This increase was moderated by the continued use of break-bulk facilities in the vicinity of former stockholding depots. Some of the increase in local delivery costs was offset by a reduction in trunking costs (from brewery to depot) of £0.01 million. The net addition to transport costs was, therefore, £0.24 million, a figure far exceeded by £1.68 million savings in facility and inventory costs.

3.3 Relative merits of contracting-out the distribution operation

In the decade preceding the distribution review there had been a sharp increase in the proportion of road freight movement in the UK contracted out to road hauliers. Between 1982 and 1992, haulage contractors increased their share of total road tonne-kilometres from 62.3 per cent to 71.2 per cent.[6] Until the mid-1980s, the vast majority of beer distribution in the UK was organised in-house. The reasons for one major brewing firm's preference for own account transport were outlined by McBeath.[7] By the early 1990s, however, several major brewing firms had entrusted local beer delivery to outside contractors.

Although Scottish Brewers decided in 1992 not to follow their example, its assessment of the externalisation option was still a very worthwhile exercise because it gave the company an opportunity to benchmark its distribution operation against the services that could be provided by outside agencies. The involvement of the S&N group's central logistics planning unit, Centre Logistics, helped to ensure the comparison of the in-house and contract options was objective. Since 1992, the company has continued to keep this issue under review.

3.4 Consequences for labour relations

A total of 50 jobs were eliminated, some by natural wastage, the rest by voluntary redundancy. No-one had to be made redundant compulsorily. Four-fifths of those volunteering to leave the company were in supervisory and management positions. An attractive severance package was available. Branch management staff were fully consulted on the depot changes and proved an invaluable source of advice on how they should be implemented at local level. Employees affected by the changes at the West of Scotland depots were involved in *kaizen* problem-solving groups which determined how the objectives were implemented locally. This employee involvement helped the company avoid any industrial relations problems. Another factor which may have contributed to the work-force's co-operation with the restructuring programme was the earlier fear that Scottish Brewers would contract out its distribution to a third-party operator and sanction much larger job

---

[6] Eibl, P., Mackenzie, R. and Kidner, D. B. (1994) 'Vehicle routeing and scheduling in the brewing industry: A case study', *International Journal of Physical Distribution and Logistics Management*, **24**(6), 27–37.

[7] McBeath, J. (1985) 'Maximising own account operations.' *Logistics Today*, **4**(4), 8–10.

losses. When the employment consequences of the in-house reorganisation became known, many staff felt a sense of relief.

SECTION 4 SPECIFIC QUESTIONS

4.1 What measures might the company have taken to 'sweat its distribution assets'?

As mentioned earlier, the two largest depots at Bellshill and South Gyle were worked much more intensively, going over to a 24-hour operation. This was tangible evidence of the firm's new commitment to 'sweat its distribution assets'. As none of the remaining depots was physically expanded, throughput per square metre increased quite substantially.

The productivity of the vehicle fleet was also improved in several ways:

1. By concentrating vehicles and drivers at fewer locations it was possible to manage the delivery operation more efficiently.
2. Vehicle productivity was further enhanced by the move to 24 hour operation and extension of the 'delivery day', with many lorries now leaving at 6 a.m. rather than 8 a.m.
3. As part of the reorganisation, fixed depot service area boundaries were abandoned and replaced by a much more flexible system of allocating customers to depots on a day-to-day basis. This 'flexing of depot boundaries', particularly between the main stockholding depots and their transit points, permitted more efficient load planning and vehicle routing.
4. Shortly after the depot restructuring, the firm introduced computerised vehicle scheduling using a package which elsewhere in the S&N group had yielded transport cost savings of around 8 per cent.[8]

4.2 How did the actual level of inventory savings compare with those predicted by the 'square root law'? What factors can undermine the validity of such a comparison?

Stock levels fell by approximately 13 per cent following the restructuring. It is possible to calculate the percentage by which safety stock levels would have fallen had the savings matched those predicted by the 'square root law'. The theoretical safety stock reduction (R) can be estimated using the following formula:

$$R = (1 - \sqrt{n_2} / \sqrt{n_1}) \times 100\%$$

where n_1 is the initial number of stockholding locations (9) and n_2 the number of locations remaining after the restructuring (4). As the square roots of 9 and 4 are whole numbers, this calculation is fairly elementary and yields a saving of 33 per cent.

This figure cannot be compared directly to Scottish Brewers' estimate of inventory savings, however, as it is not known what proportion of its inventory would be classed as 'safety stock'. It is likely, however, that the actual saving was significantly below the theoretical value. It is generally acknowledged in the distribution industry that the square root law tends to over-predict inventory reductions. It can also be very difficult to isolate the effect of centralisation as it often coincides with other inventory-related changes. In the case of Scottish Brewers, for example, the product range was diversified around the same time and, other things being equal, this would have inflated stock levels.[9]

---

[8] Department of Transport (1993) *The Transport of Goods by Road in Great Britain 1992*, HMSO, London.

[9] For a more general discussion of the 'square root law', readers should consult Maister, 1976; Das, C. (1978) 'A re-appraisal of the square root law', *International Journal of Physical Distribution*, 8(6); Sussams, J. E. (1986) 'Buffer stocks and the square root law', *Focus on Physical Distribution and Logistics Management*, 5(5); McKinnon, A. C. (1989) *Physical Distribution Systems*, Routledge, London; Zinn, W., Levy, M. and Bowersox, D. J. (1989) 'Measuring

4.3 How long was the payback period for the depot restructuring programme?

The information on Table 2 in the case study shows that the company made annual savings for £1.68. From this must be deducted the £0.25 million increase in local delivery costs, leaving a net annual saving of £1.43 million.

One-off payments comprised £1.1 million for staff redundancy payments and £0.15 million for building modifications, computing equipment and other miscellaneous items. Once allowance is made for the reduction in the amount of working capital invested in inventory (£0.4 million), it can be seen that the restructuring of the depot system required a net one-off expenditure of £0.85 million. With annual savings running at around £1.43 million, this expenditure was recouped in approximately seven months. The reorganisation, therefore, had a remarkably short payback period.

4.4 To what extent was the depot rationalisation constrained by Scotland's geography

Despite being relatively small, the two depots at Aberdeen and Inverness retained their stockholding function for several reasons:

- their distances from the brewery;
- km to Aberdeen and 252 km to Inverness);
- the low population density in the north of Scotland;
- the geographical extent of the areas served by these depots;
- the quality of the road infrastructure in these areas.

Several changes were, nevertheless, made to distribution operations in the north. The hinterlands of the two depots were marginally altered to permit a more efficient allocation of throughput. The Aberdeen depot also began to take on third-party business to help spread its overhead costs.

The depot restructuring programme was largely confined to the southern half of the country, where most of the company's sales were concentrated and where it was able to take advantage of major improvements that had been made to the trunk road network since the early 1970s when the original depot system was established.

4.5 What measures might the company have taken to ensure that the standard of customer service was maintained?

SECTION 5 POSTSCRIPT

Since the restructuring programme of 1992–3, Scottish Brewers has continued to improve the efficiency of its distribution operation. For example, computerised vehicle routing has been extended and refined and an outstation has been relocated from Ayr to Kilmarnock. None of these improvements, however, have been on the scale of the depot rationalisation project, which demanded a complete strategic reappraisal and effected a quantum change in the company's distribution system.

---

the effect of inventory centralisation/decentralisation on aggregate safety stock: The square root law revisited', *Journal of Business Logistics*, **10**(1); Ronen, D. (1990) 'Inventory centralisation/decentralisation – the square root law revisited again', *Journal of Business Logistics*, **11**(2).

SECTION 6 AUDIENCES/USES OF THE CASE

Suitable for under-graduate or post-graduate students on distribution, transport or logistics courses. As this is a strategic case is probably best suited to more advanced students.

It will also be useful on management training courses for senior or middle managers.

CASE 17

ZIMBABWE DAIRY MARKETING BOARD

Distribution Planning in a Developing Country

Stephen Errey, *Distribution Projects Limited*

SECTION 1 CASE SYNOPSIS

The case, which is real, explores the issues involved in solving a logistics problem. The study centres on the one member (the logistics planner) of a multi-disciplinary team undertaking a strategic transport review for the Zimbabwe Dairy Marketing Board (ZDMB). The case is centred on the first few days of the study, during which time the logistics planner has to plan his work for the nine-week project. The planning has to take into account:

- the limited number of tools available;
- the limited amount of information that is readily available;
- the time constraints imposed by the needs of the other members of the team.

The task which has to be addressed by the student is a project planning exercise in the context of a third world country. It requires the student to set out a work plan which shows:

- the required schedule for completing the project;
- the information required and how it might be obtained;
- what the information is going to be used for;
- the timescale for each of the tasks.

N.B. The case is *not* primarily intended to require students to propose a solution to the problem, as this would be very difficult without access to the data collected by the consultant. However more advance students may be able to make some tentative suggestions as to appropriate action.

SECTION 2 TEACHING/LEARNING OBJECTIVES

The objective of the case study is to get students to think clearly about:

- what tasks they need to complete to achieve an objective;

- what information they need to complete the tasks;
- how the information is best obtained when it is not provided in a straightforward way;
- how to place those tasks in a logical sequence;
- some of the difficulties of working in a third world environment

SECTION 3 MAIN ISSUES AND PROBLEMS RAISED BY THE CASE

The key task is to determine the optimum number and type of vehicles required by the ZDMB. All students should be able to identify this, because it is stated overtly in the objectives and the task. The other task which it would be relevant for the logistics specialist to address would be the assessment of the ideal depot network for the ZDMB. This task is not stated overtly in the objectives, but it is clearly an additional method of potentially reducing costs, and the more alert students should be expected to include this issue.

As the logistics specialist has access to a vehicle scheduling system, the main method of determining the optimum fleet size was simulation of the ZDMB requirements. The main information requirements were:

- customer location;
- customer demand (volumes and product mix);
- average driving speed;
- average drop time;
- vehicle bases;
- vehicle capacity.

This information was not held in a consistent form anywhere, and so various forms were designed to capture the basic information needed (see Appendices D; E; and F). Each vehicle base was visited to explain the requirements This sample data was to be compared with the product group data available to ensure that it was representative.

No information on driving speeds or drop times were available either, and so the logistics specialist went out on a number of delivery rounds to build up some work standards for himself.

The vehicle capacities were provided by the mechanical engineer. The assessment of the ideal number of vehicle bases was carried out by making an incremental change (i.e. assuming the closure of one base at a time), and comparing the resulting change in depot costs and transport costs.

The depot costs were provided by the accountant/economist, and the change in transport costs were assessed in two stages:

- the change in resources was simulated using the vehicle scheduling system serving the same demand from one or two vehicle bases;
- the resources required in each scenario were then costed by the accountant /economist.

The sequence of tasks is fairly obvious: collect data, analyse data, write up results. It was important to ensure that the system for collecting the sample data was set up first, and that there were activities that could be carried out during the time that it was being collected. As the assessment of the ideal depot network was not central to the project, it was left until the other tasks had been completed.

The mechanical engineer and the accountant needed details of the optimum fleet about two weeks before the end of the study so that the replacement programme could be built up.

A project structure which fulfils these requirements is:

Week 1:   visits to all locations to hand out standard forms and explain requirements
Week 2:   compile work standards for vehicle operating
           compile list of vehicles and allocations to depots (with mechanical engineer)

Week 3: compile historical sales information to compare with sample data collected from depots

update historical sales information to take account of sales forecasts.

Weeks 4 & 5: input data from returned forms to vehicle scheduling system
Weeks 6 & 7: carry out scheduling simulations*
Week 8: prepare report
Week 9: assess optimum depot network and write supplementary report.

* the scheduling was carried out in discrete geographical areas, so that the information could be passed to the Engineer progressively during this period.

SECTION 4 SPECIFIC QUESTIONS

4.1 What is the main question that Stephen Errey has to answer?

He has to calculate the optimum number and type of vehicle needed by the ZDMB to carry out their deliveries.

4.2 What information is needed to determine the optimum fleet size and mix?

The location and magnitude of customer demand; the location of the vehicle bases; the types of vehicles available; and the operating characteristics of the vehicles (average driving speed and drop time). The geography of Zimbabwe means that there are no realistic alternative locations for the main vehicle bases, but it would be possible to use hypothetical instead of actual bases.

4.3 What categories of cost are used to assess the ideal number of vehicle bases? How do these costs change as the number of vehicle bases change?

The two main cost categories are depot cost and transport costs. As the number of depots increases, the total depot costs increase. As the number of depots increased the transport costs fall. The ideal number of bases occurs when the aggregate of depot costs and transport cost is lowest.

4.4 What are the main types of activity that Stephen Errey has to carry out?

Define the data that is needed; collect the data; analyse the data; write up the results.

4.5 What information does Stephen Errey need to obtain from other members of the team, and what information does he need to provide to the rest of the team?

He needs to obtain cost information from the accountant and economist, and provide details of the ideal fleet configuration to the mechanical engineer.

SECTION 5 DESCRIPTION OF ACTUAL DEVELOPMENTS

The study was carried out in the way described in Section 3.

The first week was spent travelling round the country, visiting each depot. At each place, the survey forms were handed out, and the requirements explained. This was the only way the data on customer demand could be obtained reliably.

During the second week, Stephen Errey travelled on a number of different delivery rounds, so that the operating characteristics of the vehicles could be established. Some depots local to Harare were visited to check vehicle capacities.

In the third week, he compiled demand information from the records at the head office. The purpose of this was to have a baseline against which to calibrate the results of the survey.

By week four, the results of the survey started to arrive back at the head office in Harare. All this data had to be input into the vehicle scheduling system. This activity, together with setting-up and calibrating the system, took most of weeks four and five. There was also a little time to start writing up that part of the report concerned with data collection.

During weeks six and seven, the scheduling simulations were carried out. This was the most intensive part of the project, because there was a large volume of processing to be carried out, and the activity was on the critical path. Until this was completed, the mechanical engineer could not work out the vehicle replacement programme. There was therefore a lot of pressure to complete this as quickly as possible.

By week eight, the critical activities were being carried out by the engineer, and so Stephen Errey was then able to finish his report, covering the methodology and results of the scheduling simulations.

In week nine, there was the opportunity to add some additional sections to the report. These were not specifically required in the project brief, but the project team though they were issues which should be brought to the attention of the ZDMB and the ODA. So far as Stephen Errey was concerned, they related to the number and location of depots.

Subsequent to the completion of the report, the ODA authorised the recommended expenditure on fleet replacement for the ZDMB. An implementation team returned to Zimbabwe to carry out the recommendations of the report. The whole project won the British Consultants Bureau 'Consultants of the Year' award.

SECTION 6 POSSIBLE USES OF THE CASES

Undergraduate level course in logistics, distribution or transport planning and courses dealing with international/third world issues.

APPENDIX D: SPECIMEN SURVEY FORM (MOTOR VEHICLES)

DATE :	DEPOT/DAIRY :		
VEHICLE REG NO :	TRAILER REG NO :		
TIME OUT :	TIME BACK :	DISTANCE :	

DELIVERY POINT	PRODUCT	CRATES/CARTONS DELIVERED	LITRES/KG DELIVERED

APPENDIX E SPECIMEN SURVEY FORM (BICYCLES & HANDCARTS)

BICYCLE/HANDCART DELIVERIES

DATE:	DEPOT:

ROUND NO:	TIME OUT	TIME BACK	NO. OF DROPS	PRODUCT	TOTAL QUALITY

APPENDIX F SPECIMEN SURVEY FORM (VEHICLE AVAILABILITY)

DATE :	DEPOT/DAIRY :

VEHICLES IN SERVICE	VEHICLES OUT OF SERVICE	REASON

Part 5

Warehouse Planning and Operations Management

Case 18

BRITISH AIRWAYS AVIONIC ENGINEERING
The Development of an Automated Storage and Retrieval System

David Jessop, *University of Glamorgan*

SECTION 1 CASE SYNOPSIS

This real case is concerned with the establishment and operation of a new avionics repair and re-certification facility on a greenfield sire

The key competitive advantage that the facility is expected to provide is 'responsiveness'. Units supplied by customers need to be turned round in a very short time indeed, in some cases to enable grounded aircraft to resume operations.

It is has been necessary in planning the storage and internal distribution activities at the new site to pay close attention to the possibility of delay in providing materials to the workshops, and to the elimination of any such delays.

SECTION 2 TEACHING/LEARNING OBJECTIVES

The case may be used as a general scenario to provide a background for discussions on or consideration of stores management topics and themes such as:

- stock rotation;
- stock-turn;
- location systems;
- differing ambient needs of various commodities;

- issues arising from 'automation' of stores;
- provision of materials for independent demand arising;
- storage density v. accessibility;
- what functions should the a warehouse computer system corneal?
- what information over and above that given in the case would you need to effectively plan the storage and retrieval facility?
- are there any features of avionic parts which differentiate them from more commonly stocked items, and if so how would these features impact on the design and operation of a warehouse?

(There are many other general issues)

Following study and discussion of the case students should be able to contribute to decisions in relation to the provision and organisation of storage and internal distribution systems, and should have an understanding of some of the compromises and 'trade offs' that are, inevitably, necessary.

SECTIONS 3 & 4 MAIN ISSUES AND SPECIFIC QUESTIONS

The following specific questions should be useful to the tutor employing this case. In the development and implementation of the Llantrisant facility, BAAE have encountered and dealt with numerous problems, amongst them are the following:

1. What type of storage facility should be employed, bearing in mind the fact that there is a very large range of items to be carried, that an ability to retrieve items quickly is essential and that many of the items stocked are small electrical or electrical parts of high value, requiring careful handling? In many cases there will be no 'back up' component of a stock item is lost or damaged. The cost of failure to supply when required may exceed the cost of ownership, storage and handling by a large factor, especially if an 'Aircraft on ground' situation is being faced.

The principal issues are whether a manual, semi-automated or fully automated system should be employed, the configuration of the selected system, and how items should be located within the store (see question 2).

2. The location of items within the central store is organised primarily on a 'random' basis. Random in this context should not, of course, be taken to mean disorganised or chaotic. What it does mean is that there is no fixed location allocated for each part. On arrival each part, or batch of parts, is allocated by the computer to the next available suitable bin. When the contents of a bin are exhausted, that bin then becomes available to the system and may have allocated to it any part of the appropriate shape, size or weight.

The use of a random location system in the storage and retrieval system brings many advantages, but there are also some disadvantages associated with this approach. A particular problem is connected with the need for rapid response from the system, and the fact that a fully random system might allocate arbitrarily materials to a point in the warehouse either close to, or remote from the order picking point, the decision being taken by taking only the physical shape/size and storage needs of the item.

(a) Discuss the 'pros and cons' of random location.
(b) Suggest ways in which responsiveness in the form of shorter average picking times might be enhanced.

3. What systems might be adopted for intra company transportation, and what would be the advantages and disadvantages of each one?

4. Because the work of BAAE is concerned with Civil Aviation, several stringent controls are applied, most of them being ultimately concerned with passenger safety. One requirement is 'traceability'. In the event of the failure of an item of avionic equipment serviced at Llantrisant, it is a requirement that the origin and history of every component used in the overhaul should be known. This means of course that as well as having a part number or catalogue number, identifying

the specification of an item, the item must also have a unique identifier, indicating which particular item it is, not just its general specification. Movements of the item require to be recorded, and it is desirable that the item should be clearly labelled or marked with its unique reference.

(a) How might information technology be applied in connection with a traceability system?
(b) What problems do the need for traceability present for the stores department?

SECTION 5 DESCRIPTION OF THE ACTUAL DEVELOPMENTS

5.1 The storage and retrieval system

An Automated Storage and Retrieval System (ASRS) has been designed and installed with the aim of making available to the user stocked parts within three minutes of demand. A key element in the system is the automated central store, which is organised into two aisles of storage racking, comprising 2,400 tray locations. Within this store, the unit of storage is the tray, but the tray is effectively the sub store for bins. Altogether, the trays can accommodate some 67,000 bins. The trays are all of the same external dimensions, but can be configured internally in a variety of ways so that parts of different shapes and sizes can be accommodated. They are carried between the store and pickup and deposit points by two automatic cranes which operate under computer control by means of an optical link. Essentially, the store is a fully automated 'robotic' facility, though the insertion and extraction of items to and from the trays is undertaken manually, the trays being extracted from their location in the warehouse and presented to the operator at the picking area, the focal point of which is essentially a 'counter' at which the machine serves its customers.

The system, which was developed and installed by AEG (UK) Ltd. and AEG Softwaretechnik GmbH of Berlin, operates under two DEC system 5000/133 computers with disk shadowing and configured to provide a standby capability. The application software is AEG's Logis-B running under the UNIX (ULTRIX) operating system and an embedded Oracle relational database.

In the picking area the conveyors are organised to allow the picking function to be operated by one or two people, depending on the level of work. Under control of the system, a tray arrives from its storage location to the picking workstation, and a video monitor beside the tray indicates which bin is required for picking, and the quantity to be picked. The workstation is equipped with counting scales, a bar code reader and a label printer for the delivery docket; after picking the tray automatically returns to the store. The picked components are available for distribution to the demand originator, accompanied by the delivery docket, though of course the point of use is a workshop, which may be some considerable distance from the picking location.

5.2 Random location system

A random system has been adopted by BAAE. This has enabled the establishment of a stores which, whilst occupying a relatively small area, thereby releasing site space for productive activity, nevertheless provides accommodation for a large range of parts. The main contributing factors are:

- No dedicated empty locations waiting for replenishment.
- Stock rotation is 'forced' under computer control.
- Part number and location number of issued items is referred to on picking. This provides greater protection against incorrect issues.

There is, however, a difficulty arising from a fully random system. Items which are in frequent demand are just as likely to be placed in a tray remote from the issuing point as they are to be placed 'handily'. This means of course that the picking crane may, in response to a large number of demands, then spend a lot of time travelling to and from the remote location, thereby impairing response time, crucial in this organisation.

An alternative approach to location would be to arrange the store on a 'popularity' basis, with a fixed location system arranged according to the probability of a given item being picked. Unfortunately of course, such a system would negate the other advantages of the random system.

In dealing with this problem, BAAE have adopted a commonly encountered and slight compromise. Whilst retaining the random approach they have identified three classes of component, and categorised them as those which will e needed frequently, those which are of 'intermediate' popularity, and those which will be needed only infrequently. On receipt of a component or batch of components the system will pace the consignment somewhere near to the issuing point if it is a frequently used item, and further away if it is less likely to be demanded. The locations are not fixed though, the effect is really that the storehouse is divided into three zones, with each zone accommodating items according to the frequency of issue. There is of course no physical separation between the zones, and the relative size of each can easily be varied under software control.

5.3 Internal transportation system

What BAAE did was to install, at the time of commissioning of the plant, a pneumatic tube system of the kind frequently encountered in departmental stores. There are three such delivery systems, normally working together in an integrated way, but each capable of operating as a stand alone system available for use from either picking workstation.

When an issue from stock is made, a printed issue label is generated and this is placed with the component(s) in an empty carrier and loaded into the appropriate pneumatic system. The operator keys in the destination at the load station control panel and as soon as the required route is confirmed as available the loaded carrier is despatched. Transit times are very short, and can be measured in seconds. The empty carriers are returned to the store through the pneumatic system, though outbound (loaded) carriers take precedence.

It may be worth noting that until it could be demonstrated to the satisfaction of the mechanics and fitters that the ASRS and the associated pneumatic delivery system was reliable, there was a tendency to maintain local, informal, workshop stocks of commonly used items. This of course gave rise to difficulties connected with inventory carrying costs, non availability to a given workshop of an item held outside the ASRS, and the 'masking' of real information on system performance. This difficulty has now been overcome, and staff are prepared to rely on the system.

As a point of interest, a technical problem which was encountered following installation of the air tube system was the adverse effects of static electricity on the electronic components being moved. The static was generated as a result of the friction between the carriers and the pneumatic tubes in which they move. The problem was overcome by paying further special attention to the earthing of the conveyor tubes.

5 4 Traceability

Traceability is a necessary requirement, imposed by the Civil Aviation Authority and by other bodies and agencies with an interest in the kind of work undertaken at BAAE. Traceability needs to extend from the point and time of origin of an item, through its supply chain to point of application or use, and backwards through the system in the event of an item being sent for repair or overhaul. Naturally, this requirement gives rise to the need for appropriate systems and controls throughout the entire manufacturing, distribution, installation and use sequence, though for the purposes of this case we concentrate on just the 'stores' implications.

Some of the salient features of the BAAE traceability system are:

- Bar coding is employed, each component being identified uniquely
- Returns to store are not simply treated as reverse transactions; each returned item must be considered with a view to the need to guarantee its condition and serviceability

- The identification of parts is connected closely with the need for certification. Avionics items are returned to customers with paperwork indicating that all required standards and other criteria have been met. The store staff have a part to play in ensuring that appropriate identification is carried with items issued.
- There may be a requirement for inspection, maintenance or checking of items whilst in stock. The system may be required to make items available for this purpose, temporarily 'issuing' items without necessarily raising a charge on a job or user department.

Table 5.1 BAAE Llantrisiant ASRS Stores: Specification of installed system

Store size	40m long, 9m high, 8m wide
Store layout	2 Aisles with 4 rows of racks, 2 cranes
Trays	2,436 (600 mm x 1,300 mm) with 6 different arrangements of bins
Bins	67,140 bins of 8 types, 48 of the smallest type per tray
Parts	40,000 part numbers
Operator stations	3 operator stations (2 picking points)
Availability	97%
Throughput	75 demands per hour
Delivery	80% within 3 mins; 15 mins max. Delivered to 16 workshop units across 3 buildings

SECTION 6 AUDIENCES/USES OF THE CASE

This case can be used on courses in distribution and logistics dealing specifically with issues of warehouse planning and design.

Case 19

BRITVIC SOFT DRINKS LTD

Development of a major distribution centre

David Taylor, *University of Huddersfield* and **Martin Green**, *Touche Ross Management Consultants*

SECTION 1 CASE SYNOPSIS

Britvic Soft Drinks Ltd (BSD) is a leading manufacturer and supplier of soft drinks to the retail sector in the UK. In the early 1990's an increasing proportion of BSD's output was being supplied to the major supermarket chains which were becoming increasingly demanding in terms of service requirements. As a result the company undertook a major review of their distribution strategy and decided to create a new centralised warehouse to supply major retails on a quick response basis.

94 Warehouse Planning and Operations Management

The new distribution centre was to be built and operated by a third party contractor. The case presents the requirements specification which constituted the main part of the invitation to tender.

The case can be used to consider the high level strategic issues involved in such a development but also contains sufficient information to undertake a detailed warehouse planning exercise if so required.

SECTION 2 TEACHING OBJECTIVES

1. To illustrate the extent and nature of a contract distribution specification and 'invitation to tender' document.
2. To give an opportunity to identify and consider the main strategic issues that must be addressed in the development of a contract proposal for a modern, quick-response distribution centre.
3. To present an opportunity to undertake detailed analysis of the many specific operational issues that must be considered in developing a large distribution centre.
4. To consider how a third party contract distribution company should approach the early phases of a contract bidding process.
5. To illustrate the nature of the partnership that must be developed between the principal and the contractor in the development and management of a major distribution facility.

SECTION 3 MAIN ISSUES AND PROBLEMS

3.1 An approach to using the case

The case can be used to replicate the contractor selection procedure that might be used in such a situation.

The normal procedure is for an Invitation to Tender document to be issued to a number of major contractors. The first phase would be to reduce this to a shortlist of 2 or 3 by asking contractors to make an initial verbal presentation to the company backed by a short preliminary report.

Students using the case can be put in the position of one or more contract distribution companies (preferably in teams) that have been invited to attend a meeting at Britvic to make the initial presentation. Specifically the task given to students could be as follows:

You are the managers at a large contract distribution company and have been invited by Britvic to attend a meeting to present your initial response to the Invitation to Tender.

You have 30 minutes to impress the client that you:

1. *understand the importance of the proposal to the client's business;*
2. *have identified the major operational, technical and implementational issues that will need to be considered in undertaking this project;*
3. *have a preliminary recommendation;*
4. *are a company with which Britvic can do business.*

NB. At this stage contractors would not be expected to provide a detailed technical assessment/proposal, but to show a clear logical approach and an appreciation of the issues involved.

3.2 The main issues

3.2.1 The importance of the proposal to the client's business

There is a need to show an appreciation of the market background to this distribution development i.e.:

- The growing importance of the major multiple retailers in the soft drinks market.
- The increasing demands of multiples for higher service levels in terms of: quick response, single vehicle, daily deliveries.
- The importance of EDI links for ordering, stock visibility, invoicing, etc.
- In servicing multiple retailers and indeed other customer groups, quality, reliability and flexibility in the distribution service are increasingly a pre-requisite. Britvic need confidence that a contractor fully appreciates these business realities.

3.2.2 The main technical operational and implementational issues

Contractors would be expected to include consideration of five groups of factors:

- technical issues;
- systems control;
- management structures;
- finance;
- implementation.

3.3 Technical issues

Key factors to consider include:

- Warehouse location:
  - 'ideal' site relative to customers and factories;
  - availability of suitable sites;
  - obtaining local authority planning approval
  - availability of workforce – in some areas of the UK there is a shortage of labour;
  - possible future uses of the building – if Britvic's distributions requirements change.
- Warehouse design and operation:
  - type of storage system to use, e.g.:
    (i) block stacking;
    (ii) wide v narrow aisle;
    (iii) high bay automated;
    (iv) live storage (flow racking);
  - degree of automation;
  - MHE requirements;
  - initial size and spare capacity;
  - barcoding.
- Transport:
  - vehicle numbers using the DC;
  - vehicle type and capacity;
  - loading methods;
  - vehicle standing and manoeuvring areas adjacent to the warehouse.

3.4 Systems control

1. Warehouse management system – stock location etc.
2. Movement control system in the warehouse.
3. Links between systems (i.e. retailers, warehouse, company).
4. Information flows – within the warehouse, between warehouse and external organisations.

3.5 Management issues

1. Operational management structure.
2. Management information specification.
3. Quality management: is there a requirement for ISO 9000?
4. Procedures for contract management to liaise with the client company.
5. Liaison with retailers.

3.6 Finance

1. Capital cost
2. Operating cost
3. Land cost
4. Financing and Ownership of the DC – contractor or client

3.7 Implementation

- Project management (cost, quality, timing).
- Timescales.
- Staffing:
  - for development and implementation phase and
  - for continuity of management from development through to operation.
- Training and start up procedures.

3.7.1 The key issues in practice in development of the britvic distribution centre were:-

1. Information systems
This was probably the most critical single issue.
 The Distribution Centre was being placed in between the Multiple Retailers – each of which had their own information systems (EPOS, etc.) and the manufacturer, Britvic – with its own computer systems.
 Interfacing of the DC's computer systems with the organisations on either side was critical to the successful implementation and operation of the distribution system. Efficient information management was absolutely essential. Any contractors that were not strong and convincing on this issue were disqualified.

2. Obtaining a suitable site
The preferred solution was an automated high-bay warehouse.
 There was some difficulty in finding a suitable location.

- Modern DC's are large, visually obtrusive buildings which generate large amounts of heavy traffic and create relatively low levels of employment and, as such, are often not popular with local planning authorities.

- Added to which a high bay warehouse needs solid geographical ground conditions to support the racking systems. Such ground conditions are not found in all locations.
- A further factor was that typically, manual workers employed in a DC were rarely prepared to travel distances of more than 5 or 6 miles to work and thus the warehouse needed to be located close to a population centre.

These factors mean that often an 'ideal' location generated by computer modelling may in practise not be available.

The DC was in fact located on the Magna Park industrial/distribution area close to Lutterworth in the English Midlands.

3 Financing/ownership

There was considerable difficulty in determining the most suitable arrangement for financing the capital cost of the DC The two basic options were:

- financing by the contractor with the capital cost recouped from the client through the annual operating charges. In such circumstances clear arrangements have to be in place for the client to take over the facility if the initial contractor loses the contract at some future point.
- Financing by the client at the outset, but with the development and on-going operation in the hands of the contractor.

After much negotiation – the latter option was adopted – which in practice can leave a contractor in a weaker position.

3.8 Establishing the credibility of the contractor

In client presentations such as this to Britvic, contractors normally give information on the following issues to establish their credibility:

- previous clients as references;
- size, stability and financial resources of the company;
- similar operations they manage- including the offer of site visits;
- management credentials – experience of managers: – an important issue here is whether a contractor already has the implementational/operational managers for the proposed contract in house, or whether they would have to employ new staff if they were successful in winning the contract.

SECTION 4 SPECIFIC QUESTIONS

In addition to identifying the major strategic issues involved in warehouse development, as outlined in Section 3, the case can be used at a more operational level. In this respect other questions that could be used are:-

1. Develop a full warehouse operational plan including size, layout, operating procedures, etc .

There is sufficient information in the case for students to attempt a detailed warehouse planning exercise.

Where gaps in information do exist assumptions should be made.

2. Demand Analysis and distribution requirements planning.

Use the current demand data ,seasonality information and demand forecasts to develop a Distribution Requirements Plan.

3. Analyse the practical manifestations and requirements of the relationship between the contractor and the client that will be necessary in developing and operating this warehouse.

4. Identify the factors which would make such a relationship a 'partnership' rather than a more traditional business agreement.

SECTION 5 ACTUAL DEVELOPMENTS

The Britvic National Distribution Centre was built at Magna Park, Lutterworth in the English Midlands, which is a designated industrial/distribution park with very good access to the motorway network.

A highly automated, high bay warehouse was constructed and commenced operation in mid 1994. The warehouse is owned by Britvic and operated on a contract basis by Wincanton Distribution Ltd. Listed below are its main features and operational characteristics.

5.1 Operational status

- Land area 15.7 acres
- Total building area 275,000 sq. ft
- Cubic capacity 447,300 cubic metres
- Operations
    - 9 months   Receipt: 5 days, 24 hours
    -             Despatch: 6 days, 24 hours
    - 3 months   Receipt: 7 days, 24 hours
    -             Despatch: 7 days, 24 hours
- Volumes   In the first full year of operation – 65.8 million cases
- Employees on site
    - Britvic   45
    - Wincanton   85

5.2 Goods inwards

- Design capacity 340 pallets per hour
- Automatic off-loading using dedicated Hydraroll equipped trailer (24 pallets off-loaded in 90 seconds)
- Pallets automatically checked for height, weight and profile prior to transfer to the STV (Sorting Transfer Vehicle) system.

5.3 High Bay Warehouse

- Floor area   150,000 sq. ft
- Internal Height   24 metres
- External Height   27 metres
- locations in double-deep racking across 17 aisles
- Each aisle holds 2960 pallets in 74 double deep bays – 10 pallets high
- Each aisle is serviced by 1 of 17 fixed aisle cranes
- Each crane is unmanned and operates totally automatically
- The rack structure is fully protected by an in-rack sprinkler system

5.4 Sorting Transfer Vehicle system (STV's)

- This system forms the pallet transport system to/from the High Bay Warehouse
- Twenty STV's operate on oval track, each capable of carrying two pallets
- STV's travel at up to 100 metres per minute on straight sections of the track, ensuring rapid transit
- Each STV is allocated pallet collection/deposit tasks by a Sub-System Controller

5.5 Case picking area

- Floor area   35,000 sq. ft
- Internal height   26 ft
- Picking and FLT operations are carried out automatically by Radio Data Terminals (RDT's)
- Replenishment pallets are fed for picking by the STV system

5.6 Despatching

- Full pallets for despatch are assembled on powered pallet conveyors prior to despatch
- Each of the 12 despatch lanes can hold up to 28 pallets
- Design capacity 340 pallets per hour

5.7 IT management systems

- Britvic Soft Drinks System (IBM AS400)
- Wincanton Warehouse Management System (IBM RS6000)
- Morris Automation Movement Control System (DEC VAX 4000
- Direct communication between all three systems via fibre optic Local Area Network
- Programmable Logic Controllers (PLC's) manage the movement instructions for the cranes, conveyors and STV system

SECTION 6 AUDIENCES/USES

The case is suitable for students at Masters level or final year undergraduates on courses in logistics or distribution planning.

It is also very appropriate for executive management training courses.

To develop the contract presentation as per the Task outlined in Section 3:
- the case requires pre-reading and consideration of about 1–2 hours;
- students should work in groups of 3 or 4 to develop a proposal and presentation;
- presentation time 20–30 minutes;
- Different groups can take the role of rival third party contractors and either the tutor or an additional student group could take the role of Britvic management in evaluating the rival presentations and choosing a preferred contractor.

If the case is used as a detailed warehouse planning exercise it will require a significant amount of time – possibly a half to a full day in the context of a management training course or as a major assignment over a number of weeks for a student group.

Case 20

THE DISCOUNT SHOP

Warehouse Planning and Operations

David Taylor, *University of Huddersfield*, and **John Beaty**, *Royal Melbourne Institute of Technology*

SECTION 1 CASE SYNOPSIS

This is a real case dealing with a warehouse capacity problem in an Australian retail group, however the name of the company and the directors have been disguised for reasons of confidentiality.

Rapid expansion of the number of shops in the group, combined with purchasing policies which favoured bulk purchases and a marketing policy which led to a continual and rapid expansion in the number of product lines, resulted in a dramatic lack of capacity in the groups central warehouse. A warehouse consultant was brought in to advise on warehouse expansion and as a result a new larger warehouse was acquired and equipped. However within 6 months of opening, the new warehouse had reached capacity and the consultant was re-engaged to advise on how to further expand warehouse capacity.

The immediate issue in the case requires students to re-design, at a practical level, the existing warehouse layout to cope with the increased volumes.

However the situation invites students to consider more fundamentally, corporate strategies in terms of purchasing, marketing and inventory policy to determine whether the corporate objectives could be achieved more effectively by taking a more holistic view of the company's supply chain and logistics activities.

SECTION 2 TEACHING OBJECTIVES

1. To give students the opportunity to undertake a detailed warehouse planning exercise.
2. To require students to assess a warehouse capacity problem in the context of other aspects and policies in the supply chain.

SECTION 3 MAIN ISSUES AND PROBLEMS

The obvious issues raised by this case are:

1. The need in the short run to quickly re-design the existing warehouse to accommodate the existing increased throughput volumes.
2. The need to plan for increased warehouse capacity in the medium term to accommodate the increased throughput that will result from the planned store expansion programme.

However the real underlying issue is:

3. The need to review other aspects of the supply chain beyond the warehouse with a view to limiting levels of inventory and hence warehouse capacity requirements.

In common with many successful small retail groups the development and sophistication of logistics activities at The Discount Shop had not kept pace with the company expansion.

The company's main strengths were in retailing. The company's buying philosophy was based on bulk purchase at low unit price. The Buying director took little or no notice of the impact of such policies on the supply chain. When merchandise volumes and store numbers were low it was possible to get away with inadequate logistics systems, but as volumes grew and in this case grew very rapidly, the deficiencies of the logistics system quickly came to the forefront.

Again in common with many companies that lack logistics expertise, the management thought the solution to the problem was increased warehouse capacity – hence the employment of a warehouse consultant.

In practice Beaty realised at the outset that improved warehousing, no matter how good, would not solve the problem, but could only alleviate it for a short period. He was quickly proved right. The new warehouse, opened in October 1994, was already at capacity by March 1995, and any further re-design or expansion was only going to solve the problem for a limited time.

What was required was for the Discount Shop management to understand the operational drivers and trade offs in their supply chain. Beaty thus spent considerable time (but with only limited success) trying to educate the management to some fundamental logistics principles including:

3.1 The need to reduce inventory

Inventory level was not regarded as a problem by the management. Indeed to an extent inventory was seen as an asset rather than a cost.

There was no appreciation of the true cost of holding inventory.

There was a reluctance to delete items from the range – even though in March 1995 only half the lines (3,000 out of 6,000) were active.

There was also a need to consider whether a more modest programme of adopting new lines was advisable.

3.2 Purchasing policy

As in many retailers, the Buying Director was very powerful – and his decision was usually unquestioned because 'he knew the retail business'.

Buying policies needed to be modified, because with current policies it was impossible for either the warehouse or other aspects of the logistics system to cope with up to 60 new lines per month, especially when this was combined with a policy of volume purchasing to achieve low unit price.

There was a need to calculate the true cost of such a purchasing policy in terms of the costs it imposed on the supply chain operations and in particular stock holding costs.

3.3 Retailing strategy

There is a need to question the policy of expanding the stores at such a rapid rate (a doubling in the number of stores was proposed between 1995/1997).

Without adequate logistics systems to support such an ambitious store expansion programme, particularly as stores spread to cities away from the company's Melbourne base, it is almost inevitable that service levels and product availability to customers would suffer – which could quickly damage the customers perception of the store chain.

Again this was a reflection of the lack of appreciation on the part of management of the critical importance of logistics to retailing.

3.4 Management information

There was a need to improve the information systems in the warehouse and in the supply chain in general. Even though in 1994 Beaty had recommended the need for an improved management information system in the warehouse, little of this had been implemented in the new Kensington warehouse.

In fact the need for an improvement information management system went wider than just the warehouse. What was needed was an integrated system linking the shops, the warehouse, the buying function and possibly even back to major suppliers.

SECTION 4 SPECIFIC QUESTIONS

1. Using the information supplied and the existing warehouse layout, prepare a plan to add a further 2000 pallet positions to the warehouse storage capacity.

   Indicate the types of racking which should be used. Draw a layout of the warehouse floor plan. Make recommendations for additional materials handling equipment.

For a description of the actual approach adopted see Section 5 below

2. How would you approach the inventory reduction problem?

See comments in Sections 3 and 5

3. What basic facilities and capabilities do you think The Discount Shop would require in a warehouse management system?

The basic functions that need to be addressed are:-

- on screen receipt registration and documentation;
- print bar codes for pallet and identification and location;
- allocate storage location;
- manage storage locations and identify free locations;
- record items and quantities by location;
- maintain activity data and categories items by demand activity;
- always issue oldest stock first unless over ruled by management;
- issue picking instructions to order pickers, if possible via a remote terminal;
- confirm issued items and quantities to the main computer system for invoice generation;
- generate consignment notes;
- maintain historical data on receipts, stock holdings, store orders, consignment notes, staff hours, costs;
- maintain cyclic stock taking system.

The practicality of introducing a simple bar coding system should be investigated, involving a bar coded pallet/carton number and a bar coded storage location. It may be possible to utilise the existing remote terminals in the warehouse together with some hand held laser scanners. This would give the advantage of confirming all stock put aways, referencing pallet numbers to location numbers. In addition it would be possible to maintain a perpetual inventory on each storage location. This would reduce the requirement for stock taking to those items that had not moved for a period of months.

In Beaty's opinion the development of a viable warehouse information management system was of critical importance. The company's computer system was operating at near capacity and the options to add further facilities for the warehouse were very limited. Although the company directors had some reservations about off the shelf warehouse software, Beaty suggested it was important to develop some basic warehouse information processing very quickly and the only practical way to do this was to utilise commercial software.

4. What advice would you give the Managing Director about expanding the size of the warehouse and extending the lease?

5. As a logistics consultant, rather than just a warehouse consultant, what advice would you offer to The Discount Shop?

6. There was a need to develop a procedures manual for the new warehouse. Itemise the issues that such a manual should cover.

In conjunction with the warehouse manager and staff Beaty produced a warehouse manual that dealt with the following basic procedures:

- receipt processing;
- stock location decisions;
- put away and conformation of location;
- order picking of store orders and assembly of store orders;
- process of store allocation and store allocation assembly;
- vehicle ordering, loading and documentation;
- warehouse task planning;
- house keeping procedures and responsibilities;
- safety rules and responsibilities;
- manual handling methods;
- fork lift truck and pick truck safety;
- equipment maintenance.

SECTION 5 ACTUAL DEVELOPMENTS IN THE COMPANY

5.1 The plan to provide an additional 2,000 pallet positions

The Kensington warehouse is divided into 4 sections.

- Section 1 is an open block stack area, and includes part of the receiving area.
- Section 2 has part of the receiving area, and is selective pallet racked for reserve storage.
- Section 3 is selective pallet racked and is used for order picking from pallets at all levels.
- Section 4 is the despatch assembly area, and contains drive in pallet racking for store accumulation.

To provide the additional pallet storage it was planned to provide additional pallet racking in Section 1. This was to be a mix of drive in and selective pallet racking.

The additional racking was made up as follows:

- pallet positions in selective pallet racking to provide a confectionery storage area.
- A temperature controlled area was already established in this section, this being necessary to store chocolate products in the summer ambient temperatures of up to 40 degrees centigrade.
- pallet positions in drive in racking. This was planned for the storage of high volume products where there were multiple pallets of the same item. An example would be 35 pallets of ironing boards or 20 pallets of books. This was a reserve storage area.
- pallets in selective racking for single pallet storage in reserve.

See Figure 5.1.

5.2. The inventory management problem

The plan was implemented and the additional pallet racking installed. It provided an immediate solution to the problem of storage capacity, accessibility and safety. However it did not solve the underlying problem, which was basically an inventory control problem. These particular retail buyers had difficulty in coming to terms with the concepts of stock turn and cubic storage capacity. The long term storage solution lies in the development of a supply chain management concept, a quick response philosophy and an understanding by the buying department of the physical capabilities of the warehouse. It is a classic case of the need to develop the management and information flow interfaces between the distribution function and the buying and inventory control functions. This was a long term development task.

5.3 The warehouse management system

The other pressing requirement was the need for a warehouse management system. This requirement was presented to management and in principle accepted. A proposal for a system called 'Pulse' distributed by Pulse Logistics Systems was prepared and presented. The cost was in the region of A$200,000 including RF bar code scanning equipment. Again this was accepted in principle, but was eventually rejected due to the company's requirement to seek a total replacement for the mainframe management system, which was to incorporate the warehouse management system. There was a lack of understanding by management of the importance of the warehouse system, and on the cost and efficiency impacts that resulted from not having an effective system. At the current date (March 1996) this situation has still not been resolved.

SECTION 6 AUDIENCES/USES OF THE CASE

1. Suitable for use by students at undergraduate level on distribution or logistics courses as a specific warehouse planning exercise.
2. Also suitable for students considering distribution issues in the context of retailing or marketing.
3. Suitable for more advanced students considering wider issues of logistics and supply chain strategy and its link to corporate strategy and functional power bases within companies.

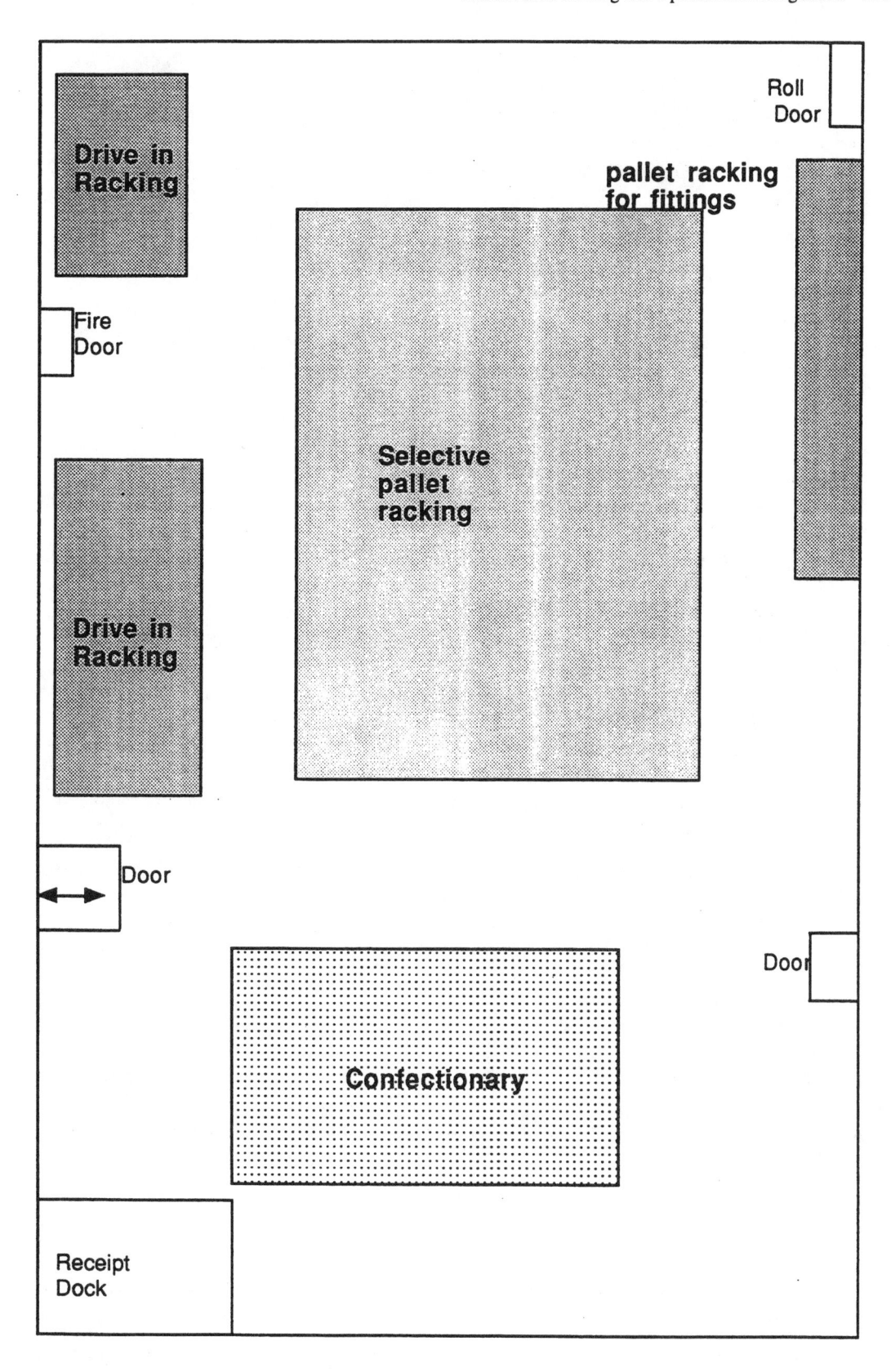

Figure 5.1 Plan of the additional 2,000 pallet spaces in Section 1 of the warehouse

Part 6

Inventory Management

Case 21

MEDISUPPLY
A Review of Stockholding Policy

Ian Black, *Cranfield University*

SECTION 1 CASE SYNOPSIS

The case is loosely based on a real company. The figures are heavily disguised and some simplifications have been made to distil the essential elements. The company was responsible for supplying medical equipment to hospitals and other medical centres. After a take-over it was required to undertake a radical review of its stockholding policy. The time is in the middle of the review when some issues have been addressed but major questions are still unresolved and it's necessary to consider how to proceed in the next phase of the review. The case therefore provides an opportunity to examine the elements that should be included in such a review together with an application of techniques that estimate optimum levels of stockholding.

SECTION 2 TEACHING/LEARNING OBJECTIVES

1. To enable students to identify the issues involved in the evaluation and design of a stock control system.
2. To enable students to identify the assumptions necessary for the production of demand forecasts and the calculation of EOQ and safety stock.
3. To allow students to critically appraise the value and relevance of such forecasts and calculations

SECTIONS 3 & 4 MAIN ISSUES AND PROBLEMS RAISED BY THE CASE AND QUESTIONS

3.1 Strategy and issues examined by the review

The exact terms of the review are not clearly specified. However given that it is concerned with the level of stockholding and its influence on costs and level of service, the review could examine a wider range of issues than merely the method used for product ordering. These issues include the range of products held, possible obsolescence of stock items, relationships with suppliers on product deliveries, relationships with customers on order delivery and co-operation with forecasting. All of these could have an effect on stockholding policy. With 5 warehouses in operation a strategic review could also consider whether there is a case for integration into a smaller number, a move which could have important implications for stockholding levels in the total distribution system. The next phase of the review ought to clearly define which of these issues are to be examined. The initial review has left most issues unresolved and the next phase needs to have specific targets including (at least) making recommendations about ordering policy for all products (not just the 'A' range), implications of any changes for cost and level of service, and implications for warehouse space requirements.

3.1.1 The sample

The sample of 10 products contributes slightly more than 10% of sales (by cases). The remaining products will have quite different profiles (demand trends, demand variation, value per case etc.). Holding and order costs will vary by product (e.g. high/low value, storage requirements). Simple projection of decision rules and cost savings from these high turnover products to other products could lead to serious errors. The next phase of the review must examine a sample of products from the whole range – not just the 'A' range. It could also consider whether the perpetual stock reorder system (using EOQ and reorder point) is appropriate for all stock items and ranges, or whether another method such as a fixed period stock ordering system is preferable.

3.2 Calculations

Recognising the limitations inherent in the sample of only high demand products, the case provides an opportunity to carry out some forecasts and estimates of EOQ and safety stocks for the 10 products.

3.2.1 Minimum balance and re-order point

The method used by the company in its re-ordering policy does have the merit of simplicity. The calculation of *minimum balance* takes account of the expected demand in the lead time (first term in the equation) plus a safety element related to demand fluctuations (second term). The alternative equation (Figure 1) found in most textbooks for the re-order point distinguishes between the variability in lead time and the variability in demand, both of which should be taken into account when estimating safety margins. Given estimates of these variabilities from previous time periods they can be incorporated into the equation which, unlike the existing method, also uses a specific probability of stock-out. The existing method cannot distinguish between products with different standard deviations of lead times. (Products 7 and 9 with large standard deviations have relatively high levels of unfulfilled orders). The minimum balance equation does take into account the fluctuations in demand over the last 6 months, but the textbook equation is more specific in its identification of demand variability and can also be used to estimate re-order points for specified levels of service.

3.2.2 Forecasting

The short period for which data is available means that formal statistical estimation of any model is difficult. The observations are sufficient to identify trends (by regression analysis for example) but with only two years data seasonal patterns are difficult to isolate. Inspection of the graphs of sales over the two years shows that any forecast should recognise the following

- a trend exists in series 3,5,6,7,10 and possibly 8 and 9;
- a seasonal pattern exists in 6,8 and possibly 7;
- special factors exist in 2 and 5.

The forecast demand shown in Exhibit 1 incorporates the trend in the data and provides a forecast for one period ahead. Although seasonal factors probably exist a run of two years data is insufficient to make accurate estimates. The forecast demand figures in Exhibit 1 are calculated from regression analysis incorporating a simple time trend (which is found to be significant for series 3,5,6,7,8,9 and 10) and projected one period ahead (i.e. January). Alternative forecasts could be produced using an exponentially weighted moving average method. In the future as more data becomes available it would be desirable to use an EWMA (Exponential Weighted Moving Average) method (such as Holt-Winters) in order to take explicit account of trends and seasonal factors. Recognition should be given to the need to take account of the effect of 'special factors' such as promotions, initiatives and competitors' practices on statistically based forecasts using regression analysis or similar methods.

3.2.3 Economic order quantity

The textbook form of the equation is given in Figure 6.1. The forecast demand can be used in the equation. Of the two cost elements the case provides an estimate of the *fixed* cost of an order. This cost only refer to the company's costs; it needs to be confirmed that charges for delivery will not change if typical order size varies. The holding cost is assumed to include the interest costs. The short run warehouse costs of holding stock are low but in the long term changes in stock levels may affect those costs related to the size of the warehouse, such as depreciation and rates. The initial review particularly noted that the storage area of the warehouse could be adjusted and it therefore seems correct to include these long run costs in the estimate of holding costs and the subsequent calculation of EOQ.

Table 6.1 shows the results of the EOQ calculation for interest only and interest plus storage charges included in the estimate of holding costs (H). For all of the 10 products the results suggest that an order size equivalent to less than one month's demand is desirable. If long run storage costs are included, the reduction is much greater. Based on these product lines, therefore, there does seem to be an opportunity to save warehouse space. As argued above these results cannot be projected simply to other products – a sample of other products must be examined in the next phase in order to determine whether these products also provide the opportunity for reductions in order quantities and hence storage requirements.

> **Figure 6.1**
>
> Reorder point
> $$B = M + Z\sigma$$
> $$M = DL$$
> $$\sigma^2 = L\sigma_D^2 + D^2\sigma_L^2$$
>
> Economic Order Quantity
> $$Q = \sqrt{\frac{2CD}{H}}$$
>
> Optimum Stockout Probability
> $$P(m > B) = \frac{HQ}{HQ + AD}$$
>
> where:
> - Q Order Quantity (cases)
> - C Ordering Cost (per order)
> - D Average demand (cases per time period)
> - H Holding Cost (per case per time period)
> - B Reorder point (cases)
> - M Average Lead Time Demand (cases)
> - L Average Lead Time (time period)
> - Z Standard Normal Deviate
> - σ Standard deviation of lead time demand (cases)
> - σ_D Standard deviation of demand (cases per time period)
> - σ_L Standard deviation of lead time (time period)
> - A Stockout Cost (per case)
> - m Lead Time Demand (cases) – a stochastic variable
> - $P(m>B)$ Probability of Stockout given Reorder Point B
> - $E(Z)$ Partial expectation

3.2.4 Safety stock

The calculation of the optimum stockout probability depends critically on the correct estimation of the trade-off between the increasing costs of holding stock and the decreasing cost of lost sales as the level of safety stocks rises. Again the issue of whether holding costs should refer to short-run (interest only) or long-run (including warehouse storage) costs needs to be addressed. A similar issue arises in the estimation of the cost of a lost sale. The average profit lost is 1.7% of the sale price, but if an estimate is made of the *marginal* cost of moving an item of stock through the system then the profit on an item may rise as high as 5.1%. In the calculations all the unfulfilled orders are assumed to be lost sales.

The results of the calculations for optimum stockout probability are shown for two extreme cases in Table 6.1. Estimates of standard deviation are derived from the last 12 months observations. This is probably higher than the true standard deviation for a month ahead forecast as it includes seasonal variations and the time trend over the previous year. The equations must be applied using consistent units of month or day; demand must be converted to per day or lead times to per month. The calculations assume 30 days per month.

When the cost of holding stock is assumed to be high and the profit margin to be low then the optimum probability of stockout can exceed 50%. With the higher profit margin the stockout probabilities are in the range 0.08-0.16. These levels will be reduced further if the cost of a lost sale is assumed to carry with it not only the immediate profit margin but also goodwill and the possibility of future lost profit. Accurate estimates of these future profits are clearly elusive and the company may wish to adopt the alternative strategy of defining target levels of stockout probability. The word *target* is important because it is based on data concerning forecasts of mean demand, mean lead time, their variances and an assumption of near Normal distributions in these variances. Table 6.1 shows estimates for the expected demand in the mean lead time and the level of safety stock for a target service level of 97.5% (i.e. stockout probability of 2.5%). Note that this is probability per order period and the Z value is 1.96 standard deviations. The associated reorder point for this service level is shown. It is possible by rearranging the optimum stockout equation and make the cost of a lost sale a function of the probability of stockout. With a service level of 97.5% the implied cost of a lost sale is £22 (interest only included) or £29 (interest and long term storage cost).

An estimate of lost sales can be made for a service level assuming again that the variability in demand is accurately forecast and the distribution is approximately Normal. For the 97.5% service level the partial expectation $E(Z)$ is 0.0097 which can be inserted into the formula to obtain the proportion of lost sales. (Strictly this calculation should only include integer values of safety stock levels.) The *estimates* of stockout probabilities and lost sales for these high safety stocks are critically dependent on the assumption that the distribution of demand in the lead time has the shape of the Normal distribution in the tail, which refers to the high levels of demand and lead time. Given the limited sample on which the standard deviation of lead time (only integer figures provided and no indication of shape) and demand are based, the estimates need to be treated with extreme caution. In practice they could easily be wrong by a factor of two or more.

It is clearly important that the next phase of the review comes to a firm decision on the level of safety stock and the implied probability of stockout. The decision is intimately influenced by the assumption about loss of profit due to unfulfilled orders. The next phase could consider gathering further evidence on the importance customers attach to unfulfilled orders and what effect it has on their attitude towards the company. The decision about the level of safety stock will also influence to some extent the size of warehouse required. The safety stock at a stockout probability of 2.5% is equivalent to between 14 and 42% of monthly sales. Reducing the probability can therefore have a significant influence on storage requirements. Tentatively (given the uncertainty about the figures used in the calculations) it appears from reported levels of unfulfilled orders over the last 2 years (Table 2 in case), that a probability of stockout of 2.5% would provide a higher level of service (Exhibit 1) and, by implication, require a higher level of safety stock than provided previously.

3.2.5 *Estimating overall costs and warehouse storage requirements*

The calculations show how estimates of EOQ and safety stocks can be made for individual products. In order to estimate total cost savings and the size of warehouse needed further information and analysis will be required. This will involve

- estimation of EOQ and safety stocks for a broad sample of products
- consideration of obsolete stock
- combining these to obtain average and maximum stock requirements for all products
- grossing-up these estimates to provide estimates for all 'A', 'B', 'C' and 'Z' categories
- storage methods to be used in the warehouse in order to convert cases to square (and cubic) metres.

Given the data provided in the case it is clearly not possible to carry out these calculations even in outline. The next phase of the review must aim to provide some estimate of the implications for annual cost and warehouse space.

Exhibit 1 Relevant Calculations

		1	2	3	4	5	6	7	8	9	10
Product		SU15	GP07	GP09	NS42	NS44	SU09	SU05	NS22	SU17	NS08
Forecast demand - cases/month		100	45	137	100	180	100	105	210	235	80
Forecast standard deviation		6	6	17	22	43	24	15	80	9	9
Value per case		71	101	66	211	29	43	129	50	21	179
Cost lost sale - margin	1.7%	1.21	1.72	1.12	3.59	0.49	0.73	2.19	0.85	0.36	3.04
- margin	5.1%	3.62	5.15	3.37	10.76	1.48	2.19	6.58	2.55	1.07	9.13
Interest - per case month		0.89	1.26	0.83	2.64	0.36	0.54	1.61	0.63	0.26	2.24
Storage - per case month		0.70	0.70	0.70	1.50	1.50	1.10	1.20	0.40	1.10	0.90
Lead time-mean days		5	7	8	5	5	8	15	10	20	5
Lead time-standard deviation		2	2	2	1	1	2	4	1	4	1
EOQ interest only (fixed £17)		62	42	73	36	140	79	49	108	177	34
EOQ interest +storage		46	34	54	29	62	45	37	84	78	29
P- (interest only) (margin5.1%)		0.13	0.14	0.12	0.08	0.14	0.16	0.10	0.11	0.15	0.10
P-(interest+storage)(margin1.7%)		0.45	0.42	0.43	0.29	0.72	0.64	0.36	0.38	0.74	0.31
Lead time - cases		17	15	34	17	35	26	57	72	161	13
Lead time safety @97.5%		14	10	24	19	37	27	36	92	65	9
Reorder Point @ 97.5%		30	26	58	36	72	54	93	163	226	22
Lost sales E(Z)=	0.0097	0.15%	0.15%	0.22%	0.32%	0.30%	0.30%	0.48%	0.54%	0.41%	0.15%

Figures may not add due to rounding

SECTION 6 AUDIENCES/USE OF CASE

The main audience for the case is under- or post-graduate students who have been introduced to the principles of forecasting and stock ordering policy. It can be used at different levels.

One possibility is for students to read the case for half an hour in small groups and then asked to make recommendations about how to proceed in the next phase of the review. What has been achieved so far and what should be the specific targets be in the next phase of the review? This requires an appreciation of methods to be used and at the same time the effect of the output from these methods on the cost and service performance of the business as a whole.

Alternatively the case can be used to enable students to apply the principles of forecasting and stock ordering policy using the data provided. This requires much more time and may be appropriate as a major assignment. It can be seen just as an opportunity to calculate EOQ and safety stocks, and understand the sensitivity of these to input assumptions. More broadly it can also incorporate the wider issues of how to translate these findings into an overall policy for all products and estimate warehouse space requirements. Finally, like the first alternative, it can require a specification of targets and procedures for the next phase.

Case 22

ST JAMES'S HOSPITAL AND LUCAS ENGINEERING SYSTEMS
A BPR Collaboration

Valerie Bence, *Cranfield University*[1]

SECTION 1 SYNOPSIS AND CASE STRUCTURE

This case illustrates an innovative collaboration between St James's Hospital, Leeds and Lucas Engineering Systems Ltd (LES). It examines how the two organisations (one public sector and one private) worked together to design and implement what are essentially manufacturing methodologies to within an NHS hospital undergoing huge process changes.

Two Business Process Redesign (BPR) projects were undertaken by the joint Lucas/St James's teams. This case examines Project B, the re-organisation and rationalisation of purchasing and supplies throughout the hospital, concentrating mainly on operational issues. The BPR Project team examined the ordering, storage and delivery of hospital supplies and recommended a move from a haphazard ordering and storage system towards a structured materials management process, with both cost savings and improved resource use. This entailed the introduction of what were essentially manufacturing methodologies to the hospital organisation e.g., a new order system built around 'Runners, Repeaters and Strangers'. The team also instigated a product rationalisation system via a Product Selection Group and developed a 'kanban' delivery system for ward supplies. The case outlines the rationale behind the collaboration and looks at how the final projects were chosen, the design of new processes and their implementation.

There is a demand for *real* cases and not just academic advice on how to 'do' BPR. Following a real case from inception, through design and implementation, analysing the problems and discussing the next steps, will hopefully prove a valuable learning experience.

Although the case investigates process and system change via BPR, within a public sector organisation, it covers issues that would be of interest to student/managers of different levels and from diverse industries, who could learn from this interesting and innovative collaboration.

SECTION 2 LEVEL OF ANALYSIS

This case is intended for use with MBA or Executive MBA students, either as a management of change or BPR case or to illustrate current issues surrounding public sector management. It could also be used as a stand-alone case within specialist electives such as BPR, or for senior delegates on short courses, e.g. NHS managers, logistics and distribution students or purchasing and procurement specialists.

---

[1] Copyright, Cranfield School of Management, 1995, All rights reserved.

SECTION 3 SUGGESTED STUDENT ASSIGNMENTS AND QUESTIONS

Although there is no obvious decision point for this case (and as such is really a case history) there is much content for class discussion, for students and managers with an interest in purchasing, supplies, procurement, logistics, materials management etc. It is possible to build on such discussions by setting assignments in the following areas:

1. Identify
   (a) the major problems and
   (b) the critical success factors for the implementation of the proposals.
2. To what extent are these problems and critical success factors likely to be different in a hospital environment compared to a business environment?
3. How should the supplies function develop its relationship with suppliers, including NHSSA?
4. What could be the impact on suppliers of the new approaches adopted by the hospital?
5. Develop an (alternative?) proposal as to how a materials management system could function at an operational level (this may differ from the 3 product categories actually implemented).
6. Examine the transferability of industrial methodologies, as used by LES, from the private to the public sector.
7. Discuss problems which could arise from the reorganisation of such a traditional Purchasing system?
8. How should management decide what benchmarks to use, both before and after the implementation of new processes in order to monitor success or failure?

SECTION 4 CASE USE

For some of these assignments, lecturers may decide to give out a shorter version of the case, i.e. stopping at a point before the case explains what was actually implemented (bottom of page 6). Students could then be requested to examine how the recommendations given at the end of Phase One could be met, and explore the role of the new Materials Managers (scope of activity and responsibilities etc.). The rest of the case could then be given in a later session, this would enable different methods of Materials Management to be explored in the context of the NHS and allow students to explore the system St James's actually implemented (see Appendix).

The case illustrates many logistics issues. The 'kanban' system of delivery, Just-In-Time production and delivery and other ways of inventory management can be explored as can the benefits to be gained from product and supplier rationalisation. Students can examine the costs and benefits of inventory holding; the differences between public and private sector logistics; and purchasing as a process not a function.

Student groups could be asked to approach the case in various ways, specific questions could be set as outlined above, or alternatively, small groups could take a functional approach and once they have analysed the case from a functional perspective they could meet and try the process approach that was necessary for the BPR team, who had to interact cross-functionally: i.e., Finance, Directorate, ward (users), Purchasing and Supply groups. It may be necessary to have a 'facilitator' in each group who takes the part of the BPR Project team member.

The case has been written with a number of teaching objectives in mind, the main points will be outlined in the following sections:

4.1 An overview of BPR.
4.2 Problems encountered in running and implementing the Project
4.3 Current status of the Project
4.4 Areas for further discussion.

These Teachers Notes will explore these and other issues (an investigation of the problems facing BPR projects; change management; implementation difficulties and human resource implications).

Class discussions can be built around these subject areas in the context of St James's Hospital; the NHS (public sector) in general; or student/delegate's own organisations.

4.1 An overview of BPR

There are probably as many definitions of BPR as there are projects but the following are useful:

Process Re-engineering

> The appeal lies in the simplicity of the central concept – to rethink, restructure and streamline the business structures, processes, methods of working, management systems and external relationships through which we create and deliver value.[2]

Business Re-engineering

> A strategy driven, top-down re-appraisal and re-designing of total business, with an emphasis on identifying core processes. Has to be supported and driven by the CEO with the total commitment and active participation of the Board – wide ranging, radical, fundamental.[3]

From a successful BPR project at Leicester Royal Infirmary;

> Fundamental rethinking and radical redesign of an entire or part of a hospital system, involving management, jobs, organisational structure, culture, and health care procurement. Getting down to the Whats and Hows.[4]

A hospital is a fragmented and highly complex organisation, the way things are done has usually evolved over time and for historical reasons.

> Because organisations grow organically, they tend to add to existing processes in a patchwork manner rather than take a clean piece of paper approach.[5]

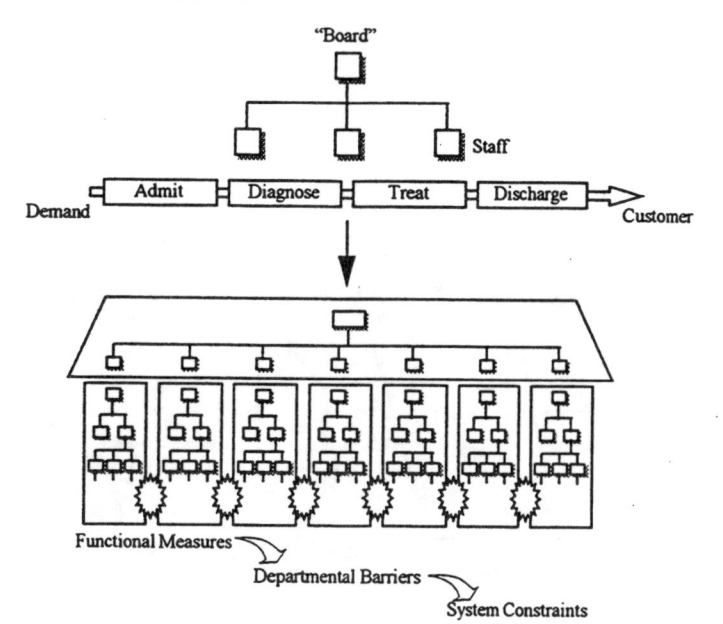

Figure 6.2

---

[2] Talwar, R. (1993) 'Business re-engineering: a strategy driven approach', *Long Range Planning*, **26**(6).
[3] Hammer, M. and Champy, J. (1993) *Re-engineering the Corporation*, Brearley Publications.
[4] Homa, P. (1994) Leicester Royal Infirmary, Institute of Health Service Managers Conference, June.
[5] Christopher, M. (1992) 'Organisational design for effective logistics', *Logistics Technology International*, Sterling Publications.

116 Inventory Management

Processes become complicated (see Figure 6.2) as demand, medical advances, patient and staff numbers, bureaucracy and technology develop and grow. Systems develop to deal with these issues usually on a functional level (e.g. Finance, Marketing) and problems arise at the functional interface, where handovers occur.

Key or core business processes directly affect the customer and account for the majority of costs, these must be managed as effectively as possible. Activities should be value-adding and the aim is to identify and eliminate non value-adding activities (see Figure 6.3). Complex wasteful tasks lead to poor service and long lead times. Cost cuts should accrue as non-value adding activities are removed and as processes increase in their level of effectiveness.

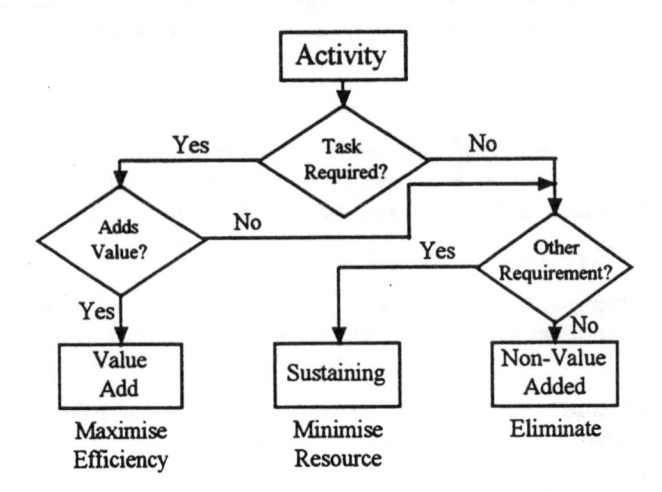

Figure 6.3

If the organisation and its processes are mapped there are often mis-matches – systems may not reflect the process flows (see Figure 6.4) it is therefore important to know where waste exists in all business processes.

THE ORGANISATION DOES NOT REFLECT THE PROCESS FLOW

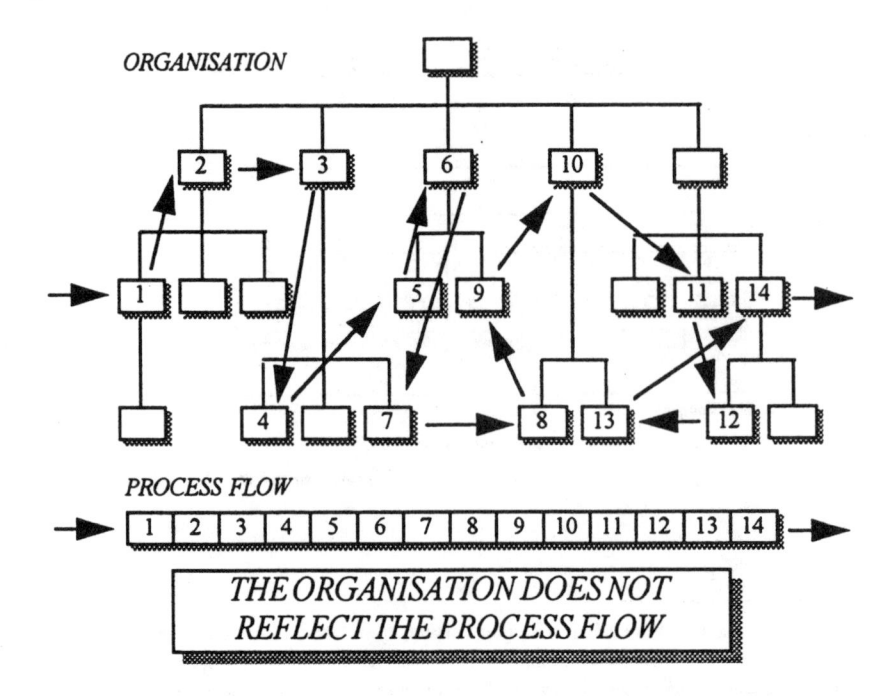

Figure 6.4

Thus the OBJECTIVES become:

- to get back to simple processes
- to understand key or core processes
- to identify who is responsible for key processes
- to strive for ideal processes (no non value-added).

A BPR approach cuts across traditional hierarchical functions (Figure 6.5) and aims to redesign improved systems to follow processes across functions, eliminate duplication, waste and overlap.

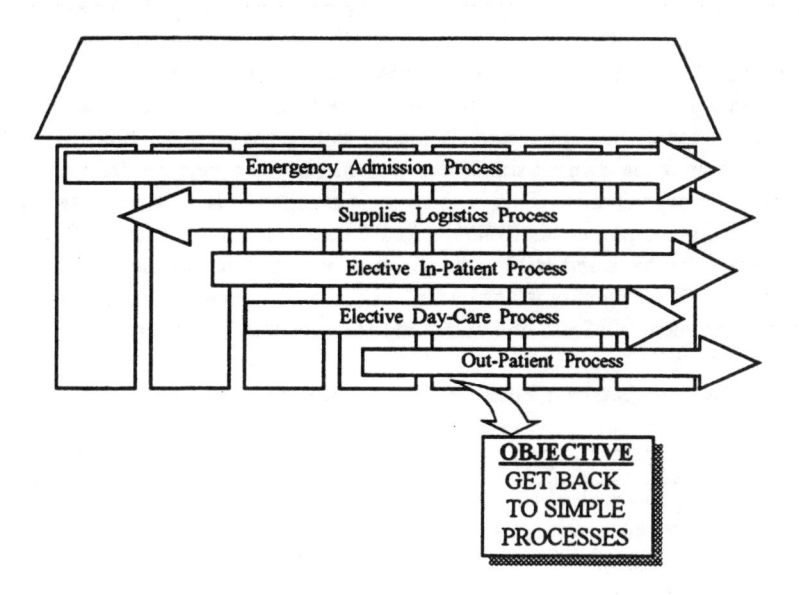

Figure 6.5

4.1.2 BPR – from manufacturing to business

LES'S approach to BPR was from a Systems Engineering perspective. It had become obvious that across all industry sectors there was a common requirement for major improvements in productivity, cost base and service quality in order to meet increasing competition. Traditional organisational structures exposed inefficiencies and the manufacturing sector was the first to realise that innovation and change would become essential for survival.

In the 1960s and 1970s Toyota in Japan pioneered Business Process Systems Engineering (BPSE) introducing the development of cross-functional organisations. This led to the introduction of team based units and showed the importance of the need to identify core business or manufacturing processes. Staff were regrouped in cross-functional teams around these key processes in order to meet customer requirements, drive costs down and performance quality up.

Many companies followed this lead and LES had been very successful in using such Systems Engineering techniques to increase efficiency in car manufacturing plants during the 1980s. It was becoming clear that many organisations, outside the manufacturing sector, could benefit from an investigation of these techniques as applied to business instead of manufacturing processes. The application of a Systems Engineering approach can be defined as follows:[6]

- take a total view of the business organisation, led by a senior management team;
- set benchmarks for system performance;

---

[6] Parnaby, J.(1994) Business process systems engineering', *Focus on Change Management*, October.

- install new effective organisational control mechanisms;
- use all available support tools and methodologies to redesign the organisation (of a process or the business) and then support its operation.

With Lucas taking this generic approach, senior management at St James's could see that some of the techniques from manufacturing (Kanban, Natural Groups, multiskilling) could be applied to the process problems found within this large public sector organisation, and hopefully produce similar success.

Increasingly, modern businesses face similar constraints, scarce resources and limited budgets, and modern managers need to demonstrate that their organisation produces value for money by focusing on performing effectively, or they will simply not survive. All organisations (manufacturers, shops, banks, universities and hospitals) process information – as well as goods, people and services. The ways in which these flows are managed – *logistics in its widest sense* – form the very substance of re-engineering. Logistics can be viewed as a holistic science and is a useful place to start since the integral supply chain management aspect, by definition, takes a cross-functional view of an organisation. This is the very view that BPR (a holistic procedure) seeks to address by moving from a functional structure to a process oriented structure. Thus there are very strong links between logistics and BPR – they both take overviews of the organisation. The same could also be said of Total Quality Management (TQM – a holistic philosophy of management[7]). Some differences between TQM and re-engineering are shown in Table 6.1.

Table 6.1 The differences between Total Quality Management and re-engineering

	TOTAL QUALITY	RE-ENGINEERING
Assumption	Basic processes are sound	Basic processes are unsound
Essence	Problem solving	Reinventing
Approach	Incremental	Radical
Goal	Enhancement	Stretching
Target	Removal of waste	Removal of non-value added
Change	Limited to individual process or department	Holistic – across the organisation
Cost savings	Secondary objective	Significant cost reduction
Domain	Individual process	Entire departments/system
IT Role	Secondary	Fundamental
Implementation	Bottom-up	Top down

Source: IHSM Conference 1994

A process can be seen as a structured, measured set of activities designed to produce a specified output for a particular customer, with a beginning, an end and clearly identified inputs and outputs. Thus, processes provide structure for organisations to act within. Juran[8] teaches that every worker has a customer to whom their work is passed next (within a hospital this is within or between departments/functions). When the work passes out of the organisation it goes to the organisation's external customers (hospital stakeholders, sub-contractors, patients etc.).

Core business processes cross functional boundaries (see Figure 6.5); address the needs and expectations of the marketplace; and drive organisations capabilities. Re-engineering of these core processes takes place when operational, technical and business knowledge are applied in order to eliminate waste and improve efficiency. The end to end or pipeline view of business processes is in essence managing the supply chain – whatever the organisation – not just in its accepted context

---

[7] *Focus on Change Management*, April 1994, p. 13.

[8] Juran J M. (1980) *Quality Planning and Analysis*, McGraw Hill New York.

within manufacturing or the logistics function in isolation. It is possible to take a supply chain perspective of any business process, examine the logistics flows within it (information, goods, people) and use this as the basis for re-engineering. Changes of the type envisaged by BPR will have potentially significant organisational impacts, primarily that of moving from functional organisational structures to one based around processes. Businesses, companies and organisations (both public and private) aim to deliver a product or service to customers and markets. In most instances no one function is able to deliver the full product or service which therefore becomes the sum of the activities within the various functions. BPR re-designs these cross-functional activities so that the organisation can deliver the service to customers in the most effective and efficient way.

Outcomes resulting from process re-engineering may or may not be known at the outset, but driving forces are mainly tied up with quality and customer service:

Output involving goods – will surround the quality of the product offering,
Output involving service – is less tangible and quality depends on the outcome of the service and on the customer's perception of the delivery system.

These outcomes could be events as diverse as the delivery of an express parcel; a successful hospital admission; a lecture on a university course. In each of these examples there are many processes leading up to the outcome and they will cross many functional areas, involve many people, operations and skills. There will be handovers, pick up points, cycle time and administration, with many opportunities for error, time lags and discrepancies. There must be very few organisations, public or private sector, that could not put their hands on their hearts and admit that individual processes could not be done, more efficiently, faster or even at all!

Another useful perspective from which to view this case is the ORDER FULFILMENT PROCESS. This can be applied to any business or organisation, public, private sector or service industry, and may not always be perceived as filling an order. *All processes work towards order fulfilment* – this is a core process, managed by logistics.

For example:

MANUFACTURER	–	order raw materials, make product, deliver, end use.
RETAILER	–	order goods, store, sell.
PUBLIC SECTOR	–	NHS (patient), local health authority (customer), admit, diagnose, treat, discharge.
EDUCATION	–	student (customer), transmit information (quality), successful exams, product – teaching.
TOURISM	–	book holiday, admin., holiday delivered.
BANKS	–	apply for loan, credit checks, admin., loan delivered, repay organisation.

BPR is not something undertaken lightly, it requires a strategy driven approach and management must have patience, commitment and tenacity to drive the projects through. They must consider whether to approach the exercise alone or whether to manage a relationship with consultants – as successfully done between St James's and LES, and then decide if they are willing and ready to change and possibly move/remove staff, products, structures, relationships and even whole departments and systems which have evolved over time.

4.2 Problem areas

There seemed to be relatively few problems during the running and implementing of this project. Difficulties that were encountered have been outlined below:

1. It is necessary to involve and keep staff informed at all stages of process redesign. This was essential in the supplies function itself where there were worries over the changing roles of buyers and the introduction of Materials Managers. There were inevitable worries over jobs.
2. Political problems, such as

(a) unwillingness to consider corporate views or needs (which could influence the ability to bulk purchase).
(b) protectionism/ring fencing – unwillingness to share scarce resources. This can be 'played off' to get a toe hold, the divide and conquer principle well known to Company Sales representatives.
(c) parochialism – (It's my budget, I'll do what I want), risk of establishing 'mini-trusts'.

There are some areas within the hospital where it is difficult to make progress, e.g. large powerful Directorates such as Pathology. This has 8 different departments all with different responsibilities, they still want to purchase and order independently, under the old system.

3. Adjustment to individual budgets became necessary during the change from the old to the new ordering process, i.e. – to prevent ordering whilst the overstocking was used up and to enable all budget holders to purchase the necessary shelving equipment to implement Materials Management. This meant that close liaison between supplies, budget holders and the Finance function was essential.

NB. St James's Hospital merged with Seacroft Hospital in April 1995 and as such has become a 5th Wave Trust (instead of a first). There were concerns that St James's would lose the advantages of not having to be part of NHSSA, but at this point it seems that provision has been made for them to retain their current supplies structure.

4.3 Current status of the project

4.3.1 Did it meet its aims?

There are still difficulties over evaluation in order to know this. Most problems will never be apparent until a new system is up and running and addressing these implementation problems take the focus from evaluating how successful the project has been/is being.

The purchasing and supply project has been totally assimilated into the organisation – is ongoing and very successful, it quickly achieved the original aim of financing the collaboration with LES and has gone on to make bottom line savings for the hospital each year.

In order to build on what has been learned from the collaboration and to utilise the expertise that they now have in this area, the hospital hopes eventually to develop a process manual (a set of written model procedures) which will be used to audit practices in all clinical areas. This will investigate what is actually being done against standards required by the hospital. All departments, wards and clinics will have their processes looked at against these models and fixed points and targets will be set (with some flexibility). It should pinpoint areas/opportunities for change, identify mismatches and suggest future action (if any). One Directorate has agreed to act as pilot.

Although this project did not take such a radical approach as many BPR projects, it has been a very real attempt to change things for the right reasons, build on what has been learnt and use the enthusiasm generated internally to eliminate non-value added activities in order to get the basics right.

4.4 Areas for further discussion

The following headings are often seen as critical re-design problem areas. An interesting class discussion could be formed around how the St James's project tackled each one.

- Overcoming middle management (all staff?) resistance to change.
- Maintaining momentum throughout the re-design process.
- Using changing customer/organisational needs as a catalyst for BPR.
- Tackling the fear of change within the organisation.

- Redefining staff/management roles as process owners and change managers.
- Successfully changing corporate (or even individual) culture towards a more effective workforce or systems efficiency.
- Effectively using benchmarking to monitor and focus progress before/during and after the change programme.

The **MANAGEMENT OF CHANGE** is an important element of the case, discussion could centre around any or all of the following areas:

Organisations and their environments
- the NHS/public sector in context: its place in society, changes to a market based system, public/private health care ethics. There has been a profound change in the culture of the service, from an organisation that had its roots in social welfare to one that is embracing the principles of a managed market.
- This can cause much anxiety for staff struggling to maintain what Charles Handy describes 'a sense of connection'[9] in effect a loss of culture.
- initiate discussions on public vs. private sector organisations approach to change – differences and similarities (based on the experience of participants).

Power, politics and conflict
- internal and external to the organisation. The case can be used to illustrate the role that groups with entrenched interests can play in facilitating or impeding the change process. *Dinosaurs vs. new management thinking!*

Organisational mission and conflict
- discussion based around organisational cultures, accepted beliefs and values, Missions statements etc.

Who has the vision?
- how important is visionary leadership, different management styles, ownership of BPR projects. Commitment from the top down, involvement from the bottom up.

Communication
- different methods
- collecting/collating information between functions,
- problems over benchmarking
- between different staff levels
- causing problems in process mapping, cross functional involvement.

BPR in public sector context
- how easy/difficult is it for staff to change ways of thinking and doing things, from being functionally biased to being process oriented – teamwork.
- HR issues – the importance of involving the actual people who will be implementing the new processes, worries over job losses etc.
- Beware of change for the sake of change.
- Outcomes are unknown at the beginning, this brings in an element of risk. One way to reduce risk is through greater use of protocols – effectively even greater standardisation of process, which is ironically a move towards greater bureaucracy.

Lessons from private/public sector collaboration
- similarities and differences

---

[9] Handy, C. (1994) *The Empty Raincoat*, London 1994.

- how transferable were the methodologies used (from industry and manufacturing)
- should BPR be approached differently in public/private sector organisations.

As well as all the potential problem areas it should be remembered that there are positive sides to process change and that the main reasons for implementing such projects are to improve service quality and resource use, and most importantly to 'unravel' the complexities that develop within large organisations e.g.:

TO SIMPLIFY AND REDUCE LEAD TIMES
- separate complex tasks;
- change their sequence;
- eliminate bottle-neck;
- combine responsibility for similar activities;
- reduce movements (people, goods, information);
- cut out unnecessary duplication;
- improve staff collaboration/communication;
- create teams.

SECTION 6 SUMMARY AND CRITICAL SUCCESS FACTORS

Even though there were teething problems and difficulties it would seem that St James's will continue to use many of the ideas generated in this collaboration for years to come and there can be little doubt that those involved have found the whole exercise a valuable learning experience.

Below is a very basic list of critical success factors, without which an organisation's attempt at BPR would have little chance of success. The organisation *must*

- be willing to change
- recognise that change means doing things differently
- lead from the top.
- commit sufficient time and resources
- broaden individual roles
- involve staff (and customers) at all levels
- communicate, communicate, communicate
- educate and train at all levels, to facilitate the changes.

Finally these quotes seem to sum up the projects:

> I believe that the Lucas Project was the most significant thing to have been done at this hospital for years.

> The Lucas Project was brilliant. Even though I had my doubts about it in the beginning, now I have seen the effects . . . it gave us control over what we were trying to do for the patients.

NB. The author gratefully acknowledges the help given by staff at St James's Hospital, Leeds during the research for this teaching note. The case and teaching note are available from European Case Clearing House, Cranfield, Beds, UK.

Part 7

Transport Management

Case 23

ALMARAI LTD

Camels in the Desert Night – Transport Safety Analysis

Will Murray, *University of Huddersfield* and **Adrian Grey**, *Almarai Ltd*

SECTION 1 CASE SYNOPSIS

This is a real case dealing with a transport issue faced by a major company. Almarai is based in Saudi Arabia (KSA) and is the largest dairy processing company in the Middle East. To service its customers throughout the whole Middle East region it has a fleet of over 80 long haul bulk collection and delivery vehicles as well as a large number of locally based customer delivery vehicles.

The company had highlighted a growing safety problem with the long haul vehicles and had commenced putting measures in place to try to control the fleet and reduce accidents. Despite this the problem had continued to grow.

The case requires students to examine the problem in more depth, and develop an appropriate policy.

SECTION 2 TEACHING AND LEARNING OBJECTIVES

By undertaking this case students will have the opportunity to gain several learning outcomes, including:

1. understanding some of the problems and realities of operating logistics systems in the Middle East
2. the ability to analyse the causes of accidents in a transport fleet
3. developing a methodology for analysing accidents, which can be applied to a wide range of situations including trucks, vans, company cars, buses, fire engines and ambulances
4. being able to make recommendations as to how to reduce accidents, in both the KSA and in other contexts

5. experiencing some of the processes involved in data collection and consultancy projects in an unfamiliar environment.

SECTION 3 MAIN ISSUES AND PROBLEMS RAISED BY THE CASE

The main issues brought up by the case revolve around transport safety and the need for it to be addressed systematically as a management problem by companies operating vehicles.

It is a area that is often neglected for a range of reasons:

- 'the insurance will cover it', 'accidents will happen', etc. are typical comments.
- its often not part of the transport manager's budget
- responsibility crosses several departments (e.g. personnel for training, administration for dealing with claims, maintenance for repairs)
- transport is still seen as being about doing rather than systematically planning.

In recent years systematic management approaches to safety have been developed and are increasingly being applied. This case is about helping Almarai to become more systematic about safety auditing and accident reduction through management action.

One approach that has been developed is the CCSM model[1] shown in Figure 7.1. It is a basis for approaching problems faced by organisations with a similar problem to that of Almarai.

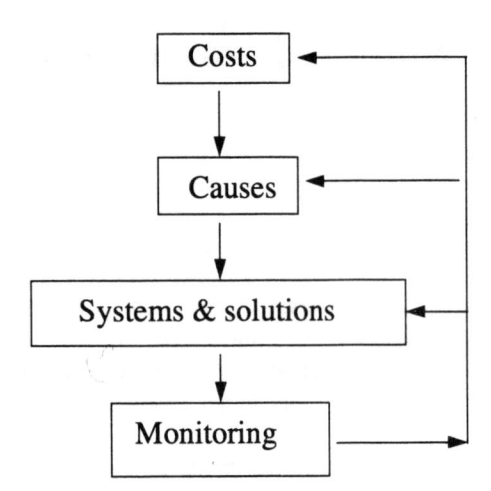

```
    ┌─────────┐
    │  Costs  │◄──────┐
    └────┬────┘       │
         ▼            │
    ┌─────────┐       │
    │ Causes  │◄──────┤
    └────┬────┘       │
         ▼            │
 ┌──────────────────┐ │
 │ Systems & solutions │◄──┤
 └────────┬─────────┘ │
          ▼           │
    ┌────────────┐    │
    │ Monitoring ├────┘
    └────────────┘
```

Figure 7.1 The CCSM accident reduction model

Any company, or consultant wishing to reduce accidents would need to collect information relating to the exact costs and causes of the accidents. Depending on these costs and causes, systems can then be developed to reduce them.

The recommendations for this case, based on applying this approach, are set out in section 5 below.

---

[1] Murray, W. and Whiteing, A. (1995) 'Reducing commercial vehicle accidents through accident databases', *Logistics Information Management*, **8** (3), 22–29.

SECTION 4 SPECIFIC QUESTIONS

Specific questions could fall into several areas:

1. Making recommendations based on the information available.
2. Requesting further information to analyse.
3. Preparing a tender for the consultancy job.

    1. From the material in the case, assume you are a consultant who has been asked by Almarai to
- assess the main causes of the company's accidents;
- suggest measures which could be adopted by the company to reduce the likelihood of accidents occurring.

    2. Assume you are a UK based consultant and have been chosen by Almarai's Personnel Manager to prepare a project proposal for the company to help them reduce their accidents. They would like you to undertake:

- initial analysis in the UK;
- a one week field visit of data collection and analysis in KSA;
- preparation of a report and recommendations on how they should reduce accidents.

To carry out this project you must initially

- Prepare a data request for the information you would need to undertake the initial UK based analysis.
- Develop an outline timetable of how you would spend the week in KSA, including what you would do, who you would wish to see/interview and why.
- By assessing what is currently best practise in your own country, explain some general recommendations you could make to the company, based on the initial information, that you feel would help them to reduce their accidents.
- As an add on the company has also told you that the price of fuel in KSA has recently increased by 300 per cent. They have requested that you make some preliminary recommendations to them about how they could reduce their fuel bills as well as their accidents.

    3. Assume you are a consultant who has been asked to tender for a contract to help Almarai improve their safety. Based on the information write a proposal for the company stating how you would undertake the project, and giving your initial recommendations based on the information available.

SECTION 5 DESCRIPTION OF ACTUAL DEVELOPMENTS IN THE COMPANY

This section describes how Almarai brought in outside consultants and also the company's initiatives since.

5.1 The consultants

The company brought in an outside consultant who reviewed the existing safety policy; undertook a series of interviews with key managers (Personnel Manager, Divisional Accountant; Fleet Engineering Manager; Workshop Supervisor and Transport Supervisor), drivers in the company and a representative from Almarai's insurers; assessed some of the drivers; collected insurance claims reports and other accident reports together; and set up a database to analyse the causes of all the previous accidents. On the basis of this several findings emerged:

- A serious accident can cost Almarai as much as 100000 to 150000 Saudi Riyals (US$30000-50000) in unrecoverable costs.
- The causes of many accidents, particularly those under the insurance excess were not being monitored.
- The main causes of Almarai's accidents fell into 4 areas: the Saudi environment, driver error, the vehicles and maintenance and poor management. Overall there was no one cause or solution for the accidents. Initiatives were required in all of these areas.

The following recommendations were among those made:

- Maintain and analyse an accident cause database. Accident reporting should be centralised and systematic for all accidents.
- Driver recruitment and induction should become more systematic, and based on a detailed person specification. It should include an interview, a practical driving skills assessment, an eyesight test, medical, written knowledge test and a safe driver test.
- Driver training and assessment of existing drivers should be undertaken. The results must be fed back to the drivers to help them improve. The best and most experienced drivers could be trained as driver trainers.
- Training for all drivers needs to include risk avoidance, defensive driving, vehicle sympathy, tachographs, accident causes and prevention, drivers' daily checks, use of brakes, night-time driving, dealing with blowouts, speed awareness and use of signals.
- Speeds, drivers' hours and the current incentive scheme should be reviewed, and brought more into line with other regions like Europe and Australia. Driver incentives for accident free years and service in Almarai should be considered. Almarai's insurers may well help to fund this.
- Ensure drivers get sufficient sleep and good facilities at points en route.
- The tyre life and replacement policy should be monitored and reviewed, to assess whether the current replacement periods are realistic.
- Service periods for the tractors are in line with UK companies. However, the tankers, trailers and their running gear are being serviced much less frequently than UK companies would consider to be safe, and should be reviewed. More emphasis should be given to defect repairs, as well as to scheduled maintenance.

5.2 Almarai initiatives

The Personnel Manager's desire for action on 3 fronts, driver selection, driver training and accident causes, had the outcomes set out below.

5.2.1 Driver selection

Driver recruitment is now undertaken to strictly adhered guidelines. Potential candidates must successfully pass a comprehensive in-house developed driving test and a laid down medical examination prior to final acceptance.

5.2.2 Driver training

A specialist driver training agency was employed to develop the skills in a cascade approach. A number of full-time driver instructors and a panel of master drivers were developed to pass on accident avoidance and defensive driving techniques. A compulsory training systems was introduced, as follows:

1. All new drivers undergo a 3 month induction programme. They are all assigned to a dedicated master driver on a 'sit with Nellie' basis. Probationers are only signed off on successful completion.
2. Annually drivers undergo a skills assessment and medical examination in conjunction with contract renewal. Training needs are identified and acted on, prior to renewal sign off.
3. Regular courses in driver skills development are conducted throughout the year by 3 full-time driving instructors.

5.2.3 Causes of accidents

The accident database that was introduced has been expended to include all accidents in the fleet since 1990 and trends on accidents are now analysed to determine accident patterns and solutions.
In addition several other steps were taken:

- The fleet has been consolidated to one site for greater management control and a specialist tachograph centre developed in-house.
- The Safety Group has been requested to further enhance the transport safety policy and to introduce a safety incentive based driver payment system.
- The company speed limit was reduced to 100 km/h, with a further reduction to 85 km/h planned for 1996. Almarai drivers were also instructed to comply with local speed limits where these are less than company imposed limits.
- Drivers operating hours are currently being reviewed, with the intention of introducing current European regulations.

5.3 The outcome

Almarai now exercises a much more structured control over the long haul fleet operations. Driver abuses have been minimised and the additional focus and enhanced transport safety policy has resulted in a greater awareness of accidents and what can be done to reduce the risks.

In 1995, the first such year, no deaths resulted from the long haul fleet's activities. This trend has continued into 1996. The pattern of accidents, with less being caused by Almarai drivers. In addition, the accidents are more generally of a less severe nature. The accident ratio for 1994/5 was 1:1.5 million km.

SECTION 6 AUDIENCES/USE OF CASE/TEACHING SUGGESTIONS

6.1 Audiences

The case is suitable for a wide range of audiences:

- undergraduates
- post-graduates
- management training courses
- in-company training
- distance learning courses.

The case is suitable for use in many different areas, including:

- transport, distribution and logistics;
- international business;
- personnel, human resource management and training;
- safety management.

6.2 Teaching suggestions and possible uses

The case is suitable for a wide variety of uses:

- written or oral presentation based assignment or examination;
- in-class discussion or brain-storming session;
- in-class role play exercise with different groups acting as consultants 'tendering' for the job, and one group evaluating the tenders;
- for in-class sessions the case requires a 2 hour session with no pre-reading, or 1 hour session with pre-reading.

Case 24

OK TEDI MINING LIMITED

Road Transport Operations in Papua New Guinea

David Taylor, *University of Huddersfield* and **George Wilson**, *OK Tedi Mining Ltd*

SECTION 1 CASE SYNOPSIS

This is a real case requiring detailed consideration of transport operations and planning issues in servicing a copper mine and its associated settlement at Tabubil in Central Papua New Guinea. The mine, operated by the OK Tedi Mining Company is located in a remote mountainous area which is subject to extreme climatic and environmental conditions. All supplies for the mine and settlement must be transported by road from the river port at Kiunga, a distance of some 137 km over unpaved, difficult mountain roads.

Readers are put in the position of George Wilson the OK Tedi Transport Superintendent who has to develop a plan to meet the 1996 transportation requirements for servicing the mine with supplies, fuel, equipment and food.

The case provides the opportunity to develop a general methodology with which to approach a transport resourcing problem, as well as giving sufficient information to undertake detailed analysis of the transportation requirements for this specific situation.

It also highlights some of in issues involved in managing transport in inhospitable third-world environments.

SECTION 2 TEACHING OBJECTIVES

1. To require students to develop a methodology with which to approach a transportation resourcing problem.
2. To allow students to identify and analyse transportation demands, resources and requirements.
3. To require students to develop alternative proposals to meet transportation requirements in both the short and longer terms.

4. To give an appreciation of the difficulties and demands of managing a transport operation in a harsh geographical and business environment.

SECTION 3 MAIN ISSUES AND PROBLEMS

3.1 Determining how to meet an increased demand for transport

The transport demand will increase in 1995/96 primarily in terms of increased fuel volumes. There is an overall increase in demand throughout the year by 10 m litres and an increase during the June to August peak. Transport resources in 1994/95 were already used to capacity.

In the short run therefore there is a need to calculate what additional resources will be required in terms of tanker capacity and drivers and what is the most cost effective way to procure these resources.

In the medium to longer term there is a need to question whether policies can be changed to reduce the demand for transport or use more efficient modes of transport for example by completing the oil pipeline from the Tabubil fuel dump to the mine on Mt Fubilan.

3.2 The difficulty of assuring adequate service to the mine given the very difficult road haulage conditions between Kiunga and Tabubil.

There is also a need to consider the extended supply lines given shipments from foreign countries and the requirement for coastal and river shipping in Papua New Guinea involving various transhipments.

3.3 Safety Requirements

The whole mine operation including the transport operations was extremely safety conscious. Any solutions must take this into consideration.

Allied to safety were the arduous road haulage conditions and the issue of driver comfort. Drivers comfort needed to be improved as this would impact on safety and in fact in 1995/96 a policy was introduced that all new vehicles would be fitted with air conditioning.

SECTION 4 SPECIFIC QUESTIONS

4.1 Planning

1. Develop a plan to meet the transportation requirements of servicing the OK Tedi Mining Company facilities at Tabubil during the 1995/96 financial year and beyond

Question 1 basically specifies the whole task: however if students require guidance through the planning process the task may be broken down into subsections using the following questions:

2. (a) Specify the main factors or issues that should be taken into account in developing a transport plan for the OK Tedi Mine.
    (b) To what extent can these factors be used as a general methodology with which to approach other transportation planing scenarios?

4.2 An approach

A general methodology with which to approach this problem and indeed other transport resource planning problems would be:

1. Categorise and quantify the transportation demands in the planning period i.e. specify the transportation task.
2. Audit current transportation resources in terms of vehicles, trailers, manpower, etc.
3. Quantify the gap (if any) between future demands and resources.
4. Identify any specific contextual factors or problems which should be taken into account in the planning process. Such factors can usefully be analysed in terms of:
   (a) internal factors e.g. company policies, objectives or requirements;
   (b) external factors e.g. aspects of the geographical, political or economic environment.
5. Develop alternative proposals to provide the resources to meet the forecast transportation demand (and bridge any gap identified in step 3).
6. Select and justify the preferred option.
7. Identify any longer term policies or improvements which should be put into place during the current period.

If required the seven steps of the above methodology could be given to students as specific questions to give more detailed guidance through the case.

SECTION 5 OUTLINE ANALYSIS OF SOME KEY ISSUES AND INDICATIONS OF POLICIES ADOPTED BY THE COMPANY

5.1 The transport task

The transport task can be split into a number of sub sections :

1. The line haul fuel task: Kiunga to Tabubil.
2. Fuel movements : Tabubil fuel dump to Mt Fubilan mine.
3. The non fuel task : line haul Kiunga to Tabubil.
4. General goods local delivery around Tabubil.

5.1.1 The line haul fuel task: Kiunga to Tabubil

(a) The increased annual fuel volume
1994/95 Situation: 60 million litres pa
                           40000 litres per tanker
                           = 1500 tanker trips
6 tankers in the fleet but with average downtime of 80-85% assume 5 tankers available on average. Tankers thus make approximately 300 trips per year.

1995/96 Requirement:
Additional 10 million litres of fuel to be transported.
The will require an additional 250 trips per year.
Therefore requires one additional tanker and one additional prime mover.

(b) The increased fuel volume in the June–August peak

June to August 1995 scheduled 24m litres	= 8 mil litre (m.l.) per month
Normal monthly volume 70÷12	= 5.8 m.l. per month
Required additional capacity (June-Aug)	= 2.2 m.l. per month

To service this addition movement
Option 1: Hire Tanktainers : (the preferred option actually selected by OK Tedi)

Tanktainer Capacity	= 20000 litres
Number required per month 2200000/20000	= 110
Number required per day 110/30	= 4

Therefore need to hire 8 i.e. four filling in Kiunga, four emptying in Tabubil

Hire cost per day US$25 x 8	= $ 200 per day

Tanktainers to be carried by the OTML fleet drop decks.
The trade-off against this is a decrease in haulage capacity for general cargo.
As is usual in the transport business this situation must be assessed regularly to reprioritise as necessary.

Option 2: Hire local tankers (not chosen)

Tanker Capacity	40000 litres
Number required per month 2200000/4000o	= 55
Number required per day 55/30	= 2
Hire cost per week per tanker K1350	= US$ 1053
Hire cost per day per tanker	= $150
Hire cost per day 2 tankers	= $300

OTML policy is not to hire local tankers unless in absolute emergency because the cost is considered to be prohibitive.

(c) Fuelling policy for line haul vehicles
The case states that all convoys were fuelled at Tabubil yet there is a refuelling facility at Kiunga. It makes no sense for tankers to haul fuel from Kiunga to Tabubil when all the convoy vehicles visit Kiunga. A policy change to refuel convoys in Kiunga would save one fuel tanker trip per week.

Convoys per week	7
Convoys average number trucks	14
Fuel usage Tabubil-Kiunga round trip	400 litres/vehicles
Total fuel usage	39200 litres/week

5.1.2 Fuel movements: Tabubil fuel dump to Mt Fubilan mine

24 m litres pa of fuel are moved from the fuel farm at Tabubil to the mine. This requires two rigid fuel tankers each with 18000 litre capacity (total of 4 trips per day).

Recommended that OTML conduct a feasibility study for completion of the partially built fuel pipeline.

The cost of completing the line to be compared to the total annual operating cost of the two trucks.

5.1.3 The non fuel task: line haul Kiunga to Tabubil

Average weekly cargo movement	1650 tonnes
Maximum weight per container	22 tonnes
Approximate number of container movements	83/week

No change in volume of these goods predicted.
Therefore assume existing transport capacity adequate.

5.1.4 General goods local delivery around Tabubil

Number of local trips per annum = 4500
Assuming 350 working days = 13 trips per day
Assume 5 drivers available therefore
trips per driver per day = 2.5
No change in local transport requirement predicted.
Therefore assume existing transport capacity adequate

5.2 The transportation resource

5.2.1 The vehicle fleet

A realistic assessment is required of the actual vehicles which will be available as opposed to the total fleet size. A key issue is vehicle downtime due either to vehicle maintenance/repair or shortage of drivers. On average 15–20% of vehicles will be off the road for maintenance or repair. Whilst on any one day approximately 12% of drivers may be unavailable either because of rest days, holidays or sick leave.

41 drivers: 3 on rest and recuperation
2 on sick leave
Tables 7.1 and 7.2 summarise the possible situation.

Table 7.1 Vehicle availability

Vehicle type	Maximum number in fleet	Vehicles available on average
Trailers		
Fuel tankers	6	5
Drop decks	15	12
Flat beds	6	5
Pipe trailers	3	3
Low loaders	2	2
Prime Movers	28	23
Convoy escort vehicles	3	3
Rigid fuel tankers	2	2
Tyre trucks	3	3

Table 7.2 Driver availability

Category	Maximum number drivers	Assumed likely number available
Line haul and tyre truck	30	27
Convoy escorts	3	3
Local delivery	6	5
Rigid fuel haul	2	2
Total	41	36

5.2.2 Addressing the issue of vehicle down-time

(a) Maintenance
The transport department has no authority to prioritise work through the Tabubil workshop which offers general maintenance services to the mine, mill and other facilities in Tabubil. Transport are just another customer of the workshop and must therefore wait their turn.

With 80–85% vehicle downtime the management finds it difficult to meet the normal haulage task with the existing fleet.

Recommendation
As transport is the biggest single customer of the workshop, the Transport department should attempt either:

1. to bring the workshop under their direct control or
2. find some way to become part of the workshop decision making process

It should be emphasised that the transport fleet is vital to maintaining the supply chain to keep the mine and all other aspects at Tabubil operational.

(b) Tyres
As a cost saving measure the transport fleet are supplied with retreaded tyres by the warehouse. The decision is made by the purchasing people in the warehouse. The transport managers argue that retreads are more prone to puncture or losing tread and therefore not only compromise safety but lead to lost transit times and also create collateral damage to the vehicle.

The policy of retreads is an unresolved and contentious issue. The nature of the roads mean tyres are subject to extremely hard wear.

Recommendation
In order to make an informal decision the transport supervisor should set up a database and start collecting information on:

- the number of flat tyres using retreads compared to normal tyres;
- accurate lost time figures in trips or hours;
- damage to components as a result of running on deflated tyres.

This must be assessed against the savings in using retreads as against new tyres.

(c) Driver unavailability
Driving conditions are extremely arduous because of unmade roads, mountainous terrain, heat and humidity, dust in the dry season, mud in the wet season.

Recommendation
Improve driver conditions and comfort by introducing air conditioned vehicles. This may impact on safety and may indirectly help to reduce driver absenteeism/sick leave.

5.3 Longer term policy developments

5.3.1 Ageing of fuel tankers

The conditions are severe in this area of PNG and vehicles are constantly running on un-paved roads. There is a need to implement a planned vehicle replacement policy. In fact OTML initiated such a policy in 1995/96 budgeting for 2 new tankers per year. A similar policy needs to be applied to all vehicles in the fleet.

5.3.2 The safety issue

The safety issue was a major concern. Convoys using the 137 km road between Kiunga and Tabubil presented a major danger to other road users. There were regular complaints from mill/mine staff over meeting on-coming trucks particularly when not properly alerted by escort vehicles.

Radio contact with convoy trucks
One of the main problems was that escorts were not in radio contact with line haul trucks which made it difficult to maintain convoy discipline i.e. speed and distance. It also meant that trucks could not be alerted to oncoming vehicles and unusual conditions e.g. road works or obstructions.

In 1996 OTML began trials of two-way radios in each convoy truck. However a factor to consider is that with a 15 gear vehicle and the tortuous road, drivers are constantly using both hands. This means that strict procedures for radio usage have to be passed to each driver and that these procedures must be observed.

Driver Training
In 1996 a driver skills analysis was carried out to ascertain driver competency levels. This was the first step in the formulation of a focused driver training programme.

SECTION 6 AUDIENCES/USES/OF THE CASE

Suitable for use at undergraduate level (second or third year) on courses specifically dealing with road transport operations and planning.

Case 25

PERFECTA BEDS

Improving Transport Productivity: The Introduction of a New Driver Incentive Scheme

Marion Court, *University of Huddersfield* and **Mark Harrison**, *Perfecta Beds*

SECTION 1 CASE SYNOPSIS

This real case examines the issues of man management, motivating and incentivising drivers within the context of Perfecta Beds, part of the Silentnight Beds Group.

The case raises issues of how the company's incentive scheme designed to enhance driver productivity within its own-account operation became out of step with the needs of the business. It allows students to evaluate methods of measuring driver productivity and raises issues of whether an in-house operation can successfully compete with third-party operations in a situation where resistance to change was the dominant culture. The case gives students the opportunity to attempt to devise a new incentive scheme that must be realistic and work within legal limits. The case also highlights the way that the old scheme had become out of touch with the needs of the business by promoting what were in reality transport objectives and not the real objectives of the business i.e. delivering more beds at a cost effective rate. It also briefly addresses the non-financial motivational factors. The case can be tackled in either a qualitative or quantitative way or both. Some analysis can be carried out using simple computer based routeing packages and spreadsheets if these are available, but this is not absolutely necessary for successful use of the case.

SECTION 2 TEACHING/LEARNING OBJECTIVES

In studying the case the students will;

1. Have the opportunity to evaluate the efficacy of measures of driver productivity.
2. Identify how the company's incentive scheme had been added to and changed over the years so that it resulted in a total transport labour cost which the business could not sustain.
3. Identify and examine alternative schemes which might more closely satisfy the needs of the business.
4. Become aware of the legal framework in which any new scheme should be developed.
5. Examine whether the own-account operation could change its performance so that a third-party take-over of the transport operation was less likely.
6. Have the opportunity to use spreadsheets and specialist routeing and scheduling software to analyse the operation.
7. Become aware of the need to find appropriate benchmark comparators when analysing the productive performance of any operation.

SECTION 3 MAIN ISSUES AND PROBLEMS RAISED BY THE CASE

3.1 The role of distribution within the Perfecta business

Perfecta was undoubtedly a sales-led organisation where distribution despite being a significant cost to the business was expected to play very much a supporting role to the sales effort. This approach is explained largely by Perfecta's strategic position in the Silentnight Group which was to help erect barriers to entry against to low-price competitors who might be in a position to threaten the more attractive market segments within the Silentnight portfolio.

3.2 Established working practices out of step with the requirements of the business

The company had a workforce with a profile of long service and a situation where the existing payment and incentive scheme meant that employees had become extremely comfortable with their lot in life. Transport productivity had become out of step with the needs of the business and the net result was that an increasingly higher proportion of the deliveries were being undertaken by outside sub-contractors. In other words the business could no longer afford the cost of low productivity within its distribution operation and had to find ways to change the workforce to supply the desired level of service and at a cost the company could afford.

3.3 Failure of the workforce to appreciate a major threat to their livelihood from third-party contracting.

The new distribution manager had established good working relations with his team of drivers but found that they failed to see that unless productivity was dramatically improved they were at risk of the operation being taken over by a third-party operator. The traffic schedulers, although highly experienced had become accustomed to working in the same old way and were operating within the culture of inertia that had infiltrated much of the department. Drivers seemed to spend an inordinate amount of time either taking vehicles down to the local garage for minor repairs or sitting about in the canteen waiting for loads to be ready, or simply accepting delays at customers either due to mis-delivery or order error without being pro-active in trying to quickly resolve any delay. Although in many cases these were situations beyond their control equally there was very little upward pressure from drivers to help speed up these processes.

3.4 The need to devise a new driver incentive scheme to meet the needs of the company and of drivers and that would avoid major industrial relations confrontation

The distribution manager was aware that a few of the drivers were more highly motivated and typically achieved a much more acceptable rate of productivity. Analysis quickly showed that if this level of productivity could be achieved across the fleet, the cost of delivering the beds could be brought down to a much more acceptable level.

Any new incentive scheme had to take into account the mixed nature of the work i.e. both long distance work combined with local deliveries at the other end, as well as the work more local to the Barnsley base. It was important that any new scheme was realistic, encouraged responsible driving within safe legal limits and was credible to the workforce. The use of tachograph analysis, benchmarking comparisons with Layeezee, specific routeing and scheduling packages and detailed monitoring of actual operations on the road all helped to contribute towards these goals.

SECTION 4 SPECIFIC QUESTIONS

1. Identify the key problem areas the business was facing in regard to its distribution activity.
2. Using the data provided compare and contrast the differing levels of performance amongst the drivers. Try to identify reasons both within and outside of the control of drivers as to why there may be such differences. Then compare the level of productivity of the Perfecta operation with that of Layeezee Beds another Silentnight company with a fairly similar distribution profile. What does this suggest?
3. Use a simple routeing package such as Autoroute to calculate times and distances between Perfecta's base in Barnsley and the major urban areas they delivered to during the representative sample periods studied. Be sure to use commercial vehicle speeds that are both realistic and legal for different road types. What size of fleet operation would be realistic in your view and how does this compare to what Perfecta were actually running? Note if a UK routeing package is not available a simple time and distance matrix is included inTable 7.3.
1. The Distribution Manager was interested in combining both individual and team bonuses. What advantages and disadvantages are there to each of these types of incentive and how might they work effectively together ?
2. If you were in the Distribution Manager's position what would you think about bringing in a totally third-party operation? Evaluate the potential gains and risks to the business if it were to take up this option.
3. Using the data and background given, attempt to outline the basis for a new driver payment scheme which would be more in line with Perfecta's real needs. Explain clearly the rationale that would be presented to:
    (a) the drivers
    (b) the company management
4. to gain acceptance of your proposals. Remember that by law, any new scheme must not encourage drivers to break either the drivers' hours regulations or to break the legal speed limits or indeed to disregard safe, professional driving practice.

Table 7.3 UK routeing information

AREA	Town location	Round trip time (hr.) for stem (decimal)	Round trip miles for stem
1. North Scotland	Inverness	20.30	757
2. Glasgow	Glasgow	10.60	521
3. Edinburgh	Edinburgh	11.50	459
5. Cumbria	Carlisle	6.30	328
6. North East	Washington	5.10	208
7. North Yorkshire	Middlesborough	4.10	164
8. North Lancashire	Blackpool	3.90	181
9. Humberside	Hull	2.90	141
10. W.Yorkshire	Harrogate	2.10	70
11. Liverpool	Liverpool	3.50	185
12. Manchester	Bolton	2.55	133
13. S. Manchester	Knutsford	2.90	106
14. S. Yorkshire	Sheffield	0.60	26
15. S. Nott'hamshire	Loughborough	2.60	130
16. Lincolnshire	Kings Lynn	6.50	227
17. Staffordshire	Shrewsbury	6.00	254
18. North Wales	Porthmadog	8.05	312
19. W. Midlands	Kidderminster	5.30	227
21. Leicestershire	Northampton	4.10	218
22. Norfolk	Ipswich	9.05	368
24. Bedfordshire	St Albans	5.75	304
25. Oxfordshire	Marlborough	8.50	364
26. Gloucestershire	Gloucester	6.25	300
27. South Wales	Cardiff	8.50	400
28. West Wales	Swansea	9.75	506
29. Essex	Southend	8.20	411
30. North London	Slough	6.55	358
31. South London	Reigate	8.30	392
32. N.Ireland	N/A	0.00	0
33. Bristol	Glastonbury	9.20	403
34. Cornwall	St Austell	14.30	674
35. Hampshire	Bournemouth	10.25	528
36. Sussex	Brighton	9.10	467
37. Kent	Hastings	10.00	471

SECTION 5 DESCRIPTION OF ACTUAL DEVELOPMENTS IN THE COMPANY.

Following extensive negotiation with the drivers and their representative Perfecta introduced a new incentive scheme on the basis of the consultants' recommendations. The benchmark comparison undertaken with the sister company, Layeezee which had a similar distribution profile, had demonstrated that it would not be unreasonable to expect a considerable increase in performance. This was a significant factor in gaining the reluctant acceptance of the new scheme by the workforce. Additionally the fact that the consultants had spent a considerable amount of time actually on the road with the drivers was also very powerful in disarming such claims as 'This is all very well in theory but you don't know what it's really like'.

5.1 The new payment scheme

The new bonus payable on top of basic pay for 55 hours worked, was to be calculated by the number of drops each driver achieved per week. The key objective was to achieve a reduction in overall cost either by ensuring that a higher proportion of the work was done by the own account fleet or alternatively to allow the same percentage own fleet/contractor mix but with a smaller fleet size. Driver payments were to be calculated using;

- the total number of actual drops made
- a number of *drop equivalents* to compensate for stem mileage out to the focal point of the delivery area and return (this was to ensure that drivers delivering further away from base were not penalised).

The bonus scheme was designed to feature both an individual and a team element both of which had starting thresholds to ensure a satisfactory minimum performance, but thereafter became open-ended to encourage maximum effort.

5.2 The individual bonus

No driver was able to earn any bonus until the basic individual performance level was reached i.e. the specified number of drops per week – say 50 (made up of an overall synthetic of actual drops plus drop equivalents). This basic performance level was set at the level of average performance that had been achieved by the driving team as a whole in the months prior to the introduction of the new scheme. The basic performance level was what each driver was expected to achieve within his normal 55 hour working week. The effect was that if all drivers achieved only this level, the whole fleet productivity would be considerably raised (because by definition, previously some drivers had performed below the average).

5.3 The team bonus

The team bonus would only come into effect once *every driver* had achieved the minimum basic performance level of 50 drops or drop equivalents. This was to reinforce the raising of overall performance by rewarding everyone if they all achieved the previous average level and to engender a team spirit.

5.4 The drop equivalent rate

To calculate the *drop equivalent rate* from the representative period studied, the consultant used a spreadsheet to calculate the number of trips into each region multiplied by the time allowed for the stem mileage (taken from a computerised vehicle roueting package) which gave a total stem mileage time. Then the total stem mileage time was deducted from the hours actually worked, which identified how much time was available for local distribution driving and delivery at the drops.

The total distribution time was divided by the number of drops undertaken by the in-house fleet which gave an average distribution time/drop rate. Students might expect to find widely differing distribution time/drop rates in different geographic areas such as inner city areas having a slow rate because of congestion. However this tended to be counterbalanced by the greater density of retail customers than was the case in smaller urban areas. Thus although drivers tended to be able to drive more quickly in less congested areas they had to drive for longer before they arrived at the next customer's premises.

This distribution time/drop rate was then reduced by approximately 20% to gain equivalent productivity to that of the Layeezee operation.

Each stem journey was then given a 'drop equivalent' based on calculated journey times multiplied by the distribution time/drop rate.

5.5 An example

Assume that the overall distribution time/drop rate was set at 2 per hour. If a driver had a load for the Nottingham area with 12 drops to make his bonus would be calculated as follows:

- Stem mileage driving time from Barnsley base to Nottingham = 2.15 hours
- Stem mileage drop equivalent = 2.15 hours x 2 = *4.3 drop equivalents*.
- This would then be added to the 12 drops actually made to estimate that the driver had made the equivalent of 16.3 drops towards his weekly bonus target.

Tachographs were analysed to determine typical drop times at customers' premises.

5.6 Calculating the new bonus

Drivers' basic pay was based on a flat 55 hours per week with any incentive coming from the number of drops (and drop equivalents) actually achieved. Within the normal 55 hour week all drivers were expected to achieve a certain number of drops and drop equivalents – say 50. Bonus was paid on a pro-rata basis for drops in excess of 50 per week. The scheme was operated within a one week cycle to maintain maximum visibility and control. Night out subsistence payments were only paid as they were actually incurred. The new scheme provided more incentive for earnings through the bonus scheme, both individual and team rather than by claiming unnecessary nights out.

In cab-phones were introduced so that a daily call could be made to every driver to establish his estimated time of arrival back at base so that distribution planning could be updated and production chased to ensure the availability of the next load. This also allowed drivers to be more pro-active at drops where difficulties or delays arose. The loading within the warehouse operation was brought under the control of the Distribution Manager which helped to improve the correct availability and accuracy of loading and the delivery order.

5.7 The outcome

The scheme was successful in bringing about some considerable change in performance by the drivers. Soon after the introduction of the scheme the marketplace started to become increasingly demanding, requiring smaller, more frequent drops. This meant that although the thresholds within the scheme had to be adjusted the basic formula for calculation remained the same.

The main focus of the new bonus scheme was that it primarily rewarded drivers for making deliveries. A critical point to remember in devising any transport incentive scheme is that the raison d'etre of vehicles and drivers is to make deliveries. Incentive schemes should be designed to maximise the number of deliveries rather than to reward any other aspect of transport activity such as hours worked, distance covered or nights out. The old scheme at Perfecta had in fact rewarded many of these non-productive transport activities.

SECTION 6 AUDIENCES/USES OF CASE/TEACHING SUGGESTIONS

This case would be suitable primarily for work with under-graduates or training courses for transport management. It has relevance for any students considering the use of incentive schemes to help change the productivity performance of a distribution activity. It also lend itself to the use of spreadsheets and simple routeing packages such as Autoroute to undertake some simple analysis of the data given.

The case would be suitable to use as an assignment for students in an under-graduate programme. Students could be expected to produce a brief report outlining the key issues within the case together with some basic analysis of the data given and summarising what steps they would take. Students should be encouraged to reflect upon the cultural and qualitative issues as well as the quantitative ones. Students might be asked to make role play presentations to the drivers and or management to explain and 'sell' their new bonus scheme.

Case 26

THE PORT OF MELBOURNE
Planning Port Capacity

David Wilson, *Monash University*

SECTION 1 CASE SYNOPSIS

This case is based on a real situation at the Port of Melbourne in 1995. A significant part of the Port, Victoria Dock, is being closed down to make way for a new freeway. Victoria Dock is one of 4 separate and distinct container terminals at the Port of Melbourne. The case asks students to take the role of planners and determine:

1. should a new container terminal be built and if so where ?
2. can the existing cargo be distributed to other terminals without incurring congestion of ships or trucks ?

The case can be used as a multi-modal design exercise where students have to decide where to build a container terminal and justify the location. It can also be used as a case in queuing theory to test the capacity of the container terminals and determine ship delays.

SECTION 2 TEACHING OBJECTIVES

1. To provide students with a logistics planning and location design problem incorporating both and land and sea transport elements.
2. To demonstrate the effects of changing terminal capacities on transport congestion.
3. To familiarise students with the technology of rail and shipping and the land-interface.

SECTION 3 MAIN ISSUES AND PROBLEMS RAISED BY THE CASE

The main issue is Port capacity. Can the Port afford to lose a container terminal which handles 93,000 containers annually without constructing a new facility ?

The key lies in the container crane unloading rates which are currently running at 14 containers per hour. It is reasonable to assume that these rates might be increased to 16 or 18 containers per hour, but this still will not be sufficient to absorb the extra boxes. The question then becomes one of the timing of ship arrivals. Some simulations (of the Monte Carlo variety) will allow students to determine the effects on ship queues. Figure 3 gives the probability of a ship arriving on any one day and this information can be used to construct a simulation.

Another issue is the extent to which rail might be used to reduce truck congestion at the Port. Although most traffic is local, it is possible to use rail to move boxes out of a congested area to a more peripheral site on the fringe of the metropolitan area.

There are no 'right' or obvious answers in this case. To a large extent it depends on the growth of trade and the importance of Melbourne as a Port in contrast to Sydney and Brisbane. However, if students opt for the 'build' option then it is clearly better to build downstream, perhaps adding on to Webb Dock. A less expensive and viable alternative is to upgrade Appelton Dock.

SECTION 4 SPECIFIC QUESTIONS

1. What are the logistics issues facing planners at the Port of Melbourne ?
2. Estimate the container movements at the Port and its various berths to 2010 if you assume a 6 % annual growth rate from 1991/92.
3. What options are available to planners to improve the logistics systems in order to cope with the closure of Victoria Dock ?
4. To what extent can greater use be made of the rail option ?
5. Is it necessary to embark on the construction of a new terminal ?
   (a) Justify your answer by examining the costs and benefits.
   (b) What is your answer if growth occurs at only 2 or 3% per year ?
6. What will be the impact of 4th generation container ships on the Port ?

SECTION 5 DESCRIPTION OF ACTUAL DEVELOPMENTS IN THE COMPANY

Planners at the Port seem to feel that the existing infrastructure is sufficient.

They will. upgrade Swanson and Webb Dock with new and larger cranes and modern container loading information systems. They are confident that they can achieve container unloading rates approaching world's best practise of around 25 to 30 TEU's per hour.

However, they may simply run out of berthing space and ship congestion could still occur.

SECTION 6 AUDIENCE/USES OF CASE/TEACHING SUGGESTIONS.

6.1 Audience

This case is suitable for under-graduates who have completed a first course in logistics or transport. It will provide them with a practical problem and get them thinking about the physical details of containers, trains, trucks, ships, loading, unloading rates , space requirements and congestion.

6.2 Possible uses

This case requires some preparation and thought. Ideally ask students to pre-read the case. It will take about an hour to discuss in class.

It might also be used as a group assignment where students might work in two's or three's and examine various scenarios.

6.3 Teaching suggestions

First, tell the students that this a design problem and that they should think conceptually. They should make reasonable assumptions or guesses if necessary when creating options. Stress that there will be no one right answer and that logic, practical solutions and cost will be important factors in evaluation.

Encourage students to work in teams of two or three. Each person could prepare a separate analysis (say forecasting, queuing and congestion, rail planning and new berth location).

Ask students to make their presentations to the class with their 'solutions'. Ask them to explain their assumptions and justify their solutions.

It is not unreasonable to turn this into a major project and make a scale model of the Port to test out various designs. It could be simulated in much the same way as a board game of monopoly with each 'turn' being a day and the players being terminal operators. The objective is to unload the ships as quickly as possible. Randomise the number and size of ships, the weather and of course strikes.

Case 27

SANTOS LTD

Oil Recovery by Truck or Pipeline?

Ian Sadler, *Victoria University of Technology*[2]

SECTION 1 CASE SYNOPSIS

'Oil Recovery By Truck Or Pipeline' explains the decisions faced by an oil and gas producer when a new oil well has been found and is ready for recovery. Conventionally pipelines have always been used for oil recovery but Santos Ltd has pioneered the use of trucks to recover oil from small wells. Trucking offers the advantages of earlier cash flow and lower capital expenditure compared to pipeline.

The case is located in the arid north of South Australia in the Cooper Basin. Santos, an oil producer with eight existing wells has to decide how to bring two new ones on stream. The decision to use trucks or pipeline will affect Santos's cash flows for the whole nine year estimated life of the

---

[2] This case was prepared by Ian Sadler as a basis for class discussion and not as an illustration of good or bad decision making. Certain data have been disguised to protect commercial interests without affecting their relative values. The case is a true representation of the situations faced by this operator.

oil wells. The case provides the estimated facts and figures available and explains the geology and climate in which operations must be carried out. It focuses on the decision between two alternatives although, in practice, there are a whole range of alternatives.

SECTION 2 TEACHING/LEARNING OBJECTIVES

1. To enable students to understand how an oil company decides the development method of an oil well.
2. To show how a decision is made between two competing modes of transport in a logistic situation.
3. To enable students to think about the risks involved in undertaking business development projects.
4. To give students an opportunity to understand how Net Present Value is used as a single measure to represent the current worth of a whole series of future cash flows.
5. To allow students access to the detailed figures of raw material reserves, capital costs, operating costs and other data which they must appreciate and analyse to take a position on the decision being made.

SECTION 3 MAIN ISSUES AND PROBLEMS (AND AN APPROACH TO USING THE CASE)

1. First run through the whole case to appreciate the variables affecting an oil well development, such as estimated reserves, geology, location, capital cost and operating cost.
2. Consider whether the Options being provided -by pipeline and truck- are the best options. Have any other important ones been omitted?
3. How do the options match up to Santos's strategic goal and development policies?
4. For the chosen options, what is the straight financial comparison on the figures estimated?
5. What is the effect of things which might go wrong; such as rain interrupting the trucking option? Students need to be coached to bring the risks of each option into perspective. They have been brought up to think of outcomes as fixed and cost figures as given, so they need prompting to take account of the variable nature of the real world in their decisions.
6. What is the effect of the true future results not being known? -The estimates could be considerably out. Which option preserves future choices?
7. Combining issues 4, 5 and 6, which options should the Engineering Manager recommend to his superiors?
8. Is the method of decision-making adequate? Are any facts or consultations missing?

SECTION 4 SPECIFIC QUESTIONS AND ANSWERS (*IN ITALICS*)

1. Describe Santos's Cooper basin development strategy. What are the advantages and risks with this strategy?

Answer: *Santos's development strategy is set out in Exhibit 3. An advantage is that it clearly sets out what Santos aims to achieve. A disadvantage is the conflict between maximising return and minimising expenditure. If the two goals are conflicting, how can a decision be resolved?*

2. Which option would you recommend to Santos Ltd and why?

Answer: *Anderson should recommend the pipeline because the opportunity to achieve greater returns, amidst differences which are quite minor compared to the possible errors in the figures available. The pipeline provides a firm basis for development which ensures future cash flows, irrespective of road conditions and a springboard for developing any other wells found in that vicinity.*

3. List the key factors which affect Santos's decision and explain the importance of each.

Answer: *Key factors are:*
1. *The importance to Santos of a positive cash flow in the next year compared to a greater cash flow over the project life.*
2. *The future selling price of oil. In the absence of artificial interference, by wars or collusion of producers, the future price of oil will remain relatively low and this depresses the value of the pipeline option.*
3. *The chance of either of the two new wells failing before their estimated life is complete. If the flow of oil were to be reduced before expected, this would favour the trucking option.*
4. *The difficulty of supporting a large number of truck drivers in a hot, dry region without facilities such as housing and entertainment.*

4. Why were the preferred pipeline and trucking options chosen?

Answer: *The preferred trucking option is to install a surface pipeline from Narooma to Bilgola and truck the combined output of both wells to Moomba. The surface pipeline over the short distance from Narooma to Bilgola halves the truck loading operation without costing any more. Trucking to Moomba rather than wakanui is justified because most of the cost of trucking is in loading and unloading, so the extra line haul adds little cost, whilst it saves installing extra storage tanks at Wakanui.*

The preferred pipeline option requires a buried pipeline from Bilgola to Wakanui and immediate pumping to Moomba. A pipeline from Bilgola to Moomba is a much more expensive than the one proposed. The omission of extra oil storage facilities at Wakanui is supported by the considerable saving in capital outlay which is not important under normal conditions.

5. What would happen if the decision was delayed for some months? How would this affect the economics of the project?

Answer: *Delaying the decision for several months would keep options open since oil recovered by truck would give a positive cash flow without blocking the ability to build a pipeline and hence enable more data to be collected about oil flow rates at both wells. However a decision to go to pipeline at a later time would lead to a reduced total cash flow (refer exhibit 8) since the same capital investment would be made, yet the higher operating cost of trucking would have been incurred for a longer period.*

SECTION 5 ACTUAL DEVELOPMENTS

Santos believes that small oil wells, producing less than 800 barrels of oil per day, will favour trucking whilst wells producing over 2000 barrels of oil per day are likely to favour pipeline installation. Oil from wells within these two production figures could be recovered either way, depending upon individual circumstances. Santos now has several wells using each oil recovery method and is pleased with the additional flexibility and earlier cash flow that the two choices provide.

Oil prices rose significantly during the last ten years to a level 100 per cent higher than they were in 1985. They have now dropped back to an identical level to that in 1985, $US 15 per barrel. If this situation were repeated over the next ten years, it would favour the pipeline option which enables a greater recovery of oil, thus capitalising on the higher oil prices.

SECTION 6 AUDIENCES/TEACHING SUGGESTIONS

This case is suitable for advanced undergraduate or early post-graduate use. It requires one hour in class after students have pre-read the case. It is simple enough to be studied individually or in groups without much teacher input.

The case is very relevant to logistics students and provides a clear example of decision-making for project management topics.

The case has been tested with groups of second year business undergraduates. The reaction was positive, with considerable interest being generated. The students were able to come to terms with the situation and answer the case questions.

Case 28

THE UNITED STATES DEPARTMENT OF THE ENVIRONMENT

Logistics Organisation in a Government Department
The Transport of Nuclear Waste[3]

Martin Dresner, *University of Maryland*

SECTION 1 CASE SYNOPSIS

This is a disguised case based on the logistics operations of a government agency and its contractors. The case involves issues of logistics organisation and control, the shipment of hazardous materials, and traffic management.

Samuel Hall, the newly appointed Logistics Division Staff Director in the United States Department of the Environment has been asked by his boss to report on the efficiency and effectiveness of logistics and transportation within the Department and to provide recommendations for change. Major problems in the logistics operation of the Department become apparent from the observations of the Department's logistics personnel, interviewed by Hall for his report. Contractors, which undertake most of the logistics activities for the Department, are not being closely monitored by Department personnel, and are being overcharged for logistics services by Department of the Environment suppliers. Department of the Environment head office staff believe logistics authority in the Department should be centralised, while field office personnel believe that the central authority is already interfering too much in logistics operations. The central logistics authority claims that carrier authorisation reports are being sent to field offices, while the field sites claim that they rarely receive these forms. The Department has no means of tracking inventories of packages, used to encase nuclear materials while in transit, nor do they monitor carrier performance, once carriers have been qualified. The Department's problems are likely to be compounded due to a projected ten fold increase in the shipment of nuclear material.

---

[3]This case is based on a real situation but for reasons of confidentiality all individuals, companies, and organizations cited in the case are disguised or fictitious.

SECTION 2 TEACHING/LEARNING OBJECTIVES

1. To highlight problems in organising logistics activities in a multi-locational setting, specifically addressing how logistics activities should be divided between the head office and the field offices.
2. To facilitate discussion of how logistics should be organised to ensure the safe handling and transportation of hazardous materials.
3. To provide students with the opportunities to determine appropriate policies for carrier selection and retention.

SECTION 3 MAIN ISSUES AND PROBLEMS RAISED BY THE CASE

1. The need to determine which logistics activities should be undertaken by the Logistics Division and which should be undertaken by field office personnel or their contractors.
2. The need to determine how a new, more efficient and effective logistics structure can be implemented.
3. The need to develop systems to monitor and control the contractors.
4. The need to develop methods of minimising the risk of a hazardous materials spill.
5. The need to determine a more efficient and effective method of carrier selection and retention.

SECTION 4 SPECIFIC QUESTIONS

1. Are the Department of the Environment's logistics activities currently organised to minimise the risks from the spill of nuclear materials? If not, why not?

Although the field offices appear to be diligent in ensuring the safe packaging and labelling of hazardous materials, the lack of carrier monitoring is bothersome. The Department relies on self reporting by the carriers on their qualification reports and computes no performance metrics related to carrier operations. An effective program of monitoring carrier performance should be an essential part of the Department's logistics procedures. As well, the lack of central control or organisation-wide standards is not acceptable for the handling and transportation of hazardous materials.

2. How should logistics be organised in the Department? Which activities should be performed by the Logistics Division and which activities should be performed in the field offices?

The following are findings from a study of the logistics practices employed by leading firms in the private sector:

- Logistics management responsibility and authority are vested in a single, mission-driven head office group.
- The head office group establishes uniform standards and practices across the whole organisation.
- The head office group aggregates shipment volumes and procurement requirements across the whole organisation to gain leverage in commercial negotiations.
- The head office group develops long term partnerships with select carriers.
- There is extensive use of performance metrics to evaluate the logistics function.
- A high degree of integration characterises information systems, and automation is widely employed to expedite orders, shipments, and payment transactions.

3. What should Hall recommend to Green?

Hall needs to provide recommendations based on the best practices of leading firms in the private sector. The Department needs a stronger central logistics organisation that can establish uniform standards and practices across the whole organisation and use the organisation's size to realise cost savings on transportation purchases. Centralised standards and control are especially important for an organisation, like the Department of the Environment, that handles hazardous materials. The Department requires an effective risk management strategy to minimise the possibility of hazardous materials spills.

SECTION 5 DESCRIPTION OF ACTUAL DEVELOPMENTS IN THE DEPARTMENT

Hall presented a report that detailed the shortcomings of the Department's current logistics organisation and recommended greater centralised control over logistics functions, along the lines of the leading private sector firms. The report was accepted politely by Hall's boss Green and then shelved. The speculation was that Green was anxious not to reveal any shortcomings in the Department for fear that these shortcomings may be leaked to the news media, that a bad report could result in reduced funds for the Department from Congress, or that the report could lead to a major Departmental reorganisation, perhaps costing Green her job.

SECTION 6 AUDIENCES/USES OF CASE/TEACHING SUGGESTIONS

6.1 Audiences

The case is suitable for undergraduate and graduate logistics courses, as well as for logistics courses aimed at managers. The case may also be used as a teaching tool in a public management course.

6.2 Possible uses

The case is designed to stimulate class discussion and is appropriate for a 1 hour time frame.

6.3 Teaching suggestions

Start with a discussion of risk management; that is whether the class believes that the Department is organised to minimise the risks of hazardous materials spills. There are those in the class who will point to the careful packaging procedures practised by the contractors as evidence that the Department's procedures are appropriate. However, other students will raise the question of carrier control and the concern over poor communication and the lack of standardised procedures among the contractors. It will become evident that the Department's procedures have left the organisation open to the risk of hazardous materials spills. After this discussion, move on to a discussion of appropriate organisational structures and systems for a multi-unit organisation. Which logistics activities should be centralised and why? Finally, discuss implementation issues. How should the Department be reorganised? At this point, bring in various possible constraints on reorganisation plans, such as the Department's method of funding programs and the extensive use of contractors.

Part 8

International Logistics/International Market Entry Strategies

Case 29

EASTMAN KODAK SINGAPORE
Managing International Logistics

Professor Peter Gilmour, *Macquarie University*

SECTION 1 CASE SYNOPSIS

Many trans-national companies are realising the potential benefit of an integrated logistics system. Some have established world wide networks; others regional networks. This case examines the logistics operation for the Pacific Region of the Eastman Kodak Company. In 1987 a CDC (central distribution centre) was set up on a free trade zone of the Port of Singapore's (PSA) Pasir Panjang port. Prior to this, product required by the Asia Pacific marketing regions was shipped direct from Kodak's manufacturing plants throughout the world. By the mid-1990s all marketing regions world wide were serviced through a network of CDCs.

But, as described by Pete Zimmerman at the beginning of the case, Kodak was not wedded to the concept of CDCs. Ever since they were established in the early 1980s the company had conducted formal evaluations of the effectiveness of the concept.(For an example of a regional supply operation in the south pacific see the Bougainville Copper case in Peter Gilmour, *Logistics Management: An Australian Framework*, Longman Cheshire, Melbourne, 1993, pp. 53-71.)

SECTION 2 TEACHING/LEARNING OBJECTIVES

It is clear that the logistics operation should be focused at helping to achieve the objectives of the company. This is not necessarily easy to establish given the desires of the marketing operations in the various individual countries, the imperatives facing the manufacturing operations and the performance criteria for world wide logistics operations group.

150 International Logistics/International Market Entry Strategies

A key purpose of this case is to have the students formally consider the relationship between the service requirements of the marketing regions and the ability of different logistics structures to provide it.

SECTION 3 MAIN ISSUES/TEACHING SUGGESTIONS

3.1 The pros and cons of centralised distribution

A good way to start this case is to ask the class why have a regional DC (distribution centre) -- anywhere. You can write up on the board a list of the advantages and the disadvantages. For example:

Advantages
1. better service:
   (a) one stop;
   (b) faster;
   (c) better support; a smaller number of customers;
   (d) better able to cope with emergencies;
2. less complex network to manage;
3. selective stocking;
4. lower stock in the marketing regions;
5. lower duties and taxes in total;
6. less administrative work for the plants;
7. transport cost savings;
8. communication easier within regions that across time zones to the US.

Disadvantages
- safety stock higher;
- double handling;
- more administration;
- more complex management of product shelf life;
- control – depends upon the autonomy of the CDCs;
- true costs hidden;

As can be seen from this listing the discussion can end with the same items on both sides. If there is sufficient time you can return to these items and discuss them in more detail.

Taking each of the items on this list in turn you can have the class discuss the extent to which the advantages would be dissipated and the disadvantages ameliorated if customers are direct shipped from the manufacturing plants.

3.2 Role of the Singapore CDC

If the discussion to this point has been in general terms you can now focus it on the particular case of the Kodak Singapore CDC. How does the Singapore CDC impact upon the operations of the Kodak business units in the Asia Pacific region?

There are a number of interesting issues. For example with a manufacturing plant in Australia does it make sense to ship the product produced at that plant up to Singapore and then across to the Asia Pacific marketing region? In order to examine this question the students will need to consider:
- the impact of the removal of the volume of the Australian product on the cost effectiveness of the operations of the Singapore CDC
- the costs involved in the double handling of the Australian manufactured product
- the vagaries of the cost allocation methods used by Eastman Kodak for their world wide logistics

operations (a useful discussion can be had on whether these should have any impact at all on logistics decision making – and if so, why).

These will need to be examined in terms of the impact on inventory holdings (duplicate locations), warehouse labour savings, facility cost savings, transport savings and management control. Impact on service levels in terms of reliability and availability also need to be considered.

This discussion can act as a lead in to the broader question as to the appropriate structure for the entire world wide logistics structure.

3.3 Performance criteria

Returning to the Singapore CDC, what criteria should be used to evaluate its performance.

Not all the information to answer this question is in the case. So start off by making a list of what might be needed regardless of what is in the case study. This list might include:

3.3.1 Costs

- freight;
- labour.

Only the costs from Singapore are known. In order to make a reasonable decision about the performance of the Singapore CDC the inbound costs also need to be known.

3.3.2 Service levels

- age of product when available to the marketing regions;
- lines filled from stock;
- stockouts;
- error free shipment;
- CDCs ability to monitor regional stockholdings.

It is important for the students to evaluate the customers' perceptions of the service being delivered by the Singapore CDC and not only the CDC's own view of their performance.

3.3.3 The impact of multi-handling

This will end up being a customer service issue but it is a direct implication of having a network of CDCs.

3.4 Balance between world wide logistics and the regional business units

Because the entire costs of the logistics chain are not included in the way that Kodak has traditionally evaluated logistics options (for example the costs of getting product to the Singapore CDC from the manufacturing plants is submerged) there has been a built in favourable bias for the CDCs.

Are there other objectives for the current logistics network which might override the objective of least total cost within acceptable service constraints?

3.5 Future structure of world wide logistics

In order to properly evaluate this, or any, logistics system the total costs of a number of options needs to be compared to the customer service that each option can provide. This requires a substantial amount of data and a thorough understanding of the requirements of the customers. To do this in practice requires a project which might take weeks or even months to complete. The data is not available in this case, and the time is not available for the students to carry out the analysis even if it were. The objective of the case study is to have the students think through what is involved. What data is needed? How could it be collected? If you allocate a reasonable amount of time to this case you can have your student dig into the detail in the case and develop either actual, approximations or educated guesses at the data required. They can make assumptions about the requirements of the regional business units. Even if many of these numbers are wildly off the mark the exercise of going through this process is valuable.

Logistics at the end of the day is a service activity. Any future role of the logistics function at Kodak should be firmly focused on meeting customer needs. (See Peter Gilmour and Robert A. Hunt, *Total Quality Management: Integrating Quality into Design, Operations and Strategy*, Longman Australia, Melbourne, 1995.) Customers needs will keep escalating; the logistics system to service them will need to keep improving.

3.6 Future role for the Singapore CDC

There are a number of roles that the Singapore CDC could play in the future and they all should relate to the strategic direction chosen by Eastman Kodak.

These may include:

- Providing a platform for future expansion in the Asia Pacific region. China and India have been targeted as substantial potential markets for some time. Other countries in the region such as Vietnam, Malaysia and Indonesia are expected to provide substantial future markets.
- Providing a co-ordinating role for direct shipments from the company's various manufacturing plants to all the large customers within the region.
- Centralised negotiation of freight rates, particularly air.
- EDI links with customers, plants and customs.

SECTION 4 SPECIFIC QUESTIONS

1. What are the advantages to Eastman Kodak of using a network of regional distribution centres throughout the world? List them. List also the disadvantages.
2. Evaluate the customer service measures used by Kodak. What can be done to improve 'order lines filled from stock'? Do you consider this to be the most important service issue for Kodak Australasia?
3. Consider the transport modes used for shipments into and out of the Singapore CDC. Can a case be made for more use of air? If you believe so, justify you position with the help of Exhibits 6 and 7 from the case study.
4. If you were Zyggy Switkowski, the Managing Director of Kodak Australasia, how would you balance the desires of Eastman Kodak's world wide logistics people and the expectations of the Kodak Australasia business units?
5. Consider the role that the Singapore CDC should play in relation to the future activities of the region's marketing companies (such as Australia).

SECTION 5 AUDIENCES/TEACHING SUGGESTIONS

This is a strategic level case and as such will be most suitable for post graduate or final year undergraduate students on courses dealing with logistics or supply chain management

It is also suitable for executive management training courses.

Discussing these issues will take about one and a half hours for a group of students who have prepared for the case session. A good preparation is, of course, to have them hand in written answers to the case questions.

It is unrealistic for the students to think that they will solve all of the outstanding issues for Kodak and its CDC in Singapore. The objective of the case is to enable them to do this if in fact they were employed by Kodak (or any other company with their international logistics system) and asked to do so.

Case 30

EXEL LOGISTICS

Internationalising a Distribution Brand

Valerie Bence, *Cranfield University*[1]

SECTION 1 CASE SYNOPSIS

This case examines the issues faced by Exel Logistics – a young company seeking to internationalise their service/product/brand. Exel Logistics was launched as a dedicated contract operator and an umbrella brand for all NFC's distribution activities, following flotation of the company on the Stock Exchange in 1988. Information on the industry background is given, both on the changing UK and European distribution markets and details of the new company structure.

This European/international entry case was developed for use on the MBA Logistics Elective; MSc International Logistics Elective and for short courses.

SECTION 2 TEACHING OBJECTIVES

It was written mainly to illustrate the company's international expansion strategy. It can also be used as a basis for class discussion in the following areas:

- the move to customer service, becoming customer driven;
- long term strategic issues;
- coping with rapid growth;
- mergers and acquisitions;
- cultural differences in business;
- the marketing of logistics as a package;
- changes in the marketplace that Exel Logistics serves;

---

[1] Copyright Cranfield School of Management, 1995. All rights reserved.

- developing the product/brand;
- moves to contract distribution;
- importance of service branding;
- early entrant – first mover with logistics;
- centralisation (retailer, manufacturer, customer changes);
- supply chain management;
- internationalisation/globalisation.

Following the first few teaching sessions both students and lecturers are of the opinion that the case is a strategy case and illustrates well the issues surrounding restructuring and organisational change, which Exel Logistics undertook in a very short period of time. It can therefore also be used to look at the strategic implications of service development and acquisitions and alliances.

The case ends at the end of 1992 when the first cycle of strategic acquisitions was virtually complete and the company had to reach a decision on the next move(s). Issues to be considered include, long term strategic planning; international marketing; questions of quality and customer service; impact of external market factors e.g. legislation and environment; are they offering the right product for the future and should they really be thinking globally?

SECTION 3 POSSIBLE QUESTIONS

1. What are Exel Logistics' strengths and weaknesses resulting from its current internationalisation strategy, with respect to it becoming a global force in logistics services?
2. Exel Logistics are a provider of European logistics services, with operations in N. America;
   (a) do they really want or need to become global?
   (b) if so, what next steps should the organisation take in order to develop its global ambitions?
3. Outline the strategic options open to Exel Logistics from the end of 1992.
4. Discuss the company's strategy of 'Exelisation' and analyse the nature of the product/service offering both in the domestic market and internationally.
5. How can Exel Logistics enter the 'value added' logistics service arena and what opportunities or threats exist on a European/global plane?

SECTION 4 EXISTING STRATEGY

- Low risk acquisition policy.
- Inconsistent pattern, customers still buying on a regional basis – not yet pan-European.
- Strategy is reactive – following existing customers/companies, are they ready to be proactive.
- Exelisation – is it working?

There are two real options facing the organisation:

1. Continue with current policy, which is to continue with the road based storage and handling of finished goods in regional or national markets – operating as an international group with a single brand image.

In this case the company should concentrate on consolidation and organic growth with selective acquisitions in geographic areas currently not represented.

2. Take an integrated supply chain approach and serve existing customers in existing market sectors but expand services to cover more links in the supply chain, and also expand activity with these customers geographically.

This should enable Exel Logistics to move towards becoming a global logistics services provider, by vertical integration within the supply chain, increasing the scope of activities and services offered to clients.

International Logistics/International Market Entry Strategies 155

In both the above cases the company must:

- focus on what their existing customers really want;
- define what global means for them *(e.g. Fed Ex, TNT??)*;
- target exploitable markets and decide where their expertise really lies;
- develop a management structure for a global business;
- expand the role of IT, essential for an international and/or global company.

SECTION 5 POSSIBLE FUTURE STRATEGIC DIRECTIONS

1. Be ruthless in addressing parts of the organisation that do not make a profit (rationalise and integrate).
2. To achieve strong organic growth, exploit the very strong world-wide customer base.
3. Possibilities of offering in-bound logistics in all markets.
4. Focus on the three distinct markets:
    (a) UK – concentrate on brand to increase market share;
    (b) USA – use good geographical and food market positioning to grow market share;
    (c) Europe – rationalise product base through disposals, acquisitions and/or co-operation to arrive at a focused European wide business. *(how successful has the process of Exelisation been?)This could be done by examining customer retention figures for acquired companies, before and after acquisition.*
5. Focus on one market or temperature range to offer a complete distribution network (food)?
6. Investigate intermodal possibilities.
7. Re-examine strategic objectives – do they want to be a global player or an international brand?
8. As environmental restrictions increase (especially in Europe) the use of sea and rail must be seriously examined. They must decide whether to remain road transport based or diversify?
9. Consolidate rather than acquire.

SECTION 6 SWOT ANALYSIS

6.1 Strengths

- Strong base in UK where it is market leader
- One of the major supply chain service providers in UK, USA and mainland Europe
- Business risk is spread across three geographical markets
- Financial backing of NFC
- Powerful brand image
- Expertise in dedicated distribution
- Expertise in food/grocery distribution
- Unique company culture in UK – *but this could be difficult to export*
- Solid customer/client base
- Local knowledge and experience
- The company is working towards the objectives of a strategic plan
- Ability to see and respond to niche markets (e.g. chilled)
- International experience, Europe, USA, Mexico, Canada and Russia
- Large size, achieved through acquisitions
- They recognise that local cultural differences have to be taken into account *(but this can become a weakness as little is actually done about it)*
- See the need to train local management in the company culture

- Food distribution has specific requirements for technical aspects including food hygiene and safety legislation, especially as relates to temperature controlled services for chilled and frozen food. Exel has expertise in this area.

6.2 Weaknesses

- Exel Logistics is a national rather than a global company, a conglomeration of businesses under a single brand.
- Fragmented organisation – becoming more difficult to control.
- The company assumes that the UK system will be transferable and can be exported, rather than addressing the distribution needs of each country.
- The storage and distribution of goods is different in UK and non-UK markets.
- Organisational expertise is primarily in grocery sector (limited experience of industrial and consumer) mainly gained via acquisitions.
- No real economies of scale have been achieved, e.g. central purchasing, central contracting.
- Less market opportunity in SEM for dedicated distribution (Exel Logistics strength), plus worries over move back to in-house operations in the UK (saturated market).
- Retailers slow to develop pan-European operations.
- Historically food distribution is operationalised on a local or national basis, and is dominated by local tastes and local markets.
- Adaptability of food distribution for global operations.
- Markets for industrial sectors are already dominated, mainly by global companies, entry is therefore difficult.
- Exel Logistics experience is limited to the retail end of the supply chain (secondary distribution) less experience with raw materials-in (primary distribution) from manufacturers.
- Incomplete strategy – the acquisitions (Europe) are not consistent in one temperature range or market.
- Growth by acquisition alone will not be sufficient to ensure global success.
- Gap between vision and reality.
- Little organic growth.
- Problems with local management after certain period of time.
- Dependence on UK retailers (M and S) as a base in Europe, makes Exel Logistics vulnerable if M and S decides to withdraw.
- Lack of links with European retailers.
- The recent BRS merger is likely to deflect senior management attention away from the stated objective of becoming a global operation.
- Customers have been bought with the companies acquired – not won.
- Intercontinental presence but not intercontinental services – (GLOBAL BADGE AND NOT GLOBAL BUSINESS).
- No evidence of innovation.
- No intermodal capability in the US at a time when a high percentage of traffic there is intermodal.
- No apparent move into S E Asia – a major growth area.

6.3 Opportunities

- SEM.
- The brand name.
- Intermodal transport should be investigated.

- Expansion of services to existing clients e.g. reverse logistics, moves along the supply chain, postponement.
- Same markets, different geographical areas (e.g. E Europe, S E Asia).
- Entry into Canada and Mexico can be developed.
- Expand on opportunities in E Europe via links in Russia.
- Integrate/rationalise some existing businesses.
- Opportunities from BRS on the in-bound logistics area.
- Go for organic growth by exploiting current world wide customer base.
- Expand on economies of scale to keep cost base as low as possible.
- Expansion of pan-European manufacturing and retailing will increase the demand for more centralised warehousing and transportation.
- There are as yet no networked operations for food distribution, Exel Logistics should build on their expertise in this area.
- Possible links with European, multi-national or global retailers.

6.4 Threats

- Changes in Government/EC legislation which affect the marketplace and industry.
- A more regulated environment which may slow the pace of, or prevent Exel Logistics achieving its objectives.
- Unclear what business they really want to be in – lack of focus.
- Cultural divisions between the various operating units.
- Increased competition from national and international companies.
- Distribution is often contracted out to owner drivers in Europe, and cheap competition with low cost operators in Eastern Europe.
- Lack of developed distribution networks in other countries (e.g. infrastructure).
- Potential to devalue the brand name.
- Difficulty in controlling such a wide spread organisation.
- Exel Logistics are still in essence 'road based'.

SECTION 7 ACQUISITION CRITERIA

Without a fully international capability, it made sense for Exel Logistics to go into mainland Europe selling national distribution to producers and market sectors that were purely national operators. It was the intention over time to string together a series of national food based networks that would ultimately form an international network as the European food market developed. There were already signs that this was changing as both manufacturers and retailers were crossing borders. Therefore, Exel Logistics needed to become proactive and acquire businesses that would create this network in each country in sequence. (Each country would be run as a separate entity until it reached a certain size, later becoming more sector oriented as in the States).

The route of growth by acquisition in specific geographical areas was chosen and strategically important grocery distribution and warehousing companies were sought, first in Spain, then Germany, France and Benelux (which was considered at this time as one entity but may later evolve in a different way).

Exel Logistics adopted the following criteria when looking for companies to acquire in their priority markets:

- The company must be operating in one of Exel Logistics' existing market sectors.
- Management must be capable of adopting Exel Logistics' ideas for further development.
- They must be operating profitably.
- They had to have a strong client list, but with no one client being more than 25% of the revenue.

- The company's management must wish to remain post-acquisition.
- Ideally the company's clients should already have warehousing and/or distribution contracts.

The only post-acquisition requirements were for regular monthly financial reporting, quarterly reviews of progress with the parent company management and agreement of the annual budget. Companies operate with a large degree of autonomy with day to day management remaining with their existing teams, at least initially.

It is important in local acquisitions to buy local management. In the USA, DCI management was very good but some original senior people have now been replaced. (Question mark over how effective this is long term).

Local company acquisition gives Exel Logistics credibility in each market/country and the following advantages:

- continuity of supply – easier to win new clients *(and keep old ones? – no information to prove this)*;
- acquisition of people with local market knowledge;
- existing client portfolio;
- establishing the brand throughout Europe.

Acquisitions were driven by geography but a by-product was being able to get into some new industry sectors.

SECTION 8 FUTURE ISSUES

Exel Logistics pioneered ways of handling complex logistics and distribution tasks for major companies like Argos and Marks and Spencer. They give individual attention to large customers e.g. 1989 Exel Logistics – Storeflow was formed to take over the Storehouse warehousing operation. All Storehouse's 900 staff at 3 locations were switched to the new company on Exel Logistics' terms of employment. Close co-operation with existing staff has led to easier transitions and acceptance of the new company culture leads to high levels of loyalty and commitment They had to come to terms very quickly with the major changes affecting the distribution industry (both in the UK and Europe) as well as grow their brand and market their service in a changing marketplace, during a recession and in many different cultures. Exel Logistics built on their strengths and ability to specialise e.g.:

- tailored requirements in vehicles;
- dedicated networks of temperature controlled fleets for fresh food;
- special fleets for hanging textiles;
- specially equipped vehicles for boxed or canned goods);
- introduction of computer stock control systems;
- monitoring the whole supply chain.

All things considered they have performed and evolved very successfully and in adopting a specific strategic approach they quickly dominated the domestic market and achieved expansion both in N America and Europe. In a relatively short period of time they have gone a long way to becoming a successful logistics operator, but they still have many questions to address, for example:

- do they continue to buy more and/or bigger acquisitions;
- strive to complete a linked network for food distribution in Europe;
- go for organic growth;
- follow existing customers into new countries;
- should they become more pro-active;
- move to non-food sectors;
- expand on a greenfield basis;
- concentrate on the home market and/or USA;

- offer shared user services;
- consider multimodal transport.

External trends must also be taken in to consideration, during strategic decision making e.g.:-

- quality and customer service in the industry as a whole;
- trend towards contracting back in of distribution;
- environmental legislation.

Following a strategic review in late 1993, NFC announced that Exel Logistics was to merge with its sister company BRS. This move, accompanied by a rights issue was aimed at giving NFC the flexibility to continue its tradition of more 'bolt on' acquisitions – possibly with greater European expansion. It is unclear whether this is a move to further the companies global aspirations, and if so, a clear strategy has yet to emerge.

SECTION 9 INDUSTRY NOTE

9.1 The single European market

In teaching sessions so far, students have shown considerable interest in discussing the possibilities offered to logistics and distribution operators by the SEM. This case provides a vehicle for class discussion in this area and a few key points are given below:

- Distribution companies initially prepared for the move into Europe, by investing in technology and mergers and acquisitions, enabling them to exploit the SEM. But the initial rush to acquire European companies has slowed and it is by no means certain what form their customer's new euro-organisations will take.
- Manufacturers in particular are showing no set patterns, some will take a pan-European approach, whilst others will simply divide the new market into 2,3 or 4 regions. Distributors need to be in a position to create a network through which goods can be moved around the continent as effectively as within their own national borders – or in jargon, a pan-European logistics capability.
- Traditionally, the European transport and haulage industry had been highly fragmented with large numbers of owner drivers providing a competitive service at low rates. It is only recently that large transport groups have emerged to offer a comprehensive range of services at all levels of the supply chain (especially integrated IT systems).
- Integrating Euro-cultures, distribution methods and infrastructure has proved more difficult than many companies bargained for. Thus the demand may not yet be for 'one stop' European logistics but for a more flexible and tailored approach and there could well be a shake out amongst distribution operators as the SEM intensifies the competition for contracts.

There are major differences between the UK and mainland Europe's logistics industries and it is very important to consider these when faced with strategic choices for the development of a pan-European logistics structure, for example:

- the differences in countries basic infrastructure and economies;
- structural differences between UK and European retailers and manufacturers;
- lower land costs in Europe means more stock can be held cheaply at the point of sale;
- owner drivers may transfer goods for several retailers, there is a predominance of autonomous self-employed drivers, unlike the UK system of employee drivers;
- fragmented nature of the logistics industry;
- cultural and language difficulties;
- the importance of considering total distribution costs and not just transport.

SECTION 10 CENTRALISATION

The centralisation of operations (manufacturing, retailing, warehousing) does away with national stockholding operations in individual European countries and instead seeks to serve the whole region from just one or two major distribution hubs or warehouse facilities.

- Some transport customers (by no means all) have been breaking down their own national boundaries in manufacturing and marketing and centralising their operations. By consolidating European operations and producing from a limited number of fixed points, these manufacturers will enjoy greater efficiencies of scale and ultimately a fall in manufacturing unit costs.
- However, with the creation of such large business units, serving in many cases more than one country, savings must be set against rising transport costs due to greater distances to bring goods to markets. *(It is therefore important to consider savings on distribution costs as a whole and not just transportation costs).*
- A recent trend has shown that for some companies, sales and marketing departments are reluctant to lose their national warehousing and management functions – believing European centralisation will mean fewer senior posts. British industry is therefore making slow progress in shifting its distribution base into mainland Europe.

10.1 Advantages of centralisation

- claims to make it easier for manufacturers (or other supplies) to exert full control over all logistics activities;
- lower transport costs by optimising the use of inbound transportation (more volume per transport operation);
- more effective management of stocks;
- faster turnover of goods and delivery times;
- better service for the end customers;
- cost reductions on distribution costs as a whole, due to economies of scale.

10.2 Disadvantages

- goods stored further away from individual markets therefore increased transport costs;
- who controls the central warehouse system?
- decisions at every stage – in-house or contract out; should the warehouse be nearer to the production plant or the main markets?
- vulnerability to local transport problems or regulations – e.g. French lorry drivers action;
- cultural/language barriers of serving more than one country.

Centralisation can put the focus on production rather than on geography, e.g. Unilever's manufacturing plants are to be streamlined, its soap factory on Merseyside, instead of producing many products for one country will produce fewer lines for all of Europe. Transport costs will rise but manufacturing unit costs will fall.

SECTION 11 FIGURES

An ILDM Europe wide survey (1991) shows how distribution expertise is improving. In 1983 distribution costs were found to be between 12-15% of sales – by 1991 companies were finding that this figure had dropped to between 4% and 7%. The Netherlands was the most efficient country in transport, distribution and warehousing at 4.62% and France the most expensive at 7.22%. In 1991/92 UK distribution costs as a proportion of sales were shown (ILDM) to be down again from

5.18 to 4.7% (the UK figure was 17% in 1980 and 8.5% by the mid-1980's). These figures show an overall improvement in the UK, in distribution service efficiency and significant cost reduction. An increasing number of companies surveyed who distributed goods in Europe, showed a general shift in short term focus to addressing longer term issues like IT and strategic planning.

The trend to contract out to 3rd party distribution operators has increased over the last few years but some companies are beginning to bring all or part of their distribution activities back in-house. This is helped by continual IT development which can give retailers tight control over some of the areas where they may not have had so much practical experience.

Other retailers are doing the opposite – seeking to establish ever closer and wider ranging partnerships with their distribution service providers. During the 1980's there was a pronounced move by retailers towards contracting out their distribution operations.

1992 figures show a move away from 3rd party distribution to own account operations (from 30% in-house to 52%) – which also continues to dominate the storage side of distribution activity. It is understood that 1993 figures will confirm this trend, although figures are not yet available.

Dedicated contract distribution is not so common outside the UK and some companies operating in both the UK and continental Europe may have to develop a dual supply chain system – one on high levels of dedicated contract distribution, based on the UK model and another on a more locally adapted shared use system.

11.1 Advantages of contracting out to a third party operator

- Allows customers to concentrate on their core business and save money through reduced stockholding and optimising their use of facilities.
- Specialist advice on total supply chain costs – not just on separate unconnected parts.
- Access to contractors with latest market knowledge.
- Since third party operations can acquire existing in-house operations, this can give a cash injection for investing in the core business.
- Flexibility – tailored contracts.

NB. The author acknowledges the assistance given by the company when writing this case and teaching note and is grateful in particular for the time and patience of the Director of Sales and Marketing (1994).

This case and teaching note is only available through European Case Clearing House, Cranfield, Beds.

Case 31

HERSHEY GOES HOME
International Market Entry Strategy

Peter Dapiran, *Monash University*

SECTION 1 CASE SYNOPSIS

Hershey Foods Corporation, an American diversified food manufacturer and marketer is one of the world's leading chocolate confectionery companies. In the US, Hershey and chocolate are synonymous. Hershey has a 21% share (c 1990) of the US confectionery market and, with the other world chocolate leader, Mars, controlling a further 19%, expansion through further acquisition domestically is unlikely. Hershey has therefore seen global expansion as a necessary strategy especially with continuing rationalisation of the world confectionery market. To this end, Hershey has employed a number of entry strategies into foreign markets.

In 1985 Hershey decided to enter the Australian market through direct exportation and distribution by a local agent. For a number of reasons distribution did not occur until November 1987. Sales did not meet expectations and in February 1989 Hershey withdrew from the Australian market.

The main issue revolves around an analysis of what went wrong and if and how to reenter the Australian market.

SECTIONS 2 & 3 TEACHING OBJECTIVES AND MAIN ISSUES

A number of interesting channel and international marketing issues can be discussed in this case including:

- standardised global products vs. locally adapted products especially with regards to foodstuffs which are oriented to local tastes and culture;
- cultural and business differences in world markets – are English speaking countries the same?
- market entry strategies;
- power relationships in channels especially the power (or lack of it) of new channel entrants attempting to access scarce supermarket shelf space;
- export price escalation;
- distributor/agent evaluation criteria;
- the marketing mix in foreign markets.

SECTION 4 SPECIFIC QUESTIONS

1. Do you believe Hershey should reenter the Australian market?
   (a) strategically important;
   (b) could form base for access to Asian markets;

(c) substantial local market (A$1.1b confectionery market with consumption per head equal to the US and substantially below European markets).
2. What major mistakes did Hershey commit in its initial efforts in the Australian market?
   (a) export price escalation and/or pricing strategy leading to considerably higher prices than competition;
   (b) no product adaptation for local tastes especially in the face of long-established, well-known locally made brands which have strong consumer taste preference (Hershey have adapted products for local tastes in other markets – see in case and also have local Canadian products);
   (c) advertising spending below the competition (A$3m compared with A$5m for Mars and A$6m for Cadbury);
   (d) low power position vis-à-vis the few strong supermarket chains (only 2 key national non-discount supermarkets – Coles and Woolworth/Safeway);
   (e) was channel choice appropriate?
   (f) was entry strategy through a local agent appropriate?
   (g) lack of understanding of channel structures and logistics in a foreign market;
   (h) through delays, the launch was in October/November; the Australian summer is December, January, February; summer is the seasonal trough for chocolate confectionery;
   (i) essentially an unknown brand needing high levels of expenditure for brand awareness and consumer tasting; research carried out on brand recognition shows a remarkably high 37% and would need to be reassessed;
   (j) test marketing was through a department store although the main channels of distribution were to be through supermarkets;
   (k) points to the need for very careful market research in foreign markets;
   (l) intensive test marketing in a small region may have been less costly in the long run.
3. What channel alternatives might Hershey consider if it chooses to reenter the Australian market?
   (a) direct exportation and local distributor;
   (b) manufacture under licence;
   (c) joint venture;
   (d) wholly owned local manufacture.
4. What recommendations would you make to the board if you were Mr Clarke?

SECTION 6 AUDIENCES/USES OF CASE/TEACHING SUGGESTIONS

The case should be useful for graduate students taking a course in distribution / marketing channel management and courses in international marketing.

It might be useful to compare this case (an unsuccessful market entry) with IKEA North America – a case of successful entry to the US market.

6.1 Teaching suggestions

As a prelude it may be interesting to have a blind chocolate tasting and ask students for their preference and the price they would be willing to pay for each type.

Note: Conversions

- kilogram (kg)   = 2.2 pound (lb)
- Australian Dollar = 0.78 US Dollar (October 1991)

Case 32

POLYMEDIC LIMITED

Modal Choice Decisions in International Transport

David Taylor, *University of Huddersfield*

SECTION 1 CASE SYNOPSIS

This disguised case presents a modal choice decision in international transport for a UK company looking to move products to Turkey. The distribution manager has to decide on the most cost effective mode of transport and schedule of deliveries to meet forecast demand during 1996. Three delivery schedules are proposed:

1. Bulk shipment of all products at the start of the year.
2. Bulk shipment of 50 % of products at the start of the year and 50 % after 6 months.
3. Regular monthly shipments.

There are three modes available; sea, road and air, with various alternatives within each category. Data on transport costs and times are derived directly from a freight forwarder as a basis for the decision. Students must determine which is the most appropriate mode of transport and delivery schedule.

The main point of the case is that the decision should be made on the basis of an assessment of total logistics cost rather than just total transport cost. In particular there is a need to identify and calculate the impact on inventory holding costs of the various modal and delivery options available.

SECTION 2 TEACHING/LEARNING OBJECTIVES

- For students to appreciate the need to calculate total logistics costs rather than just total transport costs when making a modal choice decision
- To enable students to understand the complexities of calculating a total door to door transportation cost for international freight movements.
- To enable students to identify the need to consider the impact of transport choices in terms of both modes and delivery schedules on inventory holding costs within the logistics system.
- To enable students to recognise that in reality decisions often have to be made with incomplete information and hence there is a need to make sensible assumptions.
- To enable students to identify trade offs within a transportation decision.

SECTION 3 MAIN ISSUES AND PROBLEMS

The key issue is to ensure that all relevant costs are identified and quantified. It is particularly important to calculate the effect of the modal and schedule options on the inventory holding costs to the firm. When inventory costs are included in the total logistics cost calculation, the preferred option is not the lowest transport cost option.

The three delivery alternatives have been included in order to narrow the possible options and focus students' attention on the mechanics of calculating total logistics costs, rather than first having to determine the possible delivery schedules. Clearly in practice there would be a variety of other possible delivery options, and students may be expected to point these out, even though they are not costed.

The data supplied by the freight forwarder is not entirely complete, which is often the case in reality. Students will need therefore to make sensible assumptions and cost estimates to fill in the information gaps. Poorer students often choose to ignore elements where the data is not clear and specified and it should be pointed out that this is not acceptable.

3.1 Analysis of the alternative modes of transport and delivery schedules

Choice of mode and delivery schedule depends primarily on the trade-offs between transport costs and the holding cost of inventory (please refer to the spreadsheets in the Model Answer).

1. If only delivery costs (i.e. freight charges plus unavoidable transit costs such as customs charges, insurance documentation requirements, are considered then the cheapest solution is delivery schedule option one, i.e. one shipment using one 40 foot container by sea. In this instance the size of carton (i.e. 0.1 m^3 or 0.06 m^3) makes no difference, as a full container is hired, which would have spare capacity even with the larger cartons.
2. If interest on inventory in transit is taken into account, Delivery Option 1 by sea is still the cheapest. Note that interest on pipeline stock is calculated as manufactured cost of inventory × 75% × 10% × number of days in transit ÷ 365. (See section 3.2 below.)
3. If Total Logistics Cost is calculated, taking account of transport costs, interest on pipeline stock and interest on stock in Ankara, then Delivery Option 2 (i.e. 2 shipments by sea in 20ft containers) is the cheapest alternative.

An issue here for student discussion is the sensitivity of the analysis to the values used in calculating interest on stock.

3.2 Stockholding in Ankara

The cost of holding stock in Ankara is borne by Polymedic, as Ankara is a wholly owned subsidiary. The marginal cost of holding stock in Ankara is calculated at 75 percent of the total manufactured cost of the product, because if manufacture of the product is postponed, so that stock were not held in Ankara, the company would save 75 percent of the finished cost of the product. (Raw materials account for 25 percent of product cost and the raw materials can be ignored – because the production manager had decided to buy all raw materials in bulk in October 1995. Raw materials therefore represent a sunk cost which would not be affected by choice of delivery schedule.)

Delivery Options 2 and 3 postpone the value adding (and cost adding) process of manufacture and thereby minimise the average value of stock held in Ankara. The cost of holding stock in Ankara in relation to the three options is calculated as follows.

Option	Average stock in Ankara during 1996	Cost of holding stock
1	$\dfrac{250000}{2} = 125{,}000$	125,000×0.75×0.1 = 9,375
2	$\dfrac{125000}{2} = 62{,}500$	62,500×0.75×0.1 = 4,688

166 International Logistics/International Market Entry Strategies

3 $\qquad \dfrac{20833}{2} = 10{,}422 \qquad\qquad 10{,}422 \times 0.75 \times 0.1 = 781$

NB £250,000 is the total manufactured cost of the product NOT the selling price.

3.3 The size of cartons

The use of smaller cartons is to be recommended. There is no additional cost in buying smaller cartons as they are the same price as the existing cartons. The smaller cartons give significant savings by all modes – not just air – with the exception of full container load or full truck load where the full consignment of 500 cartons did not fill either a sea container or the road trailer but the full container would in any event be hired.

If smaller cartons are adopted, Option 3 by road groupage becomes the lowest cost alternative.

In fact it would seem good policy for Polymedic to alter the size of its cartons for all its shipments (not just to Turkey) as presumably cheaper freight rates would ensue.

3.4 Other possible delivery schedules

The last statement in the case where Mason wonders if there is a better solution than the three proposed delivery schedules, invites students to consider other possible alternatives. An obvious possibility would be rapid shipments by air on a JIT basis in response to actual demand rather than to forecasts; this would minimise the risk of having too much stock in Turkey, if forecast demand did not materialise or having an inappropriate mix of product lines.

A further issue is to question the company's policy of buying raw materials in bulk.

The fact that the interest rate the company receives for money on deposit at the bank (i.e. its cost of capital) is 10 percent and this is the same as the discount for bulk purchase of raw materials, effectively cancels out the financial advantages of bulk purchase. As long as there is certainty of supply from Poppyman over 1996 the company would be better off not bulk-buying because

1. there would be less risk of being left with surplus stock of raw materials if forecast demand did not materialise;
2. Polymedic would not bear the other costs of holding stock during the year (e.g. insurance, storage space, stock monitoring).

If the company did not bulk-buy raw materials at the start of the year, but bought on a JIT basis as needed, this would require calculation of the opportunity cost of stock held in Ankara to be based on full manufactured cost rather than the 75 percent as used in the spreadsheet.

SECTION 4 SPECIFIC QUESTIONS

- Determine which mode of transport and delivery schedule should be chosen?
- Identify and justify the factors which should be taken into account in the decision.
- What alternative delivery schedules could be proposed besides the 3 options stated?
- Consider the effect that the modal choice will have on the company's marketing policy.
- Is it sensible for the production manager to bulk-buy all the raw materials for the forecast 1996 Turkish demand in October 1995?

SECTION 5 MODEL ANSWER

See Table 8.1.

5.1 Notes on the Spreadsheet model answer

- Number of Cartons – it is assumed all cartons contain £500 worth of instruments.
- Transport Options – the various possible journey legs have been listed. Where information from the Turkish Freight Agent was not forthcoming, best estimates have been made.
- Where the number of cartons transported falls between the quoted bands, the cost per carton has been calculated on a pro-rata basis. For example 42 cartons sent by road groupage is calculated at the 40 rate

$$\text{i.e. } (633 \div 40) \times 42 = £665$$

Total logistics costs is : Total Delivery Cost
plus interest on stock in the transport pipeline
plus interest on stock held in Ankara.

SECTION 6 TEACHING SUGGESTIONS

1. Suitable for undergraduate courses in logistics, distribution or transport planning – for classes considering the issue of modal choice.
2. It is particularly amenable for analysis using a computer spreadsheet and provides a good opportunity for practice in methodically constructing a spreadsheet.
3. For weaker students or if time is limited or if inventory costing has not been covered, it is possible to:
   (a) ignore the inventory issues;
   (b) ignore the issue of smaller cartons.

Table 8.1 Polymedic Ltd spreadsheet model answer

POLYMEDIC MODEL ANSWER	Option 1 Sea 40' Cont	Option 1 Road FTL	Option 2 Sea 20'Cont	Option2 Road Group cartn. 1	Option 3 Road Group cartn. 1	Option 3 Sea Group cartn 1	Option 3 Air Group cartn. 1	Option 3 Road Group cartn .06	Option 3 Sea Group cartn. .06	Option 3 Air Group cartn. .06
Value of Shipment	250,000	250000	125000	125000	20833	20833	20833	20833	20833	20833
No Cartons	500	500	250	250	42	42	42	42	42	42
COSTS OF TRANSPORT										
Transport options										
Sheff to Istanbul						412			273	
Istanbul to Ankara subsid						100			100	
Sheff to Ankara Airport							1210			888
Ankara Airport to Ankara subsid							50			50
Sheff direct to Ankara subsid	1935	2975	1290	1710	665			453		
Transport Cost /shipmt	1935	2975	1290	1710	665	512	1260	453	373	938
Insurable Value	277,129	278,273	138,919	139,381	23,648	23,480	24,302	23,415	23,327	23,948
Insurance cost/shipmt	1,178	1,183	590	697	118	117	103	117	117	102
Customs clearance/shipment	40	0	40	0	0	40	40	0	40	40
EUR1/shipment	15	15	15	15	15	15	15	15	15	15
Total Delivery Cost/shipmt	3,168	4,173	1,935	2,422	798	684	1,418	585	545	1,095
No Shipments/ year	1	1	2	2	12	12	12	12	12	12
Total Delivery cost /year	**3168**	**4173**	**3871**	**4844**	**9579**	**8213**	**17019**	**7021**	**6541**	**13137**
COSTS OF STOCK										
Transit Times (in days)										
Sheff to UK port	3		3			5			5	
UK to Turkey port	21		21			21			21	
Turkey port to Ankara subsid	2		2			4			4	
Sheff direct to Ankara subsid		10		10	10		3	10		3
Customs clearance	2	1	2	1	1	2	1	1	2	1
Total Transit Time (days)	28	11	28	11	11	32	5	11	32	5
Interest on Pipeline Stock/shpmt	1438	565	719	283	47	137	21	47	137	21
No Shipments/ year	1	1	2	2	12	12	12	12	12	12
Delivry cost+pipeln interest pa	**4606**	**4738**	**5309**	**5409**	**10144**	**9857**	**17276**	**7586**	**8185**	**13394**
Cost of holding stock in Ankara	9375	9375	4688	4688	781	781	781	781	781	781
TOTAL LOGISTICS COSTS	**13981**	**14113**	**9997**	**10096**	**10925**	**10638**	**18058**	**8367**	**8966**	**14175**

Case 33

THE RWANDAN REFUGEE CRISIS 1994

The Logistics of a Third World Relief Operation

Andrew McClintock

SECTION 1 CASE SYNOPSIS

This is a real case. It presents the scenario faced by a British logistician who worked for United Nations High Commission for Refugees in Bukavu, Zaire, for three months in late 1994. It illustrates both the underlying difficulties of operation in the third world, where much of the western infrastructure is absent, and the additional problems that come with a refugee emergency. Apart from pressure for quick results, and the absence of opportunity to consider alternatives to any first working option that presents itself, the experience highlighted one central proposition of modern logistics – that information is a substitute for inventory. With poor communications and far too many data gaps, it was possible to do a satisfactory job; but there was no chance of fine-tuning the resources to the job that had to be done.

SECTION 2 TEACHING/LEARNING OBJECTIVES

1. To give an insight into the typical operational requirements, constraints and frustrations that accompany logistics operations in situations of disaster.
2. To create awareness of the difficulties of applying the underlying principles of logistics management in the absence of a normal western infrastructure, e.g. in the Third World or in a situation of emergency.
3. To require students to identify central logistical issues in the context of an emergency relief operation.
4. To require students to propose practical logistical solutions for the short, medium and long term.

SECTION 3 MAIN ISSUES AND PROBLEMS RAISED BY THE CASE

1, 2, 7, 4, 9.1/2, 3, 5.[2]

1. Absence of neat answers
2. Bridge and road maintenance poor
3. Communications, poor (internal and external)

---

[2] This strange sequence of numbers is to illustrate the different logic at work in this situation: progress straight from 1 to 10, by way of 2, 3, 4, etc. is not the way things work.

4. Corruption – frontier officials, drunken soldiers
5. Currencies – New Zaire, USD$, Uganda Shillings, Kenya Shillings, D-Mark, Fr B, Sterling £.
6. Incompetence of government
7. Fighting – risk of
8. Financial opportunity for local traders and possessors of skills
9. Inflation
10. Information, dearth of
11. Infrastructure, absence of
12. Law, uncertainty of
13. Local disadvantaged people – additional pressure
14. Personnel in relief effort – mixed motives
15. NGOs – potential rivalry
16. Objectives, uncertain
17. Personnel in the relief effort – constant change, recruitment difficulty, stress and repatriation
18. Political pressure, by angry landowners and helpless authorities
19. Politics internal, in relief agencies- e.g. use of French/English
20. Pragmatism – effectiveness before efficiency
21. Pressure for quick results
22. Sanitation and disease
23. Technical skills –
    - stock control
    - stores management
    - vehicle maintenance
    - vehicle management (4WD),
    - Western locals (e.g. missionaries) feeling overwhelmed and bypassed.

SECTION 4 SPECIFIC QUESTIONS

4.1 General Questions

1. What are the central issues facing a logistics planner in this situation? (Objectives, resources, constraints, problems, information)?
2. Develop a plan for the three-month assignment, given the situation as described, the objectives of the Logistics Unit and of the SLO's job.
3. What are and should be the objectives of the relief effort, and of the logistics unit? Develop logistics objectives for the
    - short term (to four weeks);
    - medium term (to three months);
    - thereafter.
4. What longer-term lessons can be learnt that can help the relief agencies for the next emergency? Outline a feasible contingency plan for steps to put in place immediately the emergency breaks (e.g. staff, systems, physical resources).
5. How would you, as stores manager, have dealt with the two lorries that brought 10,000 unannounced kitchen sets?
6. A political order has come from the local governor: refugees not cleared from the streets to new camps a month hence will be pushed back over the frontier at gun point. 50,000 need moving 100 km. How would you propose to deal with the problem? How would you allocate transport resources between this and other needs? Would you be confident of success?
7. What are your warehousing and storage requirements, and are they likely to be met with the resources likely to be available?

4.2 Deliberate interruptions to the students' thinking process

To replicate the situation in the field, students can be given additional problems during the course of case analysis, such as:

8. Your one fork-lift truck, in use at the airport, is to be reclaimed by the US Forces. What do you do?
9. The team leader tells you he has just heard that a straggling column of – it is said – three hundred refugees is on its way back to town on foot; they are returning dissatisfied from the camp to which they were taken the previous day. What are the consequences if you promise lorries for the following day?

4.3 Outline answers to questions

Question 1. Central issues

1. Objectives
    - Clear the town centre of makeshift camp sites;
    - Make available for collection the NFI needs of up to 200,000 people;
    - Co-ordinate inter-agency logistics activities.
2. Resources
    - Contractors, implementing partners (Exhibit 2)
    - Office and equipment (2 laptop computers)
    - Staff of unit, 5 falling to 3
    - Stocks and warehouses (Exhibit 5)
    - Standard information (all Exhibits)
    - Vehicles, own and implementing partners (Exhibit 8)
3. Constraints
    - Not so much legal regulation, as humanity and western public opinion
4. Problems
    - Lack of information and of infrastructure
    - Unsettled situation.

Question 2. Plan for three months

- Remedy the data gaps
- Establish and remedy any shortage of resources
- Consider possible developments of the situation to be catered for
- Develop links with other agencies and own supply chain.

Question 3. Objectives for different time horizons

1. Short term:
    - General familiarisation with job and people
    - Clarify needs, and success in meeting them.
2. Medium term:
3. Introduce improvements, systems and resources
4. Long-term:
    - Hope for political solution! Possible repatriation.

Question 4. Longer-term lessons

- Possible need for register of trained people available to assist in relief
- Possible need for better systems

- Political steps for provision and harnessing of resources.

Question 5. Unannounced lorries from the coast

The theoretical alternatives were either (i) to begin immediate unloading and take the consequences of other vehicles denied access to the stores yard, or (ii) to tell the unexpected lorries to wait on the road until a convenient moment. Option (ii) was a non-runner with local security as it was, and with the ability of local lorries to change their plans.

Question 6. Order to clear the town

- Calculate clearance rate from Exhibits 6, 7 and 8.
- Make notional allowance for VOR trucks and other needs.
- Journey of 3 hours out and 3 back, plus loading and unloading etc.
- Job done in 6 weeks (20 trucks carrying 50-70 people, once per day).

See Table 8.2.

Table 8.2 Calculation of vehicle requirement, to clear town centre

Type of truck	4 tonner		7 tonner	TOTAL
Capacity, people estimated	50		70	
Number of trucks	13		33	46
		Vehicles off road at any time, est. 30%		15
		Vehicles probably available on any day		31
		Proportion of fleet on other work 33%		11
		Vehicles available for refugee transfer		20
		Qty of people carriable/truck		60
		Assuming 1 journey/day, total refugees transferable/day		1,200
		CAPACITY PER 6-DAY WEEK		7,200
		NUMBER OF WEEKS TO MOVE 50,000		7

Question 7. Warehousing and storage requirements

Exhibit 5 and the table of standard rations (Exhibit 3) allow some approximation of needs (in units and space) for 200,000 people, of the extent to which they are already said to be met, and of the apparent balance expected by camp managers. Non-existent figures for goods in the pipeline made credible figures impossible. In the event, there were very few failures to supply demand on the warehouse.

Table 8.3 Warehousing and storage requirements: flow rates

First time period

	Rec'd in week ending 16 Sept.	Weekly rate of inflow	Issued in six wks to Sept. 16	Weekly rate of outflow
Blankets	36,180	36,000	55,000	9,000
Jerry cans	—	—	24,549	4,000
Kitchen sets	29,237	29,000	16,191	2,700
Plastic sheet 4x5 m^2			42,583	7,000
Soap, per month kg			25,929	4,300

Second time period

	Rec'd in 14 weeks ending 20 Oct.	Weekly rate of inflow	Issued in 10 weeks ending 20 Oct.	Weekly rate of outflow
Blankets	205,790	14,700	104,347	10,500
Jerry cans	52,553	3,700	47,970	4,800
Kitchen sets	59,256	4,200	46,172	4,600
Plastic sheet 4x5 m^2	77,514	5,500	73,289	7,300
Soap, per month kg	64,800	4,600	52,043	5,200

Figures taken from Exhibit 5.

Table 8.4 Warehousing and storage requirements: stock level and warehouse capacity predictions*

Figures from Exhibit 5	16 Sept 16	Std ration/family	Families provided for
Blankets	144,000	3	38,000
Jerry cans	4,644	2	2,300
Kitchen sets	49,809	1	50,000
Plastic sheet 4x5 m^2	19,840	1	20,000
Soap, per month kg	45,242	1	45,000

* Stock is taken from the earlier date, which is also the higher quantity.

Space requirement for standard rations for one family, of 5 members (m^3)	0.37	+ 50%	0.5
Space requirement therefore for rations for 40,000 families (m^3)*	20,000		
Covered and secure storage volume in 4 warehouses (m^3)	6000		
Goods accomodable at 25% of cube use (m^3)	1500*		

* Worst case scenario of all rations being under one roof at one time.

Question 7 Conclusion

Volume of goods being stored apparently > total warehouse volume! Some outdoor storage was indeed evident, but the amount of it was less than what was stored indoors. Equally, some quantities said already to have been issued were well in excess of the total official allocation for 40,000 families.SO: Accuracy of data too unreliable for firm planning; but evidence of falling stock quantities and inflow, coupled with general ease of meeting day to day demand, suggest that peak storage requirements were passed in September.

UPSHOT: Accept warehouse capacity as likely to be adequate.

Question 8. Fork lift truck reclaim

Shout loudly, as communication by radio and telephone is so erratic(!), but realising you may be ignored. Go the airport and hitch a lift on a plane, to go up the supply chain and see people who may be able to help. Prepare to reduce unloading capability.

Question 9. Straggling column

Say yes indeed you can help, and tomorrow – if someone will take a political decision – to reduce the full quota of lorries publicly available for the declared top priority, of clearing the town of its refugees. Six lorries is a considerable resource.

SECTION 5 DESCRIPTION OF ACTUAL DEVELOPMENTS

With a premium on operational activity, there was little planning at a strategic or tactical level. Work was reactive much more than pro-active, and within functioning systems. Much of it was a sudden response either to changing local needs in the camps, or to the consequences of supply decisions taken further up the supply chain.

Particular proactive steps made were

1. Attempts to understand the upstream supply arrangements, by visiting its different links, in Kigali, in Nairobi, and in Mombassa. This never in fact produced a good flow of advance information of goods on their way to Bukavu.
2. Pressure on the authorities to repair the runway so that there were two alternative modes of inbound transport. The matter was still unresolved when the author finished his contract.
3. Attempts to measure outstanding demand for NFIs, using camp populations and standard allowances. Various figures were put together, but none of them were ever convincing.
4. Attempts to measure the adequacy of logistics resources,
   - of warehouse space for expected inflow of goods (the same comment as in 3 above);
   - transport resources, overall (again never really answered) and for the priority of refugee transfer. This was achieved, in about six weeks and using up to twenty lorries a day that carried about a thousand people.
5. Establish co-operation between agencies, who did share information and vehicles.

Overall, the main needs were met: the town was cleared of its 50,000 refugees who were taken to proper camps, and the clear majority of camps' demands for Non-Food-Items were met. But this achievement was done with much less control of resource use than in Britain: in particular, much labour (cheap and idle) had to be on standby at airport and warehouse for unpredictable arrivals.

The lack of information that prevented lean management of the work, at the time, extended to subsequent awareness of developments since the author left. He has heard very little, certainly not enough to form a full picture.

The actual way that the job was handled is written up as *'The Goat in The Python'; this was published twice (with illustrations) in Management Consultancy, June 1995, and Purchasing, the magazine of the Chartered Institute of Purchasing and Supply, in September 1995 (pages 18–23).*

SECTION 6 AUDIENCES/USES OF CASE/TEACHING SUGGESTIONS

6.1 Typical audience

- Degree students (transport/distribution/logistics specialists);
- Master's degree students, logistics option;
- Professionals in other disciplines needing extension training for Third World operation.

6.2 Probable shape of delivery – teaching method

Typically half a day for students in groups of approximately four.

1. Give students the statement of the case The Rwandan Refugee Crisis (text with maps, tables and other appendices), that ends with the question for the students to answer.
2. Give individuals/groups 1-2 hours to digest the situation, and to prepare their responses.
3. Consider interrupting a strongly-performing group with one of the additional questions 2 A or B (in T4).
4. Full session: hear feed-back, 15-30 mins per group.
5. Review: draw general conclusions and consolidate points learnt.

6.3 Alternative teaching method

This case could also be

1. shortened to a minimum of two hours,
2. answered in writing (possibly as part of an examination), or
3. modified for role play.

Case 34

WOOLWORTHS PLC
Sourcing Retail Merchandise From South East Asia

David Taylor, *University of Huddersfield* and **Brian Shortland**, *Kingfisher Asia Ltd*

SECTION 1 CASE SYNOPSIS

This case deals with the purchasing and supply chain policies used by Woolworths, a major UK retailer in sourcing merchandise from SE Asia. In the early 1990s the company became aware of the need to improve the supply chain systems from SE Asia which was the source of approximately one third of the company's products. A new logistics manager was appointed to review the operation. A detailed description is given of the import process from SE Asia into the UK. At the most obvious level the case requires analysis and improvement of this process. However the more fundamental issue, which is implicit within the case is the need to address the company's purchasing policies and the role and approach of the Buyers within a retail organisation. It is these issues which actually create many of the logistics problems, not only in terms of international product movements, but more importantly in terms of inventory management throughout the company's supply chain.

SECTION 2 TEACHING OBJECTIVES

1. To illustrate the mechanisms of operating an international supply chain.
2. To require identification of the operational problems in an international supply chain and the development of recommended solutions.
3. To illustrate the impact of a company's purchasing policies on the efficiency of the total supply chain.

SECTION 3 MAIN ISSUES

3.1 The need to gain control over the supply chain

The company had little control over the international supply chain, primarily because the majority of goods were purchased on a C+F basis, whereby the suppliers were responsible for organising delivery from SE Asia to the UK distribution centres.

There were various consequences of the policy:

- Woolworths had little or no information about delivery schedules until the shipments actually arrived at the UK port.
- This in turn meant it was very difficult for the 2 UK DCs to effectively plan for the receipt storage and onward despatch to stores.
- As each supplier shipped products independently, there was a large number of relatively small consignments which meant economics of scale in international transport were not fully exploited.
- Transport charges were concealed within the price quoted for products, therefore Woolworths did not know what the transport costs were, nor whether suppliers were adding a margin to the actual shipping rates.

3.2 The quality control issue

The quality control system was two staged, suppliers would send samples to London for quality assessment before any orders were placed. If this test was passed, orders would be supplied and a sample of each consignment was tested for quality on receipt at the UK distribution centre. In reality however the quality of products shipped in the orders was often inferior to the original samples sent to London and it is clear that independent quality assurance agencies in SE Asia employed to act on Woolworth's behalf were not adequately fulfilling their duties. There was thus a significant amount of product in the UK over which Woolworths was in dispute with suppliers in SE Asia. There was considerable difficulty in resolving such disputes particularly where payment had already been made on Letter of Credit.

The issue of quality control on products sourced from distant suppliers is a very real problem for many companies. Once product has been shipped half way around the world, it is unlikely to be economic to return it to the supplier if it is sub-standard, as to do so would incur additional transport charges, over which there would probably be further dispute. The only way to satisfactorily avoid such problems is to undertake quality sampling of consignments before they are shipped and establish a financial system that does not release payment until quality checks have been completed.

3.3 Purchasing policy

In common with many retailer companies, the primary objective of Woolworths' buyers was to achieve high gross margin through low unit purchase cost. This policy usually resulted in bulk purchasing and often in bulk shipments.

In calculating gross margins buyers would take account of transport costs (because products were purchase C+F delivered to the UK DC's) and of budgeted distribution costs for UK warehousing etc. Providing all products were sold in accordance with forecasts this was a reasonably satisfactory system. Problems arose however where actual sales failed to match forecasts and excess inventory was left in the system. In such cases the costs of holding excess inventory (possibly for a year until the next selling season) would not be tagged back to the buyers, but would be covered either by the distribution department (e.g. warehousing costs and stock relocation costs from stores back to DC's) or in general overheads. In particular the cost of capital tied up in inventory was treated as an overhead. In fact this was always the case, even when sales progressed according to forecast, so in fact capital cost of holding inventory was never a disincentive to buyers bulk purchasing policies. The company's stock turn-over ratio of approx. 5 (£300m stock against £1500m turnover) gives some indication of this.

The root of the problem here was that the company did not fully identify and present total logistics costs in a comprehensive manner. It was therefore impossible to identify the various trade-offs within the supply chain (e.g. the trade off of bulk purchase discounts against inventory holding costs).

A further problem exacerbating the potential inventory cost penalties was the lack of reliable historic sales data and procedures for systematic demand forecasting. In the absence of good forecasts it was difficult for buyers to purchase on anything other than 'gut feelings' or for distribution managers to undertake any systematic distribution resource planning.

In summary it can be seen that the company's purchasing policies were driven by traditional buying behaviour rather than buying behaviour which took proper account of the supply chain implications of purchasing policies.

It will be seen from Section 5 of these notes that Shortland introduced a variety of policies to gain control of the supply chain and improve life efficiency of both the physical movement of goods and information availability. The issue of quality control was also addressed.

However the issue of the company's purchasing policies was not tackled. Shortland was appointed as a logistics manager to review systems for international product movements, he neither had the brief, nor the authority to question the company's buying policies. In fact in many retail organisation the power and status of the buyers means that it is very difficult even for senior management to radically alter the traditional culture and objectives of buyers, to take account of a wider supply chain perspective in determining their purchasing policies.

SECTION 4 SPECIFIC QUESTIONS

1. What are the main problems and issues in the Woolworths supply chain? Categorise problems into strategic and operational.
2. What steps should be taken to bring the international supply chain under control? If you were the logistics manager how would you 'sell' your proposed solutions within the company.
3. To what extent do the company's purchasing policies influence (a) the international supply chain operations and (b) the supply chain operations in the UK. How could purchasing policies be changed to achieve better corporate performance?
4. Improved information systems are key to controlling the international supply chain. Specify the requirements for an information system to control the company's Far East supply pipeline.

SECTION 5 ACTUAL DEVELOPMENTS IN THE COMPANY

The two main issues addressed by Shortland were information availability and supply chain control.

5.1 Systems development

Lack of information regarding order processing and tracking throughout the international supply chain is a major issue.

There is a requirement to design an on-line information system to control and monitor the international supply chain. This will involve a specification of the required data for the daily operation of the system and for the data needed to monitor and control the system efficiency (Volumes, Lead-times, Freight costs, Customs clearance times).

The specification and development of the required software and hardware systems and the integration network required in the Far East could also be undertaken by students if required.

5.2 Supply chain control

The objective here was to ensure that merchandise arrived at the UK Distribution Centres at the correct time and any relevant quality tests were made prior to shipment.

In order to gain greater control of the supply chain the following issues were addressed:

- Shipping
- Order Status Information and Ordering Procedures
- Quality Assurance
- Finance
- Customs Clearance
- Distribution Manpower Planning

5.2.1 Shipping

1. The shipping/buying terms where changed from C&F (Cost & Freight) to F.O.B. (Free on Board). This put the choice of vessel in Woolworths control thus ensuring both prior knowledge of all shipments and flexibility of service i.e. A vessel could be chosen with a sailing schedule allowing UK arrival exactly on dates predetermined.
2. Negotiations were held with a number of shipping lines covering rates and sailing schedules. Two lines were chosen to carry Woolworths cargo:
   - Line A moved cargo to the UK from Hong Kong (this also covered China & Macao).
   - Line B moved cargo to the UK from the other ports in the rest of South East Asia.
   - A rate per TEU was agreed which showed a saving of some 20% against the estimated costs of shipment which the suppliers had been charging within their C&F pricing.

5.2.2 Order status information and ordering procedures

1. It was of paramount importance that an information system was put in place which could record and report on the status of all Woolworths import orders at all times. Not only had the system to be built, it had to be managed and information collected from some 12 different countries in Europe and South East Asia.
2. A freight forwarder was chosen as a Freight Management Company (FMC) partner who could supply just such a system and who had a world-wide network of offices and associated companies.
3. The information tracking commenced with the inputting of the import order. This was the only system available to the Woolworths buyers which recorded import orders in the currency of purchase.
   - The order was then sent electronically to the relevant office of the freight management company in the country of origin. Each order had a schedule of milestones to be achieved and a timetable set to ensure that quality tested merchandise arrived in the appropriate distribution centre at the correct time. The FMC then printed the order on Woolworths stationery and passed it to the supplier. All order progress chasing was carried out by the FMC.
   - The FMC was responsible for updating the achieved milestones. Non achieved
   - milestones were shown within the system via a bulletin board.

- 'On screen' and paper based exception reports were available to ensure that
- decisions could be made by the buyers allowing immediate action to be taken to
- overcome any problems. In addition it was possible to monitor shipping volumes
- to enable the Distribution Management to plan their manpower requirements
- up to three weeks in advance.

5.2.3 Quality assurance

The basic quality assurance system was retained but more rigorous control over factory testing was introduced. The quality assurance agencies were required to issue a test certificate in relation to each consignment and this test certificate was included in the list of documents to be presented to the bank for payment against the letter of credit. This ensured that goods were not shipped until the quality had been accepted by the Q A agency. If they were then the LoC would be discrepant and no funds would be paid to the supplier

5.2.4 Finance

All currency purchases were centralised via the Import Dept. Volumes were calculated and fixed forward contracts placed.

The currency was managed on a daily basis. Unused currency was sold. There were no excess currency balances and buyers were informed of the currency exchange rates the Import Department negotiated. Because the currency requirements of all buyers were accumulated into larger contracts, much better forward rates were obtained.

Prior to Buyers leaving for an overseas buying trip an estimate would be made by the Divisional Financial Controller and the Trade Controller of the volume of business to be transacted and in what currencies. The Import Department would then place fixed forward contracts for about 80% of this total. The Buyers were informed of the rates obtained and could therefore calculate the UK Sterling prices of their transactions with certainty.

It was agreed that all payments would be on Letter of Credit Terms. This ensured the merchandise was shipped on the date required. If merchandise was shipped late this created a discrepancy in the documents which the supplier presented for payment. The Issuing Bank would not pay the supplier without Woolworths sanctioning the action. This gave Woolworths the opportunity to negotiate a discount for late shipment. If the Quality Assurance certificate was not issued this would also lead to non payment of the L/C.

In order to handle successfully the 2000/2500 Letter of Credit applications per annum, it was necessary to automate the L/C procedure. This was achieved by using the Midland Bank's electronic Letter of Credit system. One benefit of which was a reduction in the L/C commission charges as Woolworths staff inputted all the information that the Midland Bank required which considerably reduced banking costs.

5.2.5 Customs clearance

With some 6,000 consignments p.a. being imported the amount of clerical work involved in creating a manual declaration, for each consignment, for HMC & E purposes, was enormous.

Application was made to HMC & E to be allowed to use a Period Entry (PE) System. After several audits by HMC & E approval was granted. All details were recorded in the PE System Software and a monthly report submitted to HMC & E at Southend on Sea, Essex.

The fact that a PE System was being operated successfully allowed the use of another HMC&E concession (Local Import Control) to clear merchandise on Woolworths own premises. This resulted in containers being delivered to Woolworths DC's, on average 4 days after a vessel docked at a UK port, reduction in lead times of approximately 2 1/2 weeks.

5.2.6 Other benefits

Once the above was in place it was possible to reduce the shipping department from 12 to 4 people.

Improvements in the speed and particularly the reliability of the shipments from the Far East together with the greatly improved order status information, allowed much more accurate resource planning in the UK DC's and more efficient onward distribution of products to stores. This had the effect of reducing distribution costs and improving service.

5.3 Gaining acceptance of the proposed changes

Another major issue in reality was the need to 'sell' the proposed solution to managers and staff throughout the company in order to obtain approval for changes to procedures which cut across most divisions of the company. It was essential to get senior management support, in order to restructure the roles and responsibilities of everyone concerned in the international supply chain.

The need for 'diplomacy' and selling the benefits of new logistics packages are key issues which students need to consider if proposed strategies are to be successful.

5.4 Benefits achieved by implementing new importing policy

Table 8.5 Financial savings in Year One

	Saving (£)
Freight costs reduced	500,000
Employment cost reduced	100,000
Improved currency rates	250,000
Better manpower planning in DC's	47,500
Reduced demurrage	146,000
No payment to customs agents	67,500
Total	1,111,000
Less FMC management charge	235,000
Net saving	876,000

5.4.1 Other benefits

- Database available covering all aspects of overseas merchandise procurements and payment.
- Currency risk greatly reduced.
- Better delivery schedules maintained.
- Shorter lead times.
- Reduced quality issues.

SECTION 6 AUDIENCES/USES OF THE CASE

Suitable for use on under-graduate or post-graduate courses in Logistics

Also suitable for courses in Retailing, Purchasing and International Business

At first or second year undergraduate level the case would be useful to discuss the operational issues in international supply chains.

At master's level or on management training courses it could be used to consider the strategic impact of purchasing policies and their implications for the supply chain.

It could also be useful in considering the role and influence of Buyers in a retail company.